MW00465411

GOING HOME TO TEACH

GOING HOME TO TEACH

by

Anthony C. Winkler

LMH Publishing

© 1995 by Anthony C. Winkler
First edition 1995
10 9 8 7 6 5 4 3

All rights reserved. No part of this book may be reproduced in any form
or by any means without the prior written permission of the publisher;
excepting brief quotes used in connection with reviews written specifically
for inclusion in a magazine or newspaper.

Published by LMH Publishing Ltd.
7-9 Norman Road, Kingston CSO
Email: henryles@cwjamaica.com

ISBN 976-610-152-3

Cover illustration: 'The Visit' by Albert Artwell, reproduced courtesy of
the artist and the Hardingham Collection.
Typeset by Lazertec Limited
Printed by Lightning Print

To Cathy,
who lived much of this book.

CHAPTER 1

Grandfather was dogged by bad luck all his life. He inherited a successful business from his father but lost it to a junior clerk who plundered the books while Grandfather was globe-trotting on an extravagant spending spree. He travelled to America and started a pigeon farm, but the pigeons caught a disease and died, leaving him bankrupt. He met and married an American schoolteacher and carried her home in triumph to his native Jamaica, but she developed such a loathing for his homeland that for the rest of his life she tormented him with her homesickness.

Jamaica remained Grandfather's one constant love. No matter where he went or how long he stayed away, it was for Jamaica that he always longed, to Jamaica that he always returned. His life ended in a small wooden house built by a landlord on the lip of a rutted gully on Jacques Road in Kingston. Here Grandfather raised chickens, bickered with his American wife, and wrote his novel.

He began the novel in his sixtieth year. By then Grandfather had suffered three heart attacks, had been forced by his doctor to give up the pipe and custard, was enormously fat and unable to walk any distance without scratching at his shirt pocket for the small vial of nitro pills that eased the agony in his chest and helped him breathe. Before the novel Grandfather had shown neither literary ambition nor had even been a regular reader. Yet he threw himself into its writing with abandon and pecked at it every morning from the edge of a rickety chair perched behind an unpainted wooden table on which a Remington Rand typewriter sat.

When he was tired of his literary labours, Grandfather would clamber down the steps leading from the kitchen into the backyard where the chicken coops were nailed helter-skelter against the trunks of lignum vitae trees. He would settle down on the dirt in front of a coop, pause for a few minutes to catch his breath, then throw the door open and grope for the first hen.

The hens, who knew what Grandfather was up to and didn't like it one bit, would shy away from his flailing hand and flutter up the sides of the mesh wire coop to escape his grasp.

But reaching in like an oversized bear dipping into the hollow of a honey tree and waving his hand blindly about, his face so flattened against the wire that he could see only out of the corners of his eyes, Grandfather would eventually bag a fluttering hen and yank her out of the coop. He would then upend her without ceremony and, to her indignant squawking, gore his middle finger deep into her rectum.

At first I hadn't the faintest idea why my Grandfather spent his mornings buggering hens, although it seemed to my five-year-old mind a wonderful way to pass the time, but later I found out that this makeshift examination told him whether or not a hen was about to lay and so saved him from foraging through the gullies and bushes for eggs. If his probing fingertip butted up against an egg, he would lock the hen in the coop until she had laid; otherwise he would let her out for a day's scratching in the yard.

When he was done his finger reeked with an indescribable stench and oozed a thick green paste like a punctured worm. Grandmother would spy these goings-on from the kitchen window and screech at him not to dare touch the walls or furniture with the odious finger, which he would hold high like a lance as he trudged slowly up the steps and into the house, or sometimes wave menacingly in her direction from the end of a hall as though he intended to charge and plumb her own ample bowels for eggs.

Grandfather finished his novel in the last year of his life and mailed it off hopefully to an English publisher. Months later the manuscript came back in a scruffy brown package with a letter criticizing its long-windedness and overly rich descriptions but promising another reading once he had fixed these flaws. Elated, he threw himself energetically into the revision. But before he was done rewriting even the first chapter, he was felled by a massive heart attack.

He lingered for three days in the hospital then died reaching out for his long dead mother.

The day after his death grandmother tamped down the manuscript of the novel into an empty kerosene can next to a chicken coop, put a match to all thousand foolscap pages of it, and sobbed hysterically as Grandfather's last dream went up in smoke.

I had always wanted to go home. I did not wish to spend the rest of my days in the company of Americans, for as a whole I did not understand them and was certain that I never would. There were a few whom I thought I understood, but it was with the shallow grasp of book-learning rather than the deeper understanding that springs from the heart.

Living in America as an immigrant was for me like living in a vivid dream. Sometimes things were briefly clear, you saw this and that and why so-and-so was so, but then abruptly the picture would change and you would feel giddy at your own denseness. It was like walking into a movie that was half over and picking up the storyline in the middle. Some things you got from the context; others escaped you. The despair of it all was that you could never see the movie from the start and so were forever doomed only to dimly understand it.

I felt no love for the land. It did not smell right. Even after thirteen years it still had the alien, unrecognizable spoor of a foreign place. It did not smell of labouring bodies, burning cane fields, and animal dung, and smell that way whether in the windless heat of noon or in the feathery cool breezes of the evening the way Jamaica did. Instead, it had the odour of things man-made and lifeless—store bought clothes or the felt of a new hat. "Every fox likes the smell of his own hole," Grandfather used to say. I did not like the smell of America.

It did not sound right. During the daylight hours the Jamaica of my childhood had rattled like a dray cart loaded with pots and pans, giving off the constant clatter of disorder and poverty. Nights rang with the sounds of the unseen creatures that roosted in the bushes and trees—the whistling frogs, crickets, croaking lizards—mixed in with the barking of dogs, the cough of a passing car, the throb of a distant sound system pounding like a feral heart.

But the America in which I lived hummed with the orderly rhythm of an electric clock. At night it shrieked sporadically of fire, accident, heart attack, robbery and murder. Everywhere around Los Angeles, no matter where you laid your head at night, you heard a sleepless rumble from the arterial highways that lanced through the city. Sometimes at night I would awaken and hear that droning sound and my mind would turn to the thousands of cars and trucks hurtling down the highways, and I would wonder where they were going, what people rode in them, what stories they had to tell, and that would be the end of sleep for me.

"If you don't like it here, why don't you go back where you came from?" Practically every immigrant has been or will be eventually asked that xenophobic question. It implies that the freedom to criticize America is strictly a birthright and says volumes about the gratitude and humility immigrants are expected to display for the benefit of native sons. This expectation may not be a conscious one, but it is always implicit even in the mildest-mannered and least patriotic native American.

When you are an immigrant your foreignness becomes a second skin. There is always something happening to remind you of it. You can't talk the way the natives do. Yours is, they say, a guttural and anglicized accent (many claim to find it charming), but even if English is your mother tongue you still dare not use the first heartfelt expression that pops into your head because it would be most likely be incomprehensible to native listeners. You cannot understand allusions to the shared heroes and morals of their childhoods because as the son of a faraway land you learned different lessons and were taught other stories. The land for you is not and never will be invested with the enchantment of childhood past. And though you may long to return and live in the land of your birth, you know in your heart that you will probably go home only to die. Why don't you go back where you came from?

All human life is laced to the earth by the same petty familiarities: those of friendship and love, responsibilities, obligations and debts. But in my case the fetter that chained me to this foreign land was my disappointment with what I had done with my chance. I had come to America to wage war against limitations of the self, against humble upbringing and background, against the narrowness of my early years. I had come to make something of my life, to do well in the big country. To go home again with honour and glory, bloodied but unbeaten in the fight, required me to do superlatively well—much beyond the gainful job and middle-class house with two cars in the garage. But I had done well enough only to stay where I was, not to make a triumphant return. And I was too proud to surrender.

I had come to America because I wanted to be a writer. It was a dream that Grandfather and I shared except that his ambition had blossomed late in his life while mine began haunting me on the day I first stepped out of the mists of childhood.

The relatives on my mother's side, who had all been reared in the mentality of shopkeeping, thought my ambition a folly and openly said so. Only a kindly uncle on my father's side encouraged it. The Jamaican *Gleaner* had published some of my adolescent short stories; a radio station had produced one of my plays. But shortly after my twentieth birthday it was plain to me that to develop as a writer I needed to be better educated and to taste life in a big country. Yet we were poor, depended on the mercies of my mother's rich brothers in emergencies, and scrimped to make ends meet. My father had dropped dead of a heart attack at forty-four, leaving my mother pregnant and with seven children, five of whom were still in school. The only reason we had a roof over our head was that a provision in my maternal Grandfather's will stipulated that his old house should always be reserved for use by his unmarried or widowed daughters. Since it had five bedrooms and was then occupied only by an eccentric maiden aunt, we were able to move into it after my father's sudden death. There we lived for five years during which time every penny of my salary as an insurance clerk went to support the family.

Although our situation was often desperate, by the paradox of life in an underdeveloped country we seemed wealthy compared to the truly pauperized all around us. We did not wear rags on our backs. We all had shoes on our feet. We ate simple food but we had a maid to cook it. Our house was in a solidly respectable neighbourhood and looked rich enough to draw thieves and prowlers several times a year. Yet the truth was that we were living from hand to mouth and struggling to make ends meet on what I, my older brother, and my mother earned.

So it was useless to dream of going abroad to school. Jamaica of the 1950s, like many emerging colonial countries, had a lock-step education system. If you stayed in your place and tramped determinedly through the rigid curriculum with your classmates, you got for your trouble the equivalent of a British public school education. It came with floggings, harsh discipline, and numbing memorization of a thousand jingoistic lines of doggerel about dead English monarchs and adventurers.

But I had not stayed in my place: I had strayed so far from it that I had been expelled from school at fourteen. After that, aware of my enormous ignorance, I had tried to make up lost ground with home-study courses. I had taken a course in German from a correspondence school, sat for an examination in it, and failed miserably. I tried my hand next at night-school classes in accounting, but found that I had no head for figures. I threw myself into correspondence courses on insurance law and theory, sat for two exams, passed one and got a distinction in another, but by then was certain that I'd rather spend my life in purgatory than in an insurance office. At twenty, it seemed to me that I had reached the end of the line.

And then our world was shaken by four events. First, my older brother enlisted in the British army and left for England. He left behind a mountain of debts and had no sooner boarded the plane than his car was repossessed and dunning letters began to flood the house. Next, my younger brother decided that he'd had enough of school and would go to work. Since he gave more of his salary to the household budget than the brother who had left for England, our finances got better rather then worse.

Then my mother met and fell in love with an American who had come to Jamaica to bid on the construction of an oil refinery. When the dust had settled she had extracted a promise from him to put up one of her children for a week or two if and when she sent one to America. She had never liked Jamaica and was determined to transplant her loved ones to a richer land.

The fourth blow fell on me: I lost my job with the American insurance company for which I worked. Mother pounced. Before any of it had a chance to sink in, she had bamboozled a visitor's visa in my name from the American embassy, scrounged up the money for the airfare to Miami and a bus trip to Los Angeles, called in the promise from the American lover, stuffed a hundred dollars in my pocket, and hustled me onto the plane.

One month after being fired in Jamaica I arrived at the Greyhound bus station in Los Angeles.

What followed was a nightmarish grind in an unfamiliar world populated by a puzzling people. I somehow managed to get accepted into a school and set out to support myself with a succession of mean, dispiriting jobs. For five years I slaved at every imaginable menial occupation, scrimping to buy books and pay for my tuition. It was like clawing your way up a steep and shaly hillside, getting grime on your face, dust in your eyes, and gobs of dirt in your mouth. Some days I had no money for food. One whole week I ate canned beans for breakfast, lunch, and dinner. Some nights I slept in the back of my car or on a fellow student's couch.

Time always passes quicker in the telling than in the living, and this time was lived slowly and at a pace that sometimes seemed agonizing, other times interminable. But pass it did, and suddenly the days of hardship and want were over. I had accumulated three degrees in English and a mouthful of rotten teeth from years of neglect. I had married an American.

Then that was all over, too. My teeth were fixed and I was divorced and living in an apartment. The debts from my college years were repaid. There was money in the bank, furniture in the apartment, and a paid-for car in the garage. I had become a naturalized citizen and was gainfully employed.

But I still felt no love for this land, America. It was nothing more than a place where I worked. My home was Jamaica and my heart longed to return there.

Something similar had happened to Grandfather when he was a young man. He had been residing in America for some years, had married his wife in New Jersey, and could have lived out the rest of his days in the land of plenty. Instead, he chose to return to Jamaica. When Grandfather was old and failed and at the end of his life, my mother asked him what on earth had possessed him to give up America for Jamaica. It was to her as inexplicable as anything she had ever heard a human being do.

Grandfather squinted and pondered. By then he must have been painfully conscious of the poverty and unhappiness that encircled him: the rickety cottage on the lip of the gully, the shabby furniture, the homesick American wife who flew into tantrums and raged with discontent at the drop of a pin. Finally he said that it was the smell of naseberries—an aromatic and succulent fruit native to the island—that had brought him back. It had gotten so bad that he couldn't get that smell out of his nose. Everywhere he went in America it haunted him.

Mother thought his answer empty and meaningless. Where America was concerned, she was unforgiving of jocularity.

But I believe that Grandfather meant exactly what he said. The hole simply did not smell right, and he was a smart enough fox to know that he was displaced. He chose to go home and end his days in the place where his life had begun.

At thirty-three, after living nearly thirteen years in America, that was what I also made up my mind to do.

CHAPTER 2

My family had been in Jamaica for generations by the time I was born. On my mother's side they had migrated from Lebanon in the early 1900s to escape an outbreak of sectarian warfare between Christians and Muslims. The family legend is that my mother's father had a Lebanese friend in Jamaica who wrote to him describing the island as a paradise where a Catholic family could live in peace. Whether or not the friend also described the island's racial mix to this grandfather, whom I never knew, is uncertain, but it was said in the family that when he landed in Jamaica he was horrified to discover that most of its inhabitants were black. Nevertheless, there he was, craning over the guardrail of the ship with his wife at his side who carried one infant son in her arms and another in her womb, and he had to make the best of what must have seemed to him a very bad choice.

This unknown grandfather was, from all accounts, a typical unbending Middle Eastern paterfamilias, a rigid martinet obsessed with safeguarding the virginity of his girl children and shielding them from marriage to a black or brown Jamaican who might discolour his line. Since he had eight daughters, protecting them became a nearly full-time job which required merciless beatings, ruthlessly enforced curfews, and arranged marriages. He married off his eldest daughter when she was only sixteen to a suitable Lebanese gentleman thirty years her senior who lived in the country. The old country gentleman proceeded to beat her cruelly and to breed her with one child after another. Later she went mad from his brutal mistreatment. She bore him a son, to whom the old gentleman took a violent dislike and began to beat as regularly as he beat the mother. This firstborn son went berserk in his teens, was committed to the insane asylum and eventually died there. By the time I grew to know my mad aunt, the tide had turned against the tyrant. He had become old and feeble and had taken leave of his senses. My aunt, who was then in her prime and hopelessly mad, used to occasionally box him in my presence as casually as one would kick an old dog that used to bite when it was younger but had since lost its teeth.

My mother's father must have been a rancorously unpleasant gentleman. He grew to hate Jamaica and to despise its native people. In the early years he made his living in the way of many Middle Eastern immigrants to Jamaica before him: he bought a donkey, loaded it up with dry goods, and went door to door in poor neighbourhoods selling his merchandise on credit. His occupation required him to rub elbows with the very class of Jamaicans he professed to despise—the poor black people—and this experience seems to have fuelled his hatred of them. Whenever he got vexed at his customers, he had the bad habit of raging out loud for all the world to hear that the "negro is a monkey without a tail." One day he flew into a temper and screeched this insult to a black policeman, who replied by clouting Grandfather in the stomach with his billyclub, felling him senseless on the street. Shortly afterwards he contracted liver cancer and died. He was still a relatively young man—in his early fifties—and to the very end he blamed his disease on the policeman's blow.

In spite of himself, Grandfather prospered. He was gifted with the Arab merchant's instinct and must have been altogether too cunning and sharp for the poor people whom he preyed on. He trained his three sons in the business, and before long the family had climbed down off their donkeys and moved into a shop. Soon there were several shops, with a son manning each, and then more and more shops, all in the seamiest, dirtiest section of Kingston where life was at its nastiest. As the family business flourished, the sons grew rich and built mansions in the cool hills surrounding Kingston to which they retired at the end of a business day spent in the most ·squalid part of town, to be waited on hand and foot by uniformed servants.

As I came to know them, these uncles seemed to me to be the most dreamless creatures men could become. Haggling with poor

Jamaicans over pennies had made them stingy, avaricious, and incapable of understanding anything that was not visible or had no price. They owned race horses and gambled wantonly on weekends, but they were tight-fisted and mean with their riches. They lived in wonderful houses, sent their children to the best schools abroad, and no one persecuted them for their Christian beliefs. Yet they despised the country that had made all this possible and were openly contemptuous of the poor black people from whom they earned their daily bread. Although they mixed socially with monied brown and black Jamaicans, they would rather a child of theirs had been stillborn than grow up to marry into a family that was not white.

With the exception of the oldest son whom my grandmother had cradled in her arms when the ship docked in Kingston, all these uncles had been born on the island, yet to a man they looked to Lebanon as their homeland. Most of them did not speak Lebanese, had never seen the country, had only a second-hand and anecdotal idea of its customs and people, yet they all acted as though they were living in exile. To hate the land of your birth struck me then and now as unnatural and wrong. Yet all the descendants of my mother's father, male and female alike, similarly despised Jamaica.

By the time my mother's family arrived in Jamaica, my father's had already been there for two generations and were smugly encased in the prejudices and airs of the landed gentry. But in fact they owned little land. What they owned was a prosperous music business that had been started by Great-grandfather Winkler.

A native Hungarian, Great-grandfather had come to Jamaica sometime in the early 1880s to found a music import business. He was a short, fastidious, intelligent man who spoke and wrote some six languages fluently. A piano tuner by profession, he was also a virtuoso musician and seems to have had a good head for business. When my mother's family landed in Kingston, Great-grandfather Winkler was already an established and successful businessman, owner of the only music import store on the island, and in thick with Jamaican society.

Why Great-grandfather had come to Jamaica is unknown. The story passed down in the family is that he had visited the island as the pianist aboard a cruise ship and had been so smitten by its beauty that he had jumped ship and stayed. By 1884 he had launched his music business; by 1888 he had become a naturalized Jamaican citizen. Four years earlier, he had been naturalized as an American, leaving the back door ajar in case things went badly in his new island home. But the family prospered. Great-grandfather pursued his music business, played the organ in Sunday services at the Catholic cathedral, and raised his children, of whom the only son was my failed grandfather.

Great-grandfather's wife, however, found the island small-minded and oppressively hot, so her husband obligingly established a household in Philadelphia, and the family travelled back and forth between Jamaica and America for many years, seemingly unable to make up its mind where to settle. But since the music business in Jamaica provided the income for these excursions abroad and for maintaining households in two countries, Jamaica in the end always won out over America.

In 1920, after thirty-eight years in Jamaica, Great-grandfather retired from the island, leaving the music business to Grandfather, and sailed to California intending to live out his remaining years with his oldest daughter. He had by then been widowed more than eight years.

Bad luck followed him. On the day he arrived in California, his daughter died in childbirth. He took the train across the country to Philadelphia and settled in with a second daughter in whose company he lived until his death at eighty-one.

From a distance of some eighty-odd years the differences between the families of my mother and of my father do not seem great, but magnified by life on a small island, they must have appeared insuperable when my parents married. My father's family regarded my mother's as vulgar shopkeepers. It was one thing to be an importer of pianos from Europe and to sell these refined instruments to the best households in Jamaica and another to go jiggling through town hawking cloth to the poor from the back of a donkey. Nor did this impression improve when my mother's family clambered off their donkeys and settled into their dirty shops on the side of town where the poor congregated.

Then there were the obvious differences in culture. The family on my father's side took pride in their European heritage and had snobbish pretensions to learning. But in truth their cultural accoutrements were superficial (Great-grandfather excepted) and consisted of little more than the ability to name-drop about authors and to recognize a few melodies of classical music. On my mother's side, mammon and the racehorse ruled supreme over music and books, and no one made any bones about it.

There was another marked difference between the two families. My mother's family spewed over with hate and contempt for Jamaica and its people; my father's did not. Great-grandfather Winkler was not driven to the island by a fratricidal war in his homeland, but had been drawn there by its loveliness. Grandfather loved the island and its people and chose to end his days among them. My own father thought of Jamaica as his home.

When I decided to go home in 1975, I was obeying, or so I thought, an honourable impulse of love for country shown by three generations of forefathers, and it seemed to me a fitting and decent thing to do.

But it was not as easy as getting on a plane and taking a trip. To begin with, the government had recently taken a shift towards socialism under prime minister Michael Manley and an exodus of Jamaicans who felt threatened by this move had begun. I knew little about Manley or his policies beyond what I heard from relatives and friends, all of whom were unanimous in their condemnation of both, or what I had read in the American press, which my years in America had taught me to doubt. But I was neither alarmed nor surprised by his socialism.

Jamaicans, especially those who are well-off, are notorious for their callousness towards the poor. Foreigners visiting Jamaica are struck not so much by the endemic poverty as by the obscene and gaping difference between the destitute and the conspicuously rich. In this sense Jamaica is little different from many third world countries. The mansion coexists side by side with the reeking hovel, and over the centuries Jamaican eyes have become hardened to sights of misery and squalor that would horrify any American.

So if Manley was trying to right this long-standing wrong, so much the better. I wanted to be there when he did it. A howl of outrage from the well-heeled Jamaican and an exodus of the threatened privileged was to be expected.

But there was another drawback to simply going home: I was white. And that was a graver problem.

I remember distinctly the day I found out that I was white and that there was something shameful about my colour. It was the day I begged my father to let me come along for the ride when he drove Louise home.

Louise was my nanny, and even now when I think of her my nose burns with the smell of raw chicken, thyme, and scallion, for she was also our cook and her sinewy hands constantly reeked of the stew pot. She was a gaunt and bony black woman with a grim manner towards all except children, and it was to her that my brothers and I used to run crying for kisses and hugs when we were troubled or hurt. On this particular evening, Louise having missed the bus, my father offered to drive her home, and the three of us bundled into the car.

When I saw to what a horrible and nasty tenement my father took Louise that afternoon, I quailed with dismay that she could have come to us from such a dirty place and that she intended to spend the night among such squalor. I begged my father to take her back with us, but he told me gruffly to shut up about it because this was her home and the horde of ragged urchins who had flocked to greet her when she got out of the car were her own children. Up until then, it had not dawned on me that Louise had children of her own. I had foolishly thought that my brothers and I were the only children who mattered to her. And when I tried, in my six-year-old mind, to understand why Louise and her children had to live among such nastiness while we did not, the only reason that I could see was the difference in our colour. Only blacks were desperately poor. White people were not.

Many things after that became clear. There was, for example, the mystery of our landlady who seemed so scornful towards us, and of her seaman son who, when he was home from a voyage, had always made a point of inexplicably bullying me if he accosted me alone on the street or in an adjoining yard. The son was a strapping black man who was rumoured to have been a Mr. Something or another among bodybuilders and whose enormous muscles rippled threateningly under his shirt.

One day I was taking a shortcut to meet a playmate when this bully suddenly loomed in my path and began yelling at me. I had my slingshot with me and, although I was only seven, I was determined to stand my ground. While he screeched insults, I calmly loaded the slingshot with a stone from my pocket and, as he watched with disbelief, took aim at his head.

I meant to frighten him by firing a shot past his ear, but I missed, and the stone struck him squarely above his nose, cracking open his skull and splattering blood across his forehead. He gave a howl of rage and charged. I took to my heels and ran for my life, racing between trees and overhanging bushes, hurtling over roots and stones, until I careened around the corner of my playmate's house and scurried deep under the dark cellar. My playmate's mother was on the back stoop cooking dinner when she saw me plunge under the house, and before she could ask what I was doing, the bully, bloodied and bellowing, was standing there screaming for my hide. I cowered under the cellar while the two of them had a noisy argument about what I had done. An hour or so later, after she had finally gotten rid of him, the mother was able to coax me out of the cellar. I stayed at my playmate's house that night until my father came to get me in his car.

That was the last time I lifted my hand against a black Jamaican who hated me because I was white.

Later, after we moved to Montego Bay, I was often set upon by swarms of street urchins and beaten in the streets for no other reason but that I was white. Sometimes they would walk beside me and flail at my back with switches; sometimes they would pinch my arms or kick and thump me all over. But I never fought back against them. It was perplexing to a black friend who was with me one day when the urchins attacked. This time they had gotten hold of water pistols and were gleefully prancing beside me on the street and squirting me all over my school uniform and face. A stream of water splattered my friend, and he turned and doubled his fists, but the urchins quickly apologized, saying that it had been meant for the white boy. They trailed after my friend and me until we finally came to my gate, drenching me repeatedly while taking care not to splatter him again.

By the time I got into my yard I was crying, and my friend was hanging his head in shame at my cowardice. I lamely tried to mutter something in my defence, but I could not explain to him the real reason why I had not fought back against the urchins.

I could not tell him that in my heart I felt that I deserved their abuse and beating, that if I had been born black and poor in one of Jamaica's mephitic slums, I too would have hated the sight of a white skin and been just as inclined as they to kick and thump and abase me on the street.

Still, I would go home. And I would go home, perhaps not in glory and triumph, but with laurels enough to show that I had waged a good fight in America.

I was finally a published writer. I was the author of three college textbooks, two of which were selling so well that my first royalty cheque had been the equivalent of a year's salary. If my wishes had come true, I would have returned home with my novels dripping from my coat pockets, my plays appearing to rave reviews on Broadway, my poetry being recited in English classes, but it was clear that none of this was going to happen. All I had to show for my twelve years in America were three college textbooks and a year's salary in the bank. Yet it was enough. Not glory, perhaps, but workmanlike accomplishment that Louise or any of the other stalwart women of my childhood would have applauded. Older and wiser, I would settle for less, call a truce with my ambition, and go home.

I decided that I would go home to teach. There was such a desperate shortage of teachers in Jamaica that the government had lately launched an overseas recruitment programme. The recruiters had canvassed Los Angeles the year before but had fared badly because the pay was dreadful and the chief allurement—life in a sunny tourist haven for a year or two—did not have much appeal to Angelenos who had their own benign climate. Jamaica was also getting bad press at the time because of Manley and his well-publicized admiration of Castro. The island, it was said, could end up in the communist orbit. Moreover, there were rumours of an anti-white groundswell on the island that had resulted in some ugly behaviour towards tourists.

Nevertheless, my plan struck me as sensible, and I was especially proud that by teaching I could possibly do some tangible good. I would return home to give back, not to take.

I flew to Jamaica on a vacation, intending to scout around for work, and immediately saw an ad in the *Gleaner* for a tutor in a rural teacher training college, which I shall call Longstreet College. A long time ago the school had been an English hotel catering to rich European tourists desiring to escape the oppressive heat of the Jamaican plains.

The original hotel building had stood on the ridge of a commanding hill from which its innumerable windows and doors gaped at the mountain breezes. Around this venerable old structure the government had erected a perimeter of stodgy dormitories whose beehive rooms were beaded on three floors by a narrow hallway interspersed with open toilets and showers. Scattered over the grounds were stumpy classroom buildings, each with a wall of louvred windows and a single wooden door. In the middle of these ugly whitewashed structures was a cinder-block cafeteria in which some four hundred students and thirty or so tutors, as the instructors were called, ate their meals. All the students lived on campus. Some of the tutors did, too, in specially built two-flat buildings that clung to the hillside behind the original hotel.

My interview was with the principal. He was an imposing black Jamaican with a doctorate from Cornell University and the owlish squint of a cataract sufferer. His manner was measured and sonorous and gave the impression that he could, at any moment, rear up and repel impertinence by the sheer weight of his dignity. His name was Dr. Levy and during our interview he enunciated so clearly and with such proper emphasis that a long sentence crammed with sibilants and punctuated with commas and semicolons left him visibly winded.

And then during one of his pompous speeches about the history of the school, an odd incident occurred.

A small lizard squeezed out from under a mountain of official looking documents stacked on the edge of his desk, perched in the shadow of the pile for a minute or two as if relieved to have escaped the burden of the Ministry of Education's paperwork, and began to promenade across the desk with the familiarity of a creature at home.

Dr. Levy was approaching his peroration about the school's history. For proper emphasis, he had placed his large hands on the top of the desk and begun a background tapping with his knobby fingers. Attracted by the taps, the lizard cocked its head, looked at the hands, and began to stalk one of the twitching fingers as though it were an edible fly.

Dr. Levy, looking me fixedly in the eye, continued with his lecture while the lizard scaled the curled edge of a dog-eared memo. Beside myself, I nearly said something when, without interrupting his speech and with the aplomb of a bishop, the doctor discovered a need to scratch an itchy ear lobe with the threatened finger. Once he was done with the ear lobe, he folded his arms and buried his hands deep within the safety of his armpits. The lizard, put in its place without so much as a murmur, burrowed back under to the crush of official documents from which it had come and disappeared.

The doctor's close encounter with the lizard was over in an instant, yet it struck me as wonderfully revealing of the kind of ancient lower-brain axioms that make up a nation's culture. For I immediately understood why he chose to ignore the reptile, and why he didn't, as his American counterpart in a similar predicament would certainly have done, give a cry of outrage and attempt to shoo the creature off the desk. Most Jamaicans will act out their official roles with deadly earnestness even in the face of ghastly contretemps. This hard lesson about ritualistic deportment has been inbred into Jamaicans by the English, whose monarch, it is commonly believed, would sooner choose to heroically explode with dammed-up flatulence in the privacy of her palace afterwards rather than break wind during a ceremonial public function. Likewise, the doctor would have grimly endured the reptile's gnawing his finger to the bone rather than abandon his official persona.

A flash of silent understanding passed between us while the lizard slunk away, hungry, disappointed, subdued by the manners of its betters.

Dr. Levy's severe manner said, "Shut up about the lizard and pay attention."

My polite and wordless reply was, "What lizard, sah?"

The interview ended shortly afterwards with the doctor telling me that he would advise me if I had been selected for the position. But I knew that it was mine.

The telegram was waiting for me at my brother's house when I returned to Kingston the next day.

CHAPTER 3

It was easy to say goodbye to Southern California even after thirteen years, three degrees, two homes, six motorcars, and one marriage. Southern California is a vast motel into which people check in and out without a sense of attachment or sentimentality. Most of the people in Southern California really live elsewhere—in the heartland of the Midwest, in the ethnic neighbourhoods of eastern cities, in some small town from the deep south where their parents and siblings remained and to which they return for holidays, anniversaries, funerals, family reunions, and periodic doses of reality. Southern California is the geographic equivalent of a salesman's soul: fretful, insomniac, longing, ambitious, thwarted, and once in a while on a full mooned night, slightly demented.

I had lived here during the episodic convulsions of the flower children, the anti-war movement, the Manson family madness; through the SLA, the Black Power movement, Women's Liberation, Chairman Mao, Gay Liberation, Black Panthers, Grey Liberation, Open Enrollment, Watergate, and Pyramid Power; I had seen cause succeed cause, fad follow fad, manners of speech and gesture come and go, barbers become stylists, and haircuts shoot up overnight from $2.50 to $15. Where the land lays down no laws and traditions, there is vacuum; and where there is vacuum there is always an inrush of tormented ideology into people's minds. Southern California is a vast desert dominated by the ethics of "should." And what should be or shouldn't be depends on which ideologue is currently in vogue and which lately minted creed now reigns over the hungers and cravings of a population starving for the certainties of lost childhoods.

I never understood, I never liked Southern California. I never could put into words what it is I felt about the place, the people, the eternal, dreary, benighted, jittery stew. Then one day I was talking to a friend who taught at a junior college, discussing a middle-aged teacher who had been racked by feverish fads of every conceivable denomination and dogma. She had successively "been into" Zen, Transcendental Meditation, Astrology, Demonology, I-Ching, Tarot cards, Primal Therapy, Transactional Analysis, Rolfing, Colonic Irrigation, the Beatles, and Jesus Christ. When the blacks were burning down the country, she took only black lovers. When the Chicanos began their rumblings for identity, she bedded only macho Latinos. When Women's Liberation burst over the cratered Southern California landscape, she began a wild flaunting fling with lesbianism, from which she eventually returned with a dishevelled air to cull a succession of muscular, acned young men from her college classes with whom, it was slyly rumoured, she mated only on top as befitting the dignity of her professorial rank.

My friend said that she reminded him of someone suffering from incomplete abdominal surgery, someone whose bowels had been opened up and laid out on the table by a surgeon who had forgotten to close the incision. She was obliged to get up and live out the rest of her days with intestines oozing frantically through the open cut.

It was an apt image, suitable for this one anguished woman, suitable for Southern California. Guts and intestines and entrails held in check by a freshly applied gauze of Mao, Janov, Freud, Steinem, Perls, Ho Chi Minh, Marx, Blavatsky, Macrobiotics, and whichever Indian guru had lately crossed the ocean in search of a Rolls Royce.

And what I was most grateful for, when I was finally ready to sneak out one early Saturday morning, was that I had not suffered the abomination of dying in the place; that the recurring nightmare I had had of being buried in Southern California under one of those rectangular, cheesy-smooth, ivory coloured concrete plaques that resembled porcelain fillings in teeth and that dotted the undulating swards of the cemeteries had not come to pass; that I was departing the place with sound mind and healthy body, leaving behind me only a faint spoor of memories in the minds of one or two people there whom I had come to love and with whom I had sad, lingering goodbyes.

The rest was easy. One does not mourn leaving a motel, no matter how opulent and beguiling its decor.

I stole away one Saturday morning, without making a sound.

But I did not leave alone. Cathy came with me.

Cathy lived then in her hometown of Cicero, west of Chicago, and she was vacationing in Montego Bay when we met. She came into my life through a childhood friend my father had tried to murder and who to this day still bears the scars of his homicidal assault. And she came into my life so unexpectedly, with such abruptness, that only a bull-headed positivist would not have read omens into the turn of events that brought us together.

I was in Montego Bay with my two sisters, celebrating the job offer from Longstreet, and we were sitting on the balcony of our hotel watching the sheet lightning flash off a single dark cloud writhing on the horizon, wondering where we should go to dinner.

One sister had a stony virginal air that had alarmed even the good Fransciscan Sisters of the Mount Alvernia Academy of Montego Bay. The other had been born to drive men to drink and was already confirmed in her reputation as a femme fatale. Following the second about was her latest lover, an expatriate Canadian businessman whose face bore the despairing look of the fish that knows the barb is driven deep into its throat and there is nothing it can do but wiggle.

And so we were sitting and idly plotting dinner. Where would we go?

The wicked sister, who knew that the businessman was treating, expressed her desire to go to someplace opulent, expensive. Tonight, she sighed, she felt in the mood to eat money. Nothing else would satisfy her. The businessman eagerly suggested that we go to *Chez Francois,* the only French restaurant in Montego Bay.

"Is it expensive?" the lethal sister asked dubiously.

"Very expensive."

"It has to be expensive, you know," she replied, licking his face seductively with her eyes. "I have a taste for something rich. Something that costs a lot."

"It's the most expensive restaurant in town. It's twice as expensive as the hotels."

"When I eat expensive food, it always puts me in a romantic mood," the heartless one murmured. "I wonder why. I should ask my doctor."

"This might even be the most expensive restaurant in Jamaica," the poor man panted.

It was, the businessman added, owned and run by a local named John McPherson.

John McPherson. We brightened, for here was a name that had meaning for the three of us. We knew him as the victim of a terrible accident that had happened one night many years ago when we were still children. My father, in a drunken stupor, had been behind the wheel of the car in which McPherson was a passenger.

The car had rammed a telephone pole right in front of the hospital, my father had broken his back, and John McPherson, then a boy of twenty, had been hurled through the windshield with such force that his throat had been slit from ear to ear and his larynx shattered. That night, he was given up for dead by the doctor on duty and administered Extreme Unction by a priest.

Only he didn't die. He clung grimly to life, breathing through a tube stuck down his throat, muttering incoherently night and day. His fretful mother hovered over his bed with my virginal sister at her side. Eventually, after a long hospitalization, John recovered, although he never regained his normal voice and to this day can only speak in a rasping whisper.

Now John was a restaurateur, approaching middle age, and we were about to dine at his restaurant.

Just before we left for dinner I remarked that I had always felt guilty about the accident, because I was the one my father had sent on that fateful evening bicycling into town to summon John, who had no telephone.

"I wonder what John has in store for me tonight?" I joked, as we all climbed into the car.

He had two surprises in store for me that night: the revelation that my father had deliberately rammed the telephone pole because he thought John had been having an affair with my mother; and

Cathy, who went home with me.

We had a breathless, turbid love affair. We made love on the beach, in the dirt and, one memorable noon, in the green, velvety eye of a river while tourists trekked past on either bank casting occasional worried glances at the two bodies bobbing jerkily up and down as though seized by a rapacious underwater beast. For two days we were old bones in the jaws of Eros.

During those two days, I took Cathy to Longstreet and showed her the tiny mountain village which I had decided to make my home. She said she wanted to come with me. I protested that even raw Kingstonians who had lived in Jamaica all their lives found the countryside harsh and depriving. She vowed that she would adjust. It didn't take too much argument to win me over.

Cathy went back to Chicago, resigned her job, sold her car and furniture, found a home for her beloved tom-cat, endured censure from her indignant mother and disapproving brothers, said goodbye to some scolding girlfriends, and flew to Los Angeles to meet me.

She was driven to the airport by her sister-in-law and her fretful mother, who grimly refused to wish her luck or kiss her goodbye.

That Saturday morning when I pulled out of a campground nestled in a wrinkle of the Angeles mountains and started up Highway 5, north to San Francisco, Cathy was at my side.

The smog was already seeping into the San Gabriel valley, and through the rear-view mirror I got a last glimpse of a skyline that looked as if it had been fondled by a million dirty fingers.

For one long month and ten thousand miles we said a lingering goodbye to America.

We followed the highway up the spine of California, explored San Francisco, where I said my farewells to an old roommate who had come to this city to write poetry and find his soul. Then we nosed our way east with the stubborn suburbs of the Bay area tattering past our window until, finally, we shook them off like ragged cobwebs, climbed Donner Pass and started across the long, rangy breastbone of America.

Here we drifted for one long week, making love in truck stops, bathing in wild mountain streams, falling asleep in dark mysterious crevices into which we would pull when we were too weary to drive any more, and awakening every morning to find with surprise that the land which the night before had looked so menacing and forbidding was actually green and innocent, chequered with tilled fields, or showing nothing more sinister than a distant farmhouse.

During this month I wrote nothing at all. Cathy kept saying to me, "You're a writer, but you're not writing," and I would invariably answer, "I don't feel like writing."

In my mind I was too busy saying goodbye to America to write, turning over memories I had of this land to which I had come thirteen years before as a frightened twenty-year-old.

It is the ultimate inkblot test— this America—a place so vast and multifaceted that one sees in it partly what is there and partly what is in one's own mind. But I will aim my arrow at the moon and tell how I saw America for thirteen years: I saw her as a landlady.

When I was in school I had been thrown onto the mercies of so many landladies that I came to recognize them not merely as owners and renters of property but as a new species of life crawling out of the primordial economic soup, evolving God only knew into what terrifying new forms.

I had had one landlady who had come to this country as a Swedish teenager, had forgotten her Swedish and learned her English badly, and so spoke in a gibberish that only long acquaintance with her made intelligible on first hearing. I had had one landlady who had come here as a German schoolgirl, who during the daylight was fussy and exacting about where eggs should be placed in the refrigerator, where textbooks should be left in the living room, who abhorred any intestinal sounds from her roomers, and who insisted that one day out of every week I vacate my room for a thorough cleaning with antiseptic, and yet every Friday night would come hammering drunkenly at my door demanding violent lovemaking. I had had one landlady who went mad at nights, practising fellatio on her youthful lodgers while gospel music chorused in the background and she tried, vainly, to simultaneously mouth favourite biblical passages, but who in the daylight hours was an inspector of mental hospitals in Southern California.

So much like America, the quintessential landlady: simultaneously carnal, cruel, capricious and tender; demanding and exacting and sometimes unspeakably vulgar and whorish. But no matter that she may boil soup for you when you are sick and feverish, and make love to you when you are sad and lonely, or tell you lies about yourself when you are crestfallen and defeated, there is one thing, like all landladies, that she will never do: she will never forgive you if you do not pay the rent.

We drifted into the bony landscape of Chicago, where Cathy said a final farewell to some old friends and wept over her estrangement from her mother, and then we went north into Canada, caught a ferry across to Nova Scotia and roamed through backwater villages and picturesque seascapes.

One late night we passed through New York; I awoke just as we were winging through the city, which smelled pungent and sweet like a sickly old cow, and saw the carcass hanging spiny and gaunt against the dark skyline.

Then we were in the Carolinas and so bone-weary from endless driving that we had to stop. We pulled into an ugly motel consisting of dark bungalows drawn up around a green pool and took a room there. We put on our bathing suits intending to swim but instead stood hesitantly at the edge of the pool wondering whether we were wise to dive into water which looked shiny and green like the rheumy eyes of an old cat.

The motel was run by two wizened old women who gave off the odours of a hospital bed. We were circling the pool when one of the women suddenly came hurrying down the walkway, gesturing to the other, who met her eye, pursed her lips grimly, and headed for the office.

There standing before the counter was a young black man. The old woman who had been forewarned entered the office and engaged in earnest, brief conversation with the man. He wheeled and headed angrily for his car.

I heard him say bitterly to a woman in the passenger seat, "There's no vacancy!"—just before he drove off in a swirl of marl dust.

A baby was sleeping in the back seat of the car.

The sign in front of the motel, scrawled in a cursive red neon blaze, spoke volumes: it said, "Vacancy."

It was a graphic example of the trait in American society I had come to most passionately despise: The endless preaching about freedom and equality, the constant yapping about land of the free and home of the brave, accompanied by the hypocritically nasty practice. I was so enraged that I wanted to smash something in the room. Cathy was horrified and wouldn't let me. We had an ugly fight, our first.

Then we collapsed into bed, muttering.

Two nights later we pulled into Miami. Here an enclave of Jamaicans fleeing the socialist regime of Michael Manley had lately established themselves, many of them cousins and friends from my childhood days. We stopped off to see them before departing for Jamaica and were ambushed with dire prophecy about the violent end that awaited us on the island.

They came bearing grim news. Things were not the same in Jamaica as they used to be; things were bad, very bad. There was crime in the streets, senseless violence against white people; rape was commonplace; one dared not venture out after dark. You couldn't find a dog bad enough to protect you from the burglars, thieves, murderers. You slept with a gun under your pillow; you drove with your windows and doors locked; you did not pause at stop signs.

The island was haemorrhaging its middle class. Every day in Miami I'd run into another face, another name that had recently migrated. Shock, disbelief greeted me when I said that I was on my way back. Back to Jamaica? I was clearly out of my mind. Some of these new arrivals said so with looks; some said so plainly.

A dark-brown Jamaican sits me down in the living room of my cousin's house. The man does not know me personally, but being married to my childhood friend, he regards me as a distant erring relative.

"I like you," he says in a kindly, earnest voice. "Let me tell you my story. I had a farm in Spanish Town. I kept chickens there, and grew cane. Every day for the last year they come into my fields and steal my cane. Every day, mark you, not once a week, or once a month but every day. So I call the police and they say, 'What can we do?' I reason, OK, so they steal the cane in the fields, so I won't plant any fields I can't get a watchman to patrol. The next thing I know the Ministry of Agriculture sends an inspector to see me. He says, 'You don't plant cane in all your fields. You have idle land. If it stays idle, the government will take it away from you and give it to a poor man who is willing to cultivate it.' I say to the inspector, 'I must plant cane so that people off the streets can come and steal it?' He says, 'This government will not tolerate idle land. The white man day in Jamaica is done. If you don't like it, you can take the prime minister's advice, and leave. Migrate.' So I said to myself, 'Good, you brute! I'll do what you say.' And I give away my property, Tony. I sold it to a man who paid me half what it was worth, but in American money deposited in a bank right here in Miami. At least, I got my money out. Manley can't take what I have left there, because I have nothing left. And Manley can't seize my land and pay me with government bonds that I can cash in the year 2025, when I'll be dead and gone. And you want to know why I sold out? Because here is this man, an inspector with the Jamaica government, telling me that the white man's day is done in Jamaica. Now if a government official is telling me this, and this same government is supposed to be protecting me, what chance in God's name do I have?"

Cathy looks puzzled at this dark-brown man calling himself white. But here is a great deal of sagacious head-nodding and murmuring from the other Jamaicans in the room, all of whom have a similar story to tell.

And everyone in the room can tell you in an instant what's to blame for the island's fallen state: The People's National Party and its garrulous leader, Prime Minister Michael Manley.

I do not know anything about Michael Manley, but I know a little about his father, Norman Washington. He was an imposing brown man reputed to be a brilliant thinker. When I was a child his picture seemed to be in the *Gleaner* almost daily. The elder Manley was a barrister, a Queen's Counsel trained in London. He had married an Englishwoman, his cousin, and Michael was their son.

There are two major political parties in Jamaica—the People's National Party (PNP), and the Jamaica Labour Party (JLP)—and in my youth I was hard pressed to tell the difference between them. At election time there were always vague mutterings about socialism from the PNP and equally vague rumblings about capitalism from the JLP, but nobody really took the doctrinal utterances of either party too seriously. There were dirt-poor PNP members and equally dirt-poor JLP members, and since the majority of the electorate was illiterate, it was hardly to be expected that doctrine would carry the day. And doctrine never did. Personalities, however, were quite a different matter.

The PNP was always the party of the Manleys; the JLP, on the other hand, was associated with its founder, a semi-literate labour organizer by the name of Alexander Bustamante, who was the cousin and bitter rival of the elder Manley. During my boyhood, the political stage was dominated by these two feuding cousins. When I left Jamaica in September, 1962, Bustamante as head of the Labour Party had just been elected Prime Minister. Labour won again in 1967, gaining 33 seats in Parliament against 22 for the PNP. Norman Manley retired from politics in 1969, passed the leadership of the PNP to his son Michael, and dropped dead six months later. The Kingston airport at which Cathy and I would land now bore his name.

In 1972, the People's National Party finally swept into power with Michael Manley as their leader, and right away began—if the hordes of expatriate Jamaicans were to be believed—the downfall of the island. Manley announced that his government would pursue a policy of democratic socialism and instituted a series of land reform measures directed against absentee landlords. Land deemed to be "idle" was purchased by the government, paid for in bonds redeemable at a distant date, and turned over to small tenant farmers for cultivation. Squads of relief workers were organized and employed by the government to clean the streets. These "Crash Programme Workers", as they were called, were seen by well-off Jamaicans as socialist provocateurs sent into their neighbourhoods to stir up trouble. The expatriates tell of driving out of their gates and encountering knots of Crash Programme workers squatting on the shoulder of the road, glaring murderously at them.

Night after night we hear the same stories. Manley is a communist. He worships Castro. He gave money to the Rhodesian rebels. He is inciting the Jamaican poor; one day, the rabble will heed him, rise up and butcher the middle class. There are racial incidents daily in the streets. There is murder every day; no matter where you live, no matter what you do, you're not safe, your children are not safe, your wife is not safe.

These stories come from aunts and uncles and cousins and childhood friends. They sit in the living rooms of comfortable houses and tell the grim tales over and over again. Many of them have gotten their money out of the island. The signs are unmistakable: fine clothes; lavishly furnished homes; Cadillacs, Mercedes Benzes, BMWs in the driveway; jewellery dangling from the necks and ears and fingers of their wives. These Jamaicans are doctors and lawyers and dentists and managers and businessmen and veterinarians. On the island they had maids and gardeners and nannies. Their women shudder at the horror of Jamaica; their men voice outrage, anger. Some of them still have businesses on the island to which they must fly weekly: Miami is turning into a bedroom community for Jamaica.

But the poor Jamaican, you say, in defence of a government you have never lived under, a prime minister you know only through rumour, isn't Manley trying to help the poor?

"Let me tell you about the Jamaican poor," a man says sagaciously.

He is not a bad man; just this evening, we saw him playing fondly with his son, kissing his daughter. He is a husband and provider; he believes in God; he was a community leader in Jamaica, a man of substance and background.

So now he tells us about the poor Jamaican.

"You know what the poor Jamaican wants? He wants to do two things. First he wants a woman he can breed. It's important for him to have children. He likes the idea of flashing his dick around the countryside. Second, he wants rum to drink on a Saturday night. To him, that is next in importance only to a woman to breed. He'll work for you from Monday to Friday, and if you watch him like a dog, he'll do enough to get by. I don't say he'll do a good job because God knows that basically he's a lazy fellow, but if you watch him he'll do a passable job. So now it's Saturday morning and you give him his pay and he goes to his woman and gives her a few shillings for household expenses. Then after that you catch him in the rum bar."

Murmurs of assent.

"Saturday night he's drunk by nine o'clock. Stone, blind drunk. So he goes home and grinds his woman and the next morning, Sunday, he gets up and puts on his Sunday best and walks to church. After that you catch him playing dominoes all day and drinking a little rum. Come Monday morning and you call him over and say, 'Hubert, I got a little job to do. If you do it for me, it might mean a little extra money for the week. What you say?' He looks at you out of the corner of his eyes. 'Lawd, God, sah,' he bawls, 'Hard work nearly kill me already, sah. Every week me work me finger to de bone. Is all me can do to keep up wid what me already have fe do, sah.' So you argue with him. 'But look here, Hubert,' you say, 'This little extra work will mean more money for you and you family, you know man. I going give you a ten dollar a week more.' He begins to wail. 'God Almighty, sah, me could use de little extra money, but de body weak already from all de labour, sah. De sun hot 'pon me head every day and me heart feel weak from all de hard work, sah.' You can't get him to do the extra work for you. You could beg till you turn blue.

"That is how the typical poor Jamaican is. You want to know why he's poor? He's poor because as long as he can flash his dick around and drink a little rum on Saturday, and play a little domino on Sunday, and once in a while a little backyard cricket, he is a happy man, content with his life. And so help me God, if Manley will just leave this brute alone, everything would be fine in Jamaica."

"Hear, hear," the roomful of exiles murmur.

"Jamaica mash up," one says.

"Jamaica finished. Over. Done," another declaims.

"Anybody who goes back to Jamaica now is a fool. A damn fool."

The eyes in the room swing accusingly at us. Cathy squirms uneasily at the stares.

CHAPTER 4

"Everyone going, and you coming."

So my brother greets us at the airport.

We are immersed in a throng that has just deplaned, and all around us in the cavernous terminal are piles of luggage, boxes, cartons, attended by a milling crowd of passengers. My brother isn't supposed to be in the customs hall, but he has an influential friend. The customs officials, wearing the hardened look of the bored—the trademark expression of West Indian civil servants—are pawing through open suitcases, filling out declaration forms, and levying fines as the mood takes them. Here and there passengers bicker with a customs officer, and sometimes a peal of derisive laughter rings through the room as bystanders react to one of the many raging debates.

"Me is a sufferer," a man bellows. "Me have ten pickney. De radio is for me Mumma. Her heart bad. De doctor say de radio cool her nerves."

"You still must pay duty 'pon it," the official says stonily.

"Lawd God, man!" the passenger's voice rises in outrage. "Why you must be so wicked, man? Why you want to step 'pon de head of a poor sufferer? You don't know times changing in Jamaica, man! Negar man can't take any more suffering—him heart sick wid pain and suffering."

Laughter rustles in the wake of his tirade.

The enormous crowd smells of perfume, sweat, and humus. It is a sweltering night, the air heavy and sweet with humidity, the pungent tang of kerosene fuel, the fragrance of the ocean.

Only minutes ago we were flying on the edge of a menacing blackness with nothing visible through the window except the frail light on the wing-tip of the jet and occasionally, illumined by a distant flash of lightning, shoals of dark thunderheads on the horizon.

Then the plane began its descent. We knifed through a black cloud, the plane rattled and shook, and suddenly far below we saw lights that marked the presence of an invisible land.

"Jamaica," I whispered to Cathy, pointing to a light so tiny and wavering that it could have been the illumination of a lost firefly.

She squeezed my hand with excitement as the plane shuddered.

The line we now stand in snakes raggedly across the terminal, its head nudging the inspection station manned by a slouching customs officer. Voices jabber in a mixture of Jamaican patois and English. Conveyor belts rumble into the room, bearing fresh loads of cardboard boxes and battered suitcases.

The faces in the room are black, brown, swarthy, some glinting with the yellow glow of the Oriental, some an indescribable stew of races—a jumble of delicate cheekbones, puffy negroid lips, and glinting green eyes. Long dead Englishmen peer out of coal black faces; former slaves smoulder under the yellowish skins of mulattoes; an East Indian ancestor lies mummified inside the body of the half-Chinese lady resignedly waiting her turn to battle customs. "Out of Many, One People," is the Jamaican motto.

My eyes are drawn to the familiar gestures of the crowd. I see a woman to my right "cut her eyes" at a man who has ogled her. She rolls them in the corners of their sockets in a familiar Jamaican gesture and the man quails at this wordless reproof and looks long and hard at his shoes. I hear another woman kiss her teeth—making that sibilant hissing sound with her lips which, for Jamaicans, signals inexpressible contempt. When I lived in America, I couldn't use these gestures. My mind was imprisoned in conventional speech.

The crowd is peculiarly Jamaican. In America crowds are geometric things: they form straight, disciplined lines; they have shape and order like a fishbone. In Jamaica a crowd is living tissue. It throbs, stinks, and bleeds all over a room. There is no containing it in mere geometry; it will not suffer conduits or levees or postural correctness. The English for years railed against the Jamaican habit of slouching in public places, and so here and there in the throng you can see vestiges of their teachings: a grim, stout black man who shuns a nearby post, stands obdurately straight, and disdainfully eyes the horde of leaners and saggers surrounding him.

It is all here in this airport. Three hundred years of colonialism: a people who were brought here as slaves or came as plunderers, who grew into nationhood simultaneously clinging to the passive resistance mentality of the enslaved while unconsciously admiring and aping the ways of the English master; who resent and despise authority of all kinds and make a national sport of constantly haggling with it; a people mixed and hybridized in every conceivable way—racially, culturally, linguistically, spiritually—and to whom life has been so capricious and unfair that they have come over the centuries to see it as the stuff of makeshift drama.

"Lawd God Almighty, tell me who more wicked dan a Jamaica brown man? Who on dis earth more wicked and hard dan a Jamaica brown man?" a woman shrieks, as she unknots the corner of her handkerchief in which she had tied money that she must now pay out for duty.

The customs official, a brown man with a stubborn expression pasted on his face, is aloof to her shrieking and impassively continues to fill in his quadruplicate forms. The crowd chuckles at the woman's fulminations.

"Is true," a voice assents. "Brown man is de hardest man God ever put 'pon dis earth."

"Gimme a white man any day," another concurs, "no matter how him wicked, for him can't be any more wicked dan brown man."

It is the beginning of Greek chorusing that will surge through the crowd for a few minutes.

Beside me, Cathy looks bewildered, afraid.

"Everybody in Jamaica leaving, and you coming," my brother repeats gloomily.

The airport in Kingston is near the end of the Palisadoes peninsula, which bends across Kingston harbour like a claw, giving it a sheltered anchorage. The peninsula is a thin strip of land; you can stand in its middle and hear the surf thundering against the windward side that faces the open sea, and see the same ocean licking peacefully at the brown sand on the sheltered shore.

The road winds down the centre of the peninsula, past the ruins of an old blockhouse that was once part of the Port Royal fortress but now lies half buried in the sand, past fetid swamps whose mangroves tiptoe out of the darkness on thin, knobby roots. After that it plunges down a flat spit of land where the wind and surf bleat endlessly.

My brother points to a spot off the side of the road as the place where a man and a woman were murdered a month ago. The man had parked there with a girlfriend one fateful night; out of the shadows had crept a vagabond armed with a machete. Cathy shudders as we flash past the place.

Across the landlocked harbour the lights of Kingston glitter, and out of the night an enormous mountain looms, its massive flanks brooding over the city. When I was a child, this mountain was swollen with green and loveliness. Then the mining for gypsum began, and soon the face of the mountain was ripped open and pulpy white marl exposed. Now even in the darkness you can see the excavated wound, and during the daylight you can see tractors and earthmovers gnawing ceaselessly at its ragged edges.

We drive past the rotting hulks of freighters that lost their way through the shoals and impaled themselves on the windward claw of the peninsula. During the daytime, you can see the ocean licking at their open ribs, pelicans soaring above their empty wheelhouses.

Then we are on Windward Road, and nosing into the first of Kingston's thousand slums. We drive through quickly, ignoring the noises and clamour, not looking at the rows of dirty shops, the ramshackle hovels, the throngs of people who slouch and lean and sag and eye us as we pass. The stench trails after us and lingers in the open car.

It is not to be a night of celebration. The prodigal son has come home but no one is glad. A few old friends come by my brother's house; a cousin or two pops in; an odd aunt or uncle. You are mad for coming back, they all say. We're all trying to leave. Jamaica is dead. One friend I telephone is openly suspicious at my returning.

Why are you back, he asks over and over, when everyone else is leaving? Because I want to teach, I say. Teach? In Jamaica? Why don't you teach in America? I want to help my homeland, I finally blurt out, embarrassed as though I'm forced to tell a dirty secret. Help your homeland? he asks scornfully. Now that the communists are in power, he says, only communists are coming back. Everyone else is leaving.

We sit outdoors and drink rum until late. Then we go to bed. My brother's house is "grilled," like all the houses in this neighbourhood, and he must lock it up. There are cast-iron burglar bars across the windows; there are iron gates inside the front door. The bedroom area of the house where we will sleep is sealed off from the living room and kitchen by a wrought-iron gate. My brother locks it carefully.

The thief who might break into the house, he reassures Cathy, can't get into the rooms where we sleep. Sometimes thieves do try to get into the rooms where the family sleeps. Sometimes they have guns, machetes, knives, are drunk and out to do murder. But, he hastens to add, because we have this gate, we are safe from the thief.

But her fears are not allayed. She has seen the gun in his waist and worries.

We do not sleep well that first night. We do not make love. We lie in a dark room and listen to the sounds of the dark suburbs. The dogs outside stir and occasionally growl and sometimes break into a frenzied barking. That is what dogs are for in Jamaica—to warn against the footfalls of the intruder. So we lie still and listen. The mosquitoes whine around us. We doze and are suddenly snapped awake, our hearts beating wildly at unknown noises.

But eventually we fall into a fitful sleep. And sometime in the darkest and deepest part of the night we hear a terrifying sound: four shots in the night. The dogs go wild. In the distance a siren wails. We lie still, deathly still, and listen for more. But there is no more. The dogs settle wheezily on the front porch like aging watchmen, and light from a gibbous moon throws the tangled shadows of burglar bars against the wall.

Next morning my brother informs us that a man who lives down the street fired four shots at an intruder last night.

"A-good," his East Indian cooks mutters fiercely. "Me hope dey kill every one o' de damn thief in Jamaica."

CHAPTER 5

Our new home was a small backwater village on a plateau in a central parish. It consisted then of some five or six churches, two ratty shops, a dirty rum bar, a tiny post office painted battleship grey, a police station that was shuttered tight by seven o'clock, and a cubbyhole library whose collection numbered no more than a hundred dog-eared books. The road through the village was less than a half-mile long and so lightly travelled that village dogs often sunned themselves right in the middle of it. There was a market where higglers gathered on Saturdays to hawk fruits and vegetables and where a butcher sold meat hacked from the bleeding carcass of a cow dangling off a hook.

Longstreet was located in the thickly forested heart of Jamaica that has been only slightly thinned out after three centuries of logging. Acres of grazing pastures planted in guinea grass are encircled by dense woodlands that clot the mountainside in a dark wall of solid undergrowth. The village had running water, no telephone, sporadic electricity often knocked out by afternoon thunderstorms, and was so small that strangers passing through were trailed after by stares of curiosity and suspicion.

Here we went house-hunting. We could not live in the tutors' residence on the school grounds because every flat had already been claimed, so we poked around the village looking for a small house that was not too expensive. My salary as a tutor at the school could range anywhere from three hundred dollars to six hundred dollars a month, depending on where on the pay scale the Ministry of Education decided I should be placed. Assuming that we would be on the lower end, we could afford a house that rented for no more than one hundred dollars. That is what we now looked for in the narrow country lanes meandering off the main road and winding in switchbacks up to the surrounding mountain villages.

We found a house two miles from the school off a quiet country lane. It shared a hilltop with a larger house for which it had once been the servants' quarters. Both houses overlooked acres of guinea grass pastures that stretched in hummocks and dales down to a range of mountains at whose base the land lapped and wreathed in a sea of forests. Every window in our house was filled to bursting with the lushness of greenery and mountains, and the stillness of the hilltop during even the blazing heat of the day was the whisper of God in our ear. It was a setting of incomparable loveliness.

We were shown the house by a white Jamaican farmer named Jameson who owned all the land in the valley as far as the eye could see and whose family had lived on it for generations. He looked after the two houses, he explained, for a friend who now lived and worked in New York. Jameson's own grand manor house stood on a commanding hill opposite our own and was the only other dwelling in sight.

The isolation of this hill worried me, especially when I saw that all the windows of the house were stapled over with burglar bars. I circled the house nervously, surveying its sturdy frame of concrete blocks, its open cellar, its reserve water tank smothered under a rind of green scum. Behind the house a clotted bushland was held at bay by a mortarless cut-stone wall that beaded around the perimeter of the hilltop like a necklace. The layout of the house was simple: a bare concrete floor stained red, two bedrooms and a shower, a tiny kitchen, a small drawing room and a dining room. It had hot and cold running water, a gas stove, and a hook-up for a washer and a dryer.

"Have you ever had any trouble up here with thieves?" I asked Jameson, as we stood on the sloping lawn eyeing the small house.

"Thief?" Jameson seemed amused. "Up here? It too quiet up here for thief."

"I love it," Cathy whispered at my side.

"It's very lonely," I said.

"I love it," she repeated.

We took the house, paid Jameson the first month's rent and arranged for him to screen the windows. Then we went to Kingston to buy our furniture.

To drive from the country into Kingston, which Jamaicans call "town," is to travel from one half of the Jamaican soul to the other. In the countryside the pace is stately and slow and the ways and airs of the people are polite and ingratiating. Young and old are soft-spoken and calm and seem to radiate a benign patience and gentleness. In Kingston the looks of the young are suspicious and ugly. Rage and defiance seem to impregnate every gesture and glance.

When I was a child practically every home in middle-class Kingston wore an open veranda around its front like a bib, and it was to this cool spot that people retired at the end of the day to drink and chat in the night breezes. Now the verandas of many houses were enclosed behind wrought-iron cages and Kingstonians took their nightly airing and drinks behind padlocked gates. Night brushed over the city like a menacing shadow, and in the darkness you heard sirens occasionally baying in the distance.

Everywhere in Kingston we heard the same litany of doom: Jamaica was finished, doomed. Manley had instilled hatred into the hearts of the poor and set class against class. The talk was edgy and poisoned with rumour and gossip. This one was leaving because he had heard that the government intended to bring Cuban troops into Jamaica, to abolish free travel, to make the island a prison. This one had heard that soon "they" would start confiscating property and freezing bank accounts. "They" were going to do this; "they" were plotting to do that. Jamaicans have an instinctive dread of the unidentified "they" of capricious power and authority, no doubt inherited from slavery days when life and limb hung on the whimsical and unappealable word of the slavemaster. Every time Manley opened his mouth in Parliament, he evoked this ancient fear of arbitrary power and fuelled the spread of panic and suspicion.

So we ate, drank, and talked at nights under the glare of a hundred bulbs, and when the talk occasionally faltered the men peered out watchfully at the darkness and listened intently to the barking dogs for a warning against the intruder.

Thieves had stalked the Jamaican night for as long as I could remember. In the old days they carried stones, clubs, knives and machetes, and the householder armed with a pistol and a faithful dog had the advantage. But in these troubled times the thieves walked the night with guns and a murderous fire in their eyes.

Grandfather Winkler had slept all his life with a gun under his pillow, and on one or two occasions had fired a shot out of a darkened window to warn a thief in the yard that the householder was armed. My father had also slept with a pistol under his pillow. One night he heard a thief breaking into his car, which was parked under the portico beside his bedroom, and he crept to the window, took aim at the burglar who was only a few feet away, and would have killed him if my mother hadn't woken up and screamed, sending the man bolting into the night. When I was a child, a man who lived on our street was awoken by the sound of an intruder climbing through his bedroom window. He reached for his gun and fired three bullets at point blank range into the silhouette, killing the thief instantly at the foot of his bed.

And there was even the time when a thief had saved an uncle from prison and our extended family from shame.

In his travels throughout the Jamaican countryside, the uncle had discovered that many of the small mountain villages and hamlets had no theatre and that in order to see a picture show the country dweller had to travel a great distance by infrequent buses. Since he knew how fond Jamaicans are of moving pictures, he saw a golden opportunity to buy a projector, rent some old cowboy films, and charge admission to see them in the country parts. But he had no capital for this investment. Even though he made a good salary as the manager of a tyre warehouse in Montego Bay, every penny he earned was devoured by the insatiable needs of his school-age children. So he borrowed money from the company till to buy his projector and rent the films, intending to pay it back with profits from his new venture.

Then disaster. He had just bought the equipment he needed when the company, for some inexplicable reason, ordered a surprise audit of the Montego Bay branch office. Once the auditors arrived, Uncle's embezzlement would be discovered, he would be sent to prison, and disgrace and ignominy would swallow up the family. Uncle paced the floor and chain-smoked and drank endless bottles of rum but couldn't find a way out of this fix. Then, the very night before the auditors were due from Kingston, like a godsend, the thief struck.

At three o'clock in the morning the uncle was alerted to the presence of the intruder by the strident ringing of an electric bell. Uncle had rigged up an alarm the maids could ring in his room because they been complaining about being haunted by the ghost of a fisherman who used to store his nets and lines in a cave behind the maid's quarters. The fisherman had lately died, and the maids swore that every night they heard his ghost prowling outside their window. But when the bell thrilled in the sleeping house at three o'clock that morning, it was to warn against a thief whom the maids could hear rummaging through the warehouse where the company stock was stored.

Uncle got his gun, stole out into the night, caught the thief red-handed rolling a single truck tyre down the driveway, and held the terrified man at gunpoint until the police arrived. The next morning the auditors arrived to conduct inventory.

The trial was held a few weeks later. Dressed in a serge suit and silk tie and exuding the wounded indignation of a victim, uncle testified that the thief had stolen nearly a thousand pounds worth of goods. Originally, Uncle had intended to blame every penny of his own embezzlement on the thief, but he later decided that the actual amount of his peculation would have seemed suspiciously symmetrical and small, so he dipped his hand into the till for another generous second-helping of company funds and also added this new sum to the thief's account.

During the uncle's testimony, the thief at first cowered in the dock and stared with disbelief, but then he realized that something was horribly amiss and began to bawl out his innocence on top of his lungs.

"He took twenty truck tyres and two big tractor tyres," Uncle said.

"Lawd Jesus God, sah!" the thief wailed. "All me take was de one tyre you catch me wid! Lawd God, sah, no tell lie 'pon me!"

"How many other tyres did he get?" the prosecutor asked.

"A dozen or so," Uncle replied. "Plus we can't find five batteries."

"Batteries, sah!" the thief howled. "How me one to carry heavy batteries, sah! How me to take batteries, sah! Is de one tyre him catch me wid dat me take! De one tyre! Me no take no truck tyre! Me no take no battery! Me no take no tractor tyre! All me take is de one tyre him catch me wid down de road!"

Of course, no one believed the thief although he wailed and shrieked and carried on in the courtroom like a man gone mad. Convinced by Uncle's testimony that the thief must have had several accomplices who got away, the prosecutor tried in vain to have the man name them, even promising leniency if he would. But the poor thief, who had acted alone, could only blubber that the white man was telling lie 'pon him poor head and that he had taken only the one tyre he had been caught with. This unwillingness to name his partners in crime told severely against the thief, for the prosecutor cited it as proof that he was a hardened criminal and recommended that the court show no mercy. The magistrate agreed and sentenced the poor man to fifteen years at hard labour. As the handcuffed thief was roughly dragged away by two constables, he shrieked his head off in a despairing voice,

"Fifteen year hard labour for one tyre! All me thief is de one tyre dem catch me wid! Fifteen year hard labour for one tyre! Lawd God Almighty, you know how much tyre me thief! De white man tell lie 'pon me!"

We spent the next few days going from one moving sale to another, pawing over the belongings of migrating Jamaican families, buying kitchen utensils, furniture, and odds and ends for our house in the hills of Longstreet. It was the same sad story everywhere we went. People were wary of what Manley's regime intended to do next and terrified of the wave of murders and shootings. They were getting out while the getting was good and were openly astonished that we could be moving in when everyone else was trying their best to get out. We haggled over prices and slowly accumulated the things we needed for our household. All we needed now was a refrigerator. We went to a shopping plaza to buy one and came across our first street murder.

The victim was a courier on his way to lodge money at the bank, and when we arrived at the shopping centre he had just been killed and lay crumpled at the feet of a curious throng, his head partly blown off, a torn briefcase near his outstretched hand.

The jabber of the curious surrounding the dead man was excited and feverish. One man, who said he had witnessed the whole thing from the window of a bus, was going through a lurid pantomime of what had happened. It was two men on a motorcycle, he said. He showed the very spot where they had ridden up to the dead man cutting him off on the sidewalk. He demonstrated how the passenger on the motorcycle had pointed a gun at the head of the victim and demanded the briefcase. The crowd gasped and held its breath. Revelling in the attention, the eyewitness continued in a melodramatic voice.

"But instead of giving de briefcase like dem ask, he hold on to it so," and here the man clasped his arms across his breast like one protecting a treasure from a thief.

"Him shoulda give dem de briefcase!" one man moaned.

"Give it to dem, of course!" another chorused.

"Money no good in heaven!" opined a stout higgler woman.

"So, de one on de back of de motorcycle—de one wid de gun—grab de briefcase outta him hand, and dem start to ride off, but instead of staying where him was, de man run after dem, holding on to de briefcase strap. Den me see de man on de back of de motorcycle push de gun inna de man mouth so!" and here he opened his own mouth obscenely wide and stuck his middle finger deep down into his throat, "and me hear BAM! BAM! And me see de man jump back so when de shot lick him," the witness hurled himself backwards and bounced against the dense ring of people around him, "and him drop so!" which although he tried he could not demonstrate because the raptly attentive throng was so thick that there was no room for him to fall unless right on top of the dead man whose blood still seeped onto the concrete.

Cathy buried her fingernails in my arm and shuddered. People swirled and surged to get a glimpse of the dead man lying in a pool of his own curdling blood. Having finished his story, the witness began telling it all over again for a new round of faces.

"Dis is what you bring Cathy to!" my brother said to me with disgust. "Dis is de life you want to come back to! What you come back to dis damn madhouse for, eh?"

We went back to the mountains, unloaded our furniture and belongings, and began to arrange our house the way we wanted it. A breeze swept over the pastures and fanned us with the scents of wild flowers as we worked through the day, and by the time the sun was sinking below the rim of the mountain, we were finished.

Our neighbours on the hilltop, Derrick and Heather Smith who both taught at the college, invited us over to their house for a cup of tea, and we went and visited with them.

Derrick was a curious product of Jamaican migratory patterns, a coal black Jamaican who spoke with such a marked Oxfordian English accent that at first we suspected him of faking it. Later, when we got to know him, we realized that migration at a young age to England and a strict upbringing had completely robbed him not only of his Jamaican accent, but also of his ability to speak the patois. Heather was a light brown Jamaican who had spent most of her life on the island, leaving only for the usual jaunt abroad to an English university, where she had earned a Master's degree.

"You'll like the school," Derrick assured me. "Plus we need you there desperately."

Later, we walked over to the manor house in which Jameson lived and drank lemonade with him and his wife in their spacious drawing room.

"I can't tell you," Mrs. Jameson said with feeling, "how nice it is to have another white couple living here. We get so lonely up here for a white face, it's terrible!"

"You can come and play badminton at nights," Jameson promised. "We do that quite often."

"Now our children are gone back to school in England, it's so lonely here!" Mrs. Jameson wailed.

"We are the only white family in this whole village," Jameson added. "But we've been here forever, before any of them. He was the first." He pointed to a shiny oil portrait of a supercilious looking eighteenth-century gentleman dressed in riding clothes and holding a plaited crop. "He came here in 1710. Since then, a Jameson has lived in this valley. He's still here, in fact. You'll find him in the graveyard of the corner church."

"Sometimes I just long to see another white face, " Mrs. Jameson chimed in. "You know what I mean? It's not that I have anything against seeing their faces all the time, it's just that I get lonely. It's like a man who sees nothing around him all day but cow, cow, cow, after a while, he's just dying to glimpse horse."

"But now, I don't know what's going to happen to the tradition after we are gone," Jameson continued. "The children aren't going to stay here like we did. I was born just down the road from here, and I always knew that I belonged here. But the children don't feel that at all. They're interested in night life, theatre, cricket, they want to be with their own kind of people. I don't know what we'll do with the property when we get old."

"How much property do you own?" I asked.

"About six thousand acres," he said. "I raise beef. I supply all the beef to the aluminium company."

"Now when people spot a white face coming from afar, they can't just automatically say, 'There's a Jameson'," Mrs. Jameson said with a smug smile. "For it could be a Winkler."

"By the way, if you ever need anything," Jameson suggested, "see my headman, Brown. He lives in the house at the bottom of your driveway. Here, I'll introduce you to him. Brown! Brown!"

A black man in his late thirties shambled into the living room clutching his cap in his hands and exuding an air of ingrained servility.

"Yes, Missah Jameson?"

"Brown, this is Mister and Missus Winkler. They rented the Johnson house. I told them to see you if they need anything."

"How'd de do, sah!" Brown said pleasantly. "Good evening, Missus Winkler."

"Brown's a good boy," Jameson added after the headman had gone. "He's been with me for years. Absolutely dependable."

"He didn't used to be that way, but Richard trained him," Mrs. Jameson said conspiratorially. "They all have to be taught. Discipline doesn't come naturally to them the way it does to us."

The darkness came to our hilltop. On this first night we would spend in our own house in Jamaica, we sat on the stoop and watched the dusk seep into the valley with a tang of cool in the evening breeze and a flight of egrets from the fields into the darkening woods. The sky slowly drained of its searing whiteness, and in the dimming light, the mountains bled with the purple streaks of a bruise. Swallows and bats soared overhead, cattle lowed in the fields, and calves brayed for their mothers.

Then the mosquitoes descended on us with a vengeance and we had to retreat inside our screened house. In a profound and fearful silence so strange and new that it made us uneasy and talkative, we ate dinner. On the mountaintop, our house threw off a thin gauze of light on the great and bottomless beyond of darkness that enfolded the earth. After dinner we walked out into the yard and stared at constellations and stars beyond counting, at the Milky Way hanging from the black cavity of the sky like a spider's gossamer, at a night filled with clarity and beauty that took our breath away. The croaking lizards had begun their chorusing in the woodlands, and the dark pastures rang with their guttural song.

When we turned off the last light in our house, the night snapped shut like a jaw and we were swallowed up in the very mouth of death. Cathy gasped. I reached under the bed to reassure myself that the machete I had bought for protection was still there. A breeze whooshed over the pasture and a clammy coolness brushed our cheeks on the pillow.

CHAPTER 6

The next morning there was a staff meeting at the school. Expatriates and natives, the tutors gathered in an upstairs room to be addressed by the vice principal, acting for Dr. Levy who, I was told to my surprise, had gone on sabbatical. He was a severe looking black man with a head shaped like a beehive and the crimped mouth of the habitual classroom disciplinarian. We sat and listened to him while he explained in a steady voice that something sinister was afoot among the students.

We were an odd collection of Jamaicans, white expatriates, and Caribbean small islanders. Among us the five white faces shone conspicuously: Peter Matheson, a young itinerant Englishman who made a living as a globetrotting teacher in underdeveloped countries; Melissa Richardson, a homely Englishwoman who had been at the school now for eight years and seemed to be hardening before our very eyes into permanent and dishevelled spinsterhood; Mrs. Mendoza, a stylish Canadian usually dressed in an expensive frock and sporting bangles and beads which made her look as though she was on her way to a cathedral wedding; Evelyn Moon, a tall and lanky Canadian volunteer who had just moved into the village with her two small children and emitted the compliant amiability of the professional do-gooder.

We five white faces sat dispersed throughout the group listening to the vice principal give his talk.

Among the West Indians were a Trinidadian mathematics teacher, Robert Black, who sat in a corner wearing the expression of overweening aloofness characteristic of his countrymen; and a native of Nevis named Raymond Hunt, who had lately graduated from the University of the West Indies and whose rhetoric dripped with socialism, revolution, and dislike of white foreigners.

So something was afoot. We listened to hear what it was. The vice principal droned on. The students had been asked to submit two names for election as leaders of the first year and second year classes. But they had pulled a trick, submitting the names of two reprobates who were totally unacceptable to the staff. Little did they know, however, that the staff was on to their trickery. The vice principal smiled without humour.

"But they are going to find out," he said, "that they can't put one over on us, that we know what they're trying to do, and will fix their business for them."

This meant something to the older teachers and they signified it by nodding grim approval. The rest of us stared at the vice principal and tried to follow his reasoning.

"What did the students do?" I asked.

The vice principal looked sharply at me.

"They're troublemakers," he said with a smirk. "But we know all about them and their ways."

"But what have they done?"

"One of them, the boy—his name is Carlton—was involved in a disreputable incident involving the girls' washroom in which unseemly remarks were passed. The other one, her name is Mavis, is a known troublemaker. But they won't get away with this little trick."

I could tell that the older tutors thought it bumptious of the new junior English staff member to be asking questions rather than sitting and learning and keeping his mouth shut, but I was determined to know more.

"But if they're the ones the students want as their representatives," I ventured to say, "why don't we just let them have them?"

The vice principal stung me with a sharp look.

"You don't understand the minds of these students, Mr. Winkler," he said tartly. "We understand them a little better than you."

Miss Webster, one of the older Jamaican teachers, took me aside after the meeting and enlightened me on the offence of the rabble-rouser Carlton. With a solemn and scandalized face, she explained that he had been heard to pass a remark expressing his intent to bore a peep hole in the bathroom wall of the girls' dorm through which he could ogle their private parts.

"Imagine that rude brute planning such nastiness," she said with a ferocious scowl. "And dis is de boy dey want to represent the second year class. I take Adolph Hitler first!"

I have always been a bad first-time lecturer. My heart trips and hammers, my throat becomes dry, I stand before the class struggling inwardly against hysteria and paralysis. The first word must be said and said quickly to overcome this fear, and usually when I bound into a classroom on the initial meeting I come bearing buoyant platitude or hearty greeting just so I can quickly break the ice. This first time in a Jamaican classroom was no different. If anything, it was worse because I desperately wanted to make a good impression on my students.

There was the long walk down the paved walkway past the royal palms and the towering flame heart trees, and then the unnerving climb up the soiled concrete steps and into the maw of the classroom where the students were already assembled and waiting. I stepped inside and they all jumped to attention like soldiers on parade. I stopped dead in the doorway, my mind in a whirl, until I remembered that this standing at attention when the teacher enters the classroom was a courtesy drilled into all Jamaican students from infancy and one that I myself used to practice. So here was my chance to break the ice: do away with this obsolete courtesy left over by the excessively ceremonious Englishman.

I placed my books on the desk and waved the students to be seated.

"From now on," I began, hoping that my voice did not sound as croaky to them as it did to me, "don't stand up when I come into the classroom. I'm not used to that and it makes me uncomfortable. Just stay in your seats while I call the roll."

A stony silence greeted this announcement. I fumbled for the roll book and began calling off the names on the roster. With the first name, a student leapt to her feet and said, "Here, sah!"

"You don't have to stand up when I call your names," I said. "Just say, 'here'."

After I had read the roll and looked at every face and tried my best to attach a name to it, I stood up and gave an introductory speech. I told them my name, emphasized that I was a returning Jamaican, and said the usual nervous platitudes about hoping to get to know everyone and to have a good and fruitful year with the class.

The students sat ominously silent. No one moved. Hardly anyone looked in my direction. Everyone seemed engrossed in studying their desk tops or observing unseen creatures on the concrete floor.

"Are there any questions?" I asked at the end of my speech.

Please ask a question, I whispered inwardly. Please ask anything just to help me over this hump.

No one said a word. No one stirred. No one looked at me. A doomsday silence swelled in the room. I glanced at the class. It consisted of some twenty-nine brown and black women and one effeminate black man who sat in the very back row, wore a jacket and tie, and was identified on the roll book as the Reverend Hamilton. I singled him out.

"Mr. Hamilton," I said over the rows and rows of expressionless faces, "I see that you're a minister. What denomination?"

"Church of the Holy Ghost, sah," he replied timidly in a falsetto voice.

A stout woman in the front row swivelled in her seat with effort and glared at him.

"No one is to talk, Hamilton!" she snapped.

"Sorry," he whispered, looking downcast.

"Why can't he talk?" I asked innocently. "He can talk if I ask him a question, can't he?"

The stout woman stared fixedly at the floor.

"What's your name?" I asked, the panic rising to flood spate. Something was amiss. They hated me·so intensely at first sight that they had entered into a conspiracy never to breathe a word in my presence.

She did not answer.

"Why is no one to talk?"

Nothing. Not a sigh, not a whisper. Somewhere in the classroom a belly bubbled hungrily and in the deafening silence it sounded like a draining sink.

I walked from one end of the room to the other—keep moving, always keep moving in times of tension—looking them over with what I hoped was appropriate mystification and good will. Nothing. The most hideous display of deadpan.

"All right, then," I said firmly. "If we can't talk, at least we can write. This is an English class and we are going to be doing a lot of writing in it. We will write at least one composition a week. So take out your books and write a composition on your home town or village. I won't be marking it, I just want to get an idea of what kind of work you can do."

Not a single solitary soul moved. Not a finger lifted a pencil, not a hand touched an exercise book. They sat before me row after row of mummified, expressionless faces. I had made such a bad impression on them that right before my eyes they had been collectively struck dead. How would I explain that thirty students entrusted to my care by the Jamaican government had all dropped dead the moment I began lecturing? My years of teaching American pothead students in California told me that there was only one graceful and intelligent thing to do: get the devil out of there before the class started decomposing.

"Well, in that case," I said in my huffiest tone, "you can carry on without a teacher."

I walked sternly and slowly out of the room like a postman bravely and desperately turning his back on a bad dog and went home.

It was a long and fretful weekend. My class had met on a Friday afternoon and I had two days to ponder what I would do on Monday, whether to throw myself at the mercy of the vice principal and confess that I had given my students a case of terminal catatonia, or to charge once more into the classroom and do my best to shake them out of their collective stupor.

"I can't believe this is happening to me," I told Cathy over and over again. "I just can't believe it! You should have seen them. They sat there and didn't say a word. Not a word!"

"There must be an explanation," she assured me. "Did you say something to upset them?"

"I told them my name."

"Don't be silly."

"I told them I was looking forward to spending the academic year with them. Maybe that was it? Maybe they found the idea so unbearable that they all passed out on the spot?"

"Did you give them homework?"

"Homework? I couldn't even get them to do classwork, much less homework! I asked them to write an essay just so I could see a sample of their work, and they didn't move. They just sat there!"

"There has to be an explanation."

"There is! They hate me! They can't stand the sight of me! That's the explanation!"

"They don't know you. How can they hate you?"

"God, I can't believe this is happening to me! On my first class meeting, too!"

Friday night passed like a funeral cortege. Cathy tried to cheer me up, but I was inconsolable. Saturday we went to the beach, but all I could think of was thirty glum faces staring impassively at me while I vainly tried to coax signs of life out of them. On Sunday I paced and brooded and went for a walk in the pastures during a drizzle and racked my brain for any hint of what I might have said or done to alienate the class and turn them all against me. Nothing occurred to me. Not a clue, not a glimmer, nothing at all.

That night as we sat with the Smiths having a drink in their drawing room and watching the sun set, all I could think about was that tomorrow I would once again have to brave that sea of hardened faces.

"How many students do you have in your class?" Cathy asked Derrick, trying to make conversation.

He laughed.

"I'm not sure," he said. "They wouldn't answer the roll."

I nearly jumped out of my chair.

"Really?" I gasped.

"Yes. They're on strike. Cheeky! Sat there and wouldn't say a word. Wouldn't even answer when I called their names. Just sat there."

"They did!"

He seemed puzzled by the elation in my voice.

"They did the same to me, too," said Heather. "I got so mad I wanted to reach out and box one of their faces."

"They're on strike!" I gushed over and over to Cathy as we walked back to our house in the darkness. "The whole school is on strike! Isn't it wonderful?"

"I'm so happy for you, sweetheart," she murmured.

The entire school was on a silence strike. At issue was the vice principal's refusal to admit the student representatives that the first and second year classes had voted for. He stood adamantly against admitting them, the students struck for a day, sulked over the weekend, closeted in their dorms planning action, and turned out at assembly on Monday morning intending to show collective resistance against the vice principal's obduracy. After the morning singing and sermon, the students remained in their seats looking disgruntled and militant, but the vice principal lectured them sternly about the wonderful opportunity the government had given them by allowing them to be educated free in this college and reminded them that if they did not want the chance they had gotten they could drop out now and have their places taken by some of the hundreds on the waiting list. This message seemed to sink in. A few scowls wreathed the faces of the assembled throng and one or two dissenting hisses and murmurs were heard. The staff filed out of the assembly hall with offended dignity while the students remained in their seats trying to sort out what to do next.

"If I had my way," the physical education teacher, a wiry Jamaican firebrand named Fay Murphy, was declaiming in the staff room, "I'd line every one of them up against a wall with a switch in me hand, and I'd say, 'You brute, you going to class or you not going? If you not going, get off de premises and now! No if's, and's, but's or maybe's! Now!'And if dey give me argument, I'd give dem one beast lick wid de switch and drive dere backside off the premises! A-whoa!"

"But Fay!" protested Miss Walker, a soft-spoken matronly woman whose waistline bespoke her love for creamy puddings. "You can't beat dese students. You can't beat big women. Dey're not children. Dey're big women!"

"Big woman!" Fay sneered. "Big woman! You come to me wid dis big woman foolishness! When you in my class you not a big woman. Me is de only big woman in my class. If you in my class, I couldn't care less whether you old enough to have one foot in de grave, you a pickney! Only one big woman in my class, and is I! If de Holy Ghost himself in my class, him is a pickney to me! Him must behave himself like a pickney 'cause me is de teacher and him is de pupil!"

The teachers laughed.

"Give dem hell, Fay," Raymond Hunt urged her on. "Give 'em hell!"

That afternoon I met once again with my class. This time as I set out from the staff room armed with the textbooks and a writing assignment, my heart was not racing as madly as it had done on my ignominious retreat. Pompously, I reminded myself over and over again that I was a duly empowered teacher in the employ of the Jamaican government and the students, my charges, were in a state of rebellion against the constituted authority which I represented. What had been appalling before was the thought that the students might dislike me personally, but knowing that it was only the school, the Ministry of Education, and the entire staff that they detested had put me in a decidedly more cheerful mood. I had even prepared a little homily against rebellion that I intended to deliver to any stubborn holdouts. But when I entered the classroom, to my surprise, the students not only sprang to attention as before, a few of them even smiled sheepishly.

Wearing what I hoped was my severest expression, I took roll. One by one, obediently and respectfully, the students answered their names as they were called, each one standing up beside her desk.

"So," I said, pacing before the blackboard, "the strike is over now, eh?"

A few students tittered.

"Who is your class leader?" I asked.

A stout woman in the front row turned around and looked at Hamilton, the only male student, who sat cringing in a far corner.

"Hamilton!" she hissed. "You is de man in dis room. You is we leader!"

"Me say me don't want de job," Hamilton protested feebly.

The roomful of women in the room glared at him.

"You is de man! You goin' be we leader. We vote you for de job and you goin' lead!" one of them grated.

"But me don't want be no leader!" Hamilton whined.

"Hush up you mouth and lead!" another woman said.

"Man suppose to lead, woman suppose to follow!" said a third.

Hamilton withered in his seat before twenty-nine openly contemptuous female stares.

"Well, Hamilton," I pressed, "are you the class leader?"

He gave an effeminate shrug and seemed to shrink in his seat.

"Yes, sah," he whispered. "So dey say!"

"Yes, sah!" corrected a woman. "Shut up 'bout de 'so dem say'."

"Yes, sah," Hamilton said, visibly cowed.

"Yes, sah, I am de class leader!" another glowering woman prompted.

Hamilton sighed.

"Yes, sah," he said with resignation heavy in his voice. "I am de class leader."

"So, is the strike over Hamilton, as far as your class is concerned?"

"Yes, sah. It over and done wid, thank God."

"Good!" I said coolly. "Now, take out your exercise books and write an essay about your home town or village. I'm not going to mark it, I just want to see what kind of work you can do."

With a flurry of movement, the students dug out their exercise books, took out their pens, screwed up their brows, and began to write. The charged silence of academic purpose and industry fell over the classroom as the universal student symphony of weary sighs, tapping fingers, and shuffling feet sounded.

The crisis was past, the strike over. When I left the class that afternoon, I carried under my arm the booty of thirty essays laboriously scrawled in a variety of hands detailing childhoods spent in villages of almost every Jamaican parish.

Chapter 7

The essays were ghastly. It was a shock to read them. Yet one was such a grammatical nightmare that I was paradoxically encouraged. It read:

Village life put me in a whole heap of funny mood. Sometimes boredom strike. What to do but bear up? Where to go? Who to chat to? This is how my village in Manchester effect my mood. Bus don't run there. No electric light is there. When night fall, everybody may as well go to bed seeing as nothing can be done about it. One night a woman went mad in the dark and hangs herself from a tamarind tree, but it was to dark to put the rope right around her neck and instead of breaking it it allow her to hang all night breathing still.

Next morning school children finds her and call the district ·constable and he chop her off with a machete and carry her to the clinic in Sav-La-Mar. When her neck fix she send to the madhouse in Kingston where she let out three months later. Since then everybody call her "Tough Neck" and the tree call "Tough Neck Tree." Tough Neck walk with her neck hang down and mad same way if I stay in my village maybe one night I might hang too because it very boring there at night with pure ugly country man all over the place.

This essay embodied some stereotypical mistakes that any English teacher could sink his teeth into. For example, it was obvious that the writer had a point to make about her village—that it was boring—and that she had struggled to impart it. Essays that have an incipient point incompletely made give any English teacher a sense of purpose. You can show the student the main point in its inchoate form and you can impart focusing techniques for bringing it out on a later try.

But even more encouraging were the grammatical errors embodied in the essay. It contained some juicy shifts in tense—as when the student goes from "went mad" to "hangs herself from a tree"—good ripe stuff over which any English teacher would drool. It also featured errors of subject/verb agreement—"he chop"—and one plump and wonderful run-on sentence—the last.

These are veritable dragons that transform any teacher of English into a rampaging St. George.

What is stupefyingly difficult for a teacher to overcome in student writing is the error of thinking, and thankfully, this paper and the others I received that day were beyond such a worry. A grammatical error, a shift in tense or a bad pronoun reference, is like a bacterial infection to which the dispensing teacher can apply a quick antibiotic fix and usually congratulate himself afterwards on having saved a sentence. But the error of thinking is a deeply recessed brain tumour requiring surgery that is likely to kill the teacher while sparing the student. One of my former American students, for example, had begun a paper with this memorable paragraph: "Reading is an acquired taste and one that I have not lately acquired. But I first acquired it when I read *Eye of the Needle* by Ken Follett. When I acquired this taste for reading, it made me desirous of more reading and greater acquiring. But I guess I watch too much television because I lost the taste for reading that I acquired after reading Follett. I wish I could acquire it again."

I do not know how to cope with such thinking. I don't believe that anyone does. You cannot combat it with principles of grammar because as it stands the passage is not ungrammatical. You can only deal with it on grounds of rhetoric, meaning that you can criticize it as simplistic and ineffective, which is the equivalent of rapping the student's brain. But that is a bottomless exercise that gets you nowhere and, if you take such things seriously, could give you a coronary at an early age.

Thankfully, my Jamaican students suffered from the gross diseases of bad writing, not from the miasmatic subtleties of bad thinking brought about by watching countless hours of vapid television that afflicted their American counterparts. I rolled up my sleeves and set to work.

I would teach, I made up my mind, the American way. I would never teach the way I had been taught as a child in Jamaica, which is the Englishman's way. England and America practise entirely opposite pedagogy in the classroom, and I believe that why they do so is as much a reflection of their opposing political worldviews as of competing education theories.

In the Jamaican classroom of my youth, the Englishman taught mainly by rote. He emphasized practice and drilled lessons into the students' heads until they could rattle them off in their sleep. He did not encourage questioning from students because he cared little about whether or not they understood what he was teaching so long as they could parrot it back. This was the pedagogy suitable to a hoary nation encrusted in stylizations, rites, ceremonies, and rituals that ranged from the unthinking obeisance paid the monarchy to the preservation of ancient customs in Parliament. It was the teaching method you would expect from a hierarchical and rigid society where advancement and preferment were based as much on accident of birth as on talent and industry. Knowing one's place in such a society was more important than understanding how one got into that place to begin with.

When I was child attending school in Jamaica, my head spun from daily drilling in every conceivable subject by tutors trained in England. In English, we parsed hundreds, thousands of sentences without understanding how their parts were related. In arithmetic, we memorized the multiplication tables without being taught that we were learning a shortcut form of addition. In Latin, we swatted and sang out verb conjugations in unison without the faintest glimmer of what they meant. In history, we committed to memory the dates on which Lord This did that without ever being told why he had done it. And if a student was naive enough to ask, he would probably be told to shut up and pay attention and not waste the class's time with stupid questions.

The result was that my classmates and I were collectively a bunch of idiot savants. We knew facts and figures but we did not understand what they meant. Ask us to recite the principal dates of the Norman invasion of England, and we would sit back and blow you out of your chair with a blast of erudition. Ask us why the Normans invaded England and we would stare at you as though you were demented.

This state of affairs led to some peculiar misadventures when I was a student. Once, for example, my Latin class at Cornwall College got a new teacher and he proceeded to drill us in the War Commentaries of Caesar. Of course, this meant that we had to learn the whole thing by heart, which was duck's soup to the hardened memorizers the whole class had by then become. But then the lunatic decided that for our final examination we would translate the first five hundred lines of it. I remember staring at the Latin text with bewilderment, wondering how on earth I could do a translation of it, and trudging wretchedly to school on the day of the examination, painfully conscious that after four years of Latin and one solid year of Caesar's turgid War Commentaries, I could no more translate it than I could predict the future from the guano of sea birds.

By the time I got to my class, I had steeled myself to the inevitable and was reconciled to failing the exam. But then I started to talk with the boy beside me, who looked just as fretful as I, and he confessed that he'd stayed up most of the night and had been able to render only the first line, "All of Gaul is divided into three parts." The boy behind us overheard our talk and ruefully admitted that he too couldn't make head or tail of Caesar. Soon the entire class was clustered around our single text and everyone was laboriously struggling to translate verbs and nouns whose conjugations we could have rattled off as easily as "Mary Had A Little Lamb."

We were grappling with Caesar when a classmate renowned for his slyness burst into the room waving a copy of the translation which, he boasted, he had stolen from the Latin teacher's desk in the staff room. Now we were in our element! Twenty-five of us gathered around the stolen paper and began to drum it into our heads at a frantic pace. By the time the master walked into the room, we had memorized it down to the last comma. Bursting with impatience to vomit out the translation before we forgot it, we fidgeted and tapped our feet and chewed our lips while the teacher leisurely passed out the exam papers. When he said, "Begin," he must have been astonished as each boy exploded in a fury of scribbling to set down the words he had just crammed. Every jack-man of us passed, much to the surprise and delight of the dimwitted teacher, who never caught on to how we did it.

The rote method of education practised by the Englishman has left an indelible mark on Jamaican society. You will find, for example, workers in key places who do their jobs with slavish obedience to the techniques they were taught but who haven't the foggiest idea why they are doing what they do. If you ask them to explain the underlying theory behind their work they cannot because it was never explained to them.

One example stands out distinctly in my mind. I had an uncle who was terminally ill with emphysema and committed to the Chest Hospital in Kingston. One humid afternoon he was seized with a suffocating attack, and when the nurse scrambled for the oxygen, she could not get the valve to work. While we all struggled with the contraption, a desperate call went out for a man named "Henry."

"Henry! Call Henry!" one nurse screeched to another in a separate building.

The cry for Henry rang from building to building while poor Uncle, bent over and turning blue in his bed, was stifling to death before our very eyes.

"Who's Henry?" I asked the frantic nurse.

"He de only one who know how dis machine work," she said urgently.

A few harried minutes later, Henry—an old black man dressed in ragged trousers—came panting to the room.

"De oxygen tank won't work!" the nurse bawled at him.

Henry took in the situation at a glance, scurried out of the building to the driveway where he picked up a big stone, then hurried back into the room. He raised the stone and gave the tank a stout whack right below the neck of the valve. With a hiss, the tank released its precious oxygen, which Uncle gasped at through his mask like a suffocating fish.

Afterwards, in a conversation with Henry, I learned that he hadn't a clue about how the valve on the tank worked or even what oxygen was, but that someone had taught him a few years ago to hit the tank in that particular spot with a stone if it should ever jam, and he had been successfully doing this ever since. None of the other nurses had mastered the exact spot to hit and Henry was not particularly keen on revealing it because doing so would make him less important, perhaps even dispensable, to the sanatorium. Since no one knew how to fix the valve so that it would never stick and never have to be whacked, this exercise had been periodically played out in the sanatorium now for some years. Every time an oxygen tank stuck, Henry came running with his stone like a doctor summoned to save a life in a crowded theatre, and he was every bit as pompous as a real medico about it.

From the Englishman's point of view, the way Henry was taught to do his job made perfect sense. To get Henry to understand the properties of oxygen, the Englishman would have had to teach him some chemistry and a dab of physics. To get him to understand how gas behaves under pressure, he would have had to teach him Boyle's Law and Charles's Law. To grasp the functioning of the valve, Henry would have had to be taught other theories and skills that ranged far afield of the job at hand. And since Henry was illiterate, to do any of these things meant first teaching him how to read and write. The next thing you know, you have educated Henry to the point that he begins to wonder what the devil you're doing in his country and who the dickens is this bloody Queen you expect him to bow down to morning, noon, and night. Better by far, as a matter of colonial policy, to teach Henry to whack the neck of the tank with a stone and leave things the way they are.

Americans, on the other hand, do not teach by rote: they

emphasize understanding. They stress mastering the operative principle, absorbing the "why" rather than the "what" of a subject. They spend endless hours in simplifying ideas and concepts, in elucidating them with homely illustrations, in relating them to practical arts and applications. Implicit in this effort is the idea that it is better to understand than to memorize, and this primal belief seems rooted as much in their political commitment to democracy as in any pedagogical theory.

For in contrast to the Englishman, who is a slavish devotee of inheritance, Americans are more interested in what you can do than in who your parents are. To them, Providence is the croupier who randomly disperses talents without regard to age, sex, creed or national origin, as the wooden phrase goes. Whose birth canal a soul has passed through on its way to incarnation in this world—a high-born lady's or a Cockney housewife's—is not a determinant that could chart its course for the rest of its days. If it is talented or gifted in any way, the soul can achieve the full measure of its gifts depending on its drive and ambition, and whether or not its parents drop their "h's" or mispronounce their "r's" is not likely to retard this progress to fulfillment.

The downside of the American system is that it is implicitly less disciplined than the Englishman's way. To memorize something, to swat and cram and learn by rote, requires and encourages disciplined and ordered thinking. To learn and grasp a fundamental principle does not. American students therefore seem less disciplined than their English equivalents. They tend to lack a solid bedrock of memorized truths to guide them later on in their academic life. For example, it is not uncommon for American teachers to find in the papers even of superior students misused irregular verbs. It is far less common in the papers of Jamaican students because when they are still barely able to toddle they are made to sit in a classroom and bawl out conjugations such as "give, gave, given"; "bring, brought, brought"; "sing, sang, sung." To this day, such chanteys ring still in my head from my kindergarten years. We said them over and over again, we chanted them hours on end until they became as reflexive as a blink.

In any event, I would teach the American way. It would matter less to me what the students had memorized and could spit out on their papers. What I would try to teach were the fundamental reasons and principles behind even such an arbitrary Elysian mystery as grammar. When I was done with my students, even if they did not know, they would at least understand.

At the next class meeting I set down the ground rules. We would start from scratch. We would begin with what a thesis is and how you compose and use one in an essay. We would examine the kinds of specific detail writers use to make a point, study basic rules of punctuation and grammar, and emphasize the principles behind them.

The students looked up silently at me like fish in an aquarium.

We would also have a participatory class. If you had a question, ask it. If you had a doubt, ask for further explanation.

Some squirming accompanied this announcement.

I launched into my introductory lecture. I read some of their essays, extracted sentences at random, wrote them on the blackboard and tried to show what was wrong with them. After every explanation, I asked for questions. No one stirred. Everyone looked up stonily at me as though I were a preacher calling for a public confession of carnal sin. A few minutes of this and I sat down on the edge of the desk.

"That's it!" I announced. "I don't move from here until somebody asks a question."

A smirk or two lighted up the sea of dour faces.

"I mean it. I'm glued to this spot until somebody asks me a question."

Nobody asked a question. I stayed where I was, mechanically running my eyes up and down the furrowed rows of faces. A few students began to squirm uncomfortably.

"Mr. Hamilton!" I called to the only male student in the class. "You're the leader, ask a question!"

"I don't have any question to ask, sah," he said timidly.

"Did you understand everything I said?"

"Yes, sah."

"Every single, blessed thing?"

"Not everything, sah," he said dubiously.

"Tell me one thing I said that you didn't understand or I'm glued to this spot for the next week, Mr. Hamilton!"

He hesitated.

"Well, sah," he said finally, "I don't quite understand 'bout coordinating adjectives."

Coordinate adjectives! Wonderful! Just the sort of question English teachers thrive on because it can be answered with a straightforward rule and a commonsense test. How to tell the difference between the "waiting" in, "It is a waiting, silent, limp room," and "It is a silent, limp, waiting room." When you get a question of grammar that can be answered plainly without qualification by endless and knotty exceptions, you almost want to jump for joy. And here was just such a juicy one. I almost drooled as I stepped to the blackboard.

After my explanation, I scanned the faces of the students looking for that gleam, that light that flares in the eyes and says, "I've got it!" It was shining in a few faces, but others were still dark and muddy. I launched into another explanation, using different examples. Lights flashed on in faces sitting in this row, that one. But not five feet from me in a front row sat a student whose eyes were shrouded still in darkness.

I began anew, aiming my explanation at her. I scratched for fresh examples, musing to myself how much teaching grammar is like pleasing a woman during lovemaking. You search for the delicate, private spot (coordinate adjectives) that sets her afire, and when you find it you approach it gingerly, touch it carefully, withdraw coyly from it, turn and make a bold frontal assault that drives her mad, then quickly let it go with indifference and probe elsewhere until when you return to it again she is ripe and begging and this time you are so surgical and exact that with the slightest contact she explodes under you like a bomb. So I worked this student with my explanation of coordinate adjectives, watching for the flash of understanding.

But it didn't come. In fact, the lights in the other faces before me begin to dim and go out. Obdurate darkness as thick as jelly gripped this student's face.

I paused, exhausted.

A hand leaped up above the class.

"Is it right to begin a sentence with 'and', Mr. Winkler?" someone asked.

Another juicy question! This was my lucky day!

"And the Lord said, 'Let there be light'," I quoted, seeking out the darkened face of the dense one who sat before me.

Not only had she still not gotten coordinate adjectives, she now was floundering in fresh mystification. She could not understand. She could not come. A man could break his back atop such a woman and she would still rise up afterwards and make tea in an aura of discontent. The wise lover gives it up. He says, "This is a job for Superman," puts on his clothes and goes out into the street for a breath of fresh air.

Leaving her stewing in darkness not five feet from where I paced, I turned my attention to fanning the flickers of light I saw before me in the rows and rows of other beaming faces.

CHAPTER 8

The mission of our college was the training of teachers to run the elementary schools in the government system. The tutors were charged with teaching not only the content of their disciplines, but also techniques on how to teach them. So far, however, not the slightest murmur about teaching technique had come up in my classes, for my students and I were still waging trench warfare against elementary misconceptions of grammar which they tended to practice with religious viciousness. The rule of not beginning a sentence with "and," for example, had been picked up by many of them along the way from some simple-minded pedagogue and they now stubbornly refused to part with it no matter what reasoning was offered against it. While none of them was openly defiant when I suggested that perhaps they were being picky or had been misled by some former mentor, it was plain that they were politely squeamish with this blast of liberalism I was blowing over their strictured view of proper English. Always abiding by and practicing a literal and formal correctness was as important to them as to a rabbi. This trait I put down to the pernicious influence of the Englishman and his excessive emphasis on rightness in ceremony and grammar, and it is a feature so typical of Jamaicans as a whole as to be almost a national characteristic.

When Jamaica was under English rule, the colonial Englishman was every bit a caricature of what bad Hollywood movies now imagine the nineteenth century Empire-bound Englishman to be, and his speech reflected eccentric mannerisms he had picked up on the playing fields of public schools. He spoke with a precise and rigid emphasis on enunciation which included the rat-a-tat rattling of his "r's" on the tip of his tongue and the gusty aspiration of all initial "h's," said "pardon" incessantly, observed picky and knee-jerk rules based on Victorian syntax, and sprinkled his words with colloquialisms that we now see as stuffy. Because he was our colonial master, the notion spread throughout Jamaica that his English was the authentic and superior one, and that any departure from his accent, his syntactical patterns, his vocabulary, even his low-keyed and muted gestures, were barbarisms, corruptions, or simply uncouth. Once the population had swallowed this lie, everyone ambitious and eager to rise in the scheme of colonial society naturally tried to speak as the Englishman did. But the flip side of this counterfeit coin was that if you spoke like he did, unless you were a superb mummer, you often ended up thinking and behaving as he did. By getting you to ape him in his language, he succeeded in transfiguring you from a native Jamaican into a pseudo Englishman.

The hard fact, of course, was that no one born on Jamaican soil to Jamaican parents could ever be truly English. But without force of arms, without any outward act of aggression, the Englishman achieved a bloodless coup of the native mind using as his storm troopers an endless succession of stupid rules about grammar, pronunciation, ceremony, politeness, and manners.

One day I happened to be rummaging through a stack of papers on the mail desk of the college when I came upon its latest entrance examination. Out of curiosity, I sat down and read the English section. I was stunned. The questions were inanely pedantic and demanded such a hairsplitting knowledge of English grammar that I very much doubted if I could have answered them. There was a question, for example, that asked students to select the correct verb form in a sentence such as this: "Neither the man nor the women (sees, see) anything wrong with doing that." I stared at this gnarled sentence for a long moment before I could remember the fusty rule (the verb takes the form of the nearer subject: the correct answer was therefore the plural "see").

There was another that asked for the students to distinguish between the correct Victorian usage of "shall" and "will" (your great-grandmother may have had to memorize it: "I and We take Shall, all other pronouns take Will, except in case of emphasis, determination, or command.") In real life, however, only a Jamaican fatally afflicted with anglophile pompousness would ever have the nerve to either mouth or write "shall." ·

My students, who had cut their teeth on such grammatical pickiness all their lives, had less difficulty with the test than I myself would have had, and even though few of them spoke errorless Standard English, most were sophistical parlour grammarians of the most redoubtable, schoolmarmish type. Later that year, for example when the students were out in elementary classrooms doing practice teaching, I was sent to monitor one girl and found that she had scrawled this improbable sentence on her blackboard: "John saw many fishes in the market this morning." When I asked her why she hadn't simply written "fish" rather than "fishes," she frostily informed me that the plural noun meant that John had seen many different species of fishes, not merely many fish of the same species. Oh, I said lamely. Later, I looked up the rule to see whether she had buffaloed me. But she was quite right.

Jamaicans naturally speak among themselves an English patois that is peculiar to the island. It is rich in idioms and aphorisms that crisply sum up social situations with an elegant economy, and its hybrid vocabulary of Africanisms and English is spoken with an inflection that invariably strikes the foreign ear as sing-song. As with any language, it contains idiosyncrasies that cannot be explained by logic. Break your ankle, and the Jamaican will say that you've broken your foot. Break the thighbone, and he'll still insist that you've broken your foot since "foot" designates the entire appendage from the waist down. "Leg" is nonexistent in the patois. When a Jamaican changes his mind about going somewhere, he will say "I'm not going again," even though he never went in the first place.

When I lived in America, not being able to speak Jamaican patois was what I missed the most. But now, among my own people, with the language of my childhood ringing daily in my ears, I felt as if an overwhelming burden had passed from me. No longer did people crane to listen to me as I spoke. Now I could say what was in my heart in the most natural and instinctive way without filtering my speech of those idioms and catch-phrases an American listener would not have understood. The force of my native language came flooding back in all its habitual and familiar expressions, and I wallowed in my childhood tongue for the first month I was back in Jamaica like a mute who had miraculously regained his tongue.

One day in class, the students and I were swapping tales about idiomatic expressions and phrases, discussing their untranslatable meanings and reflecting on the power of language that often defies the explanations of text books. One student said she had a funny story to tell about an old woman and proceeded to tell this tale which, except for the punchline, I have rendered into Standard English from the patois:

An old woman lived in a tenement, and on this particular morning, as she stepped outside her hut, the neighbour's dog rushed up and bit her the ankle. Nursing the dog bite, she stepped back into her hut and promptly broke her only pair of spectacles. She went to draw water from the standpipe with a basin, but on the way back with the basin of water balanced on her head, she stepped straight onto a cow pat and got doodoo all over her one pair of shoes. Grumbling to herself about what a horrible start the day had taken, she put on her clean frock and went out into the street to catch the bus that would take her to her work as a domestic. She was waiting for the bus and peacefully minding her own business when a madman with a machete went berserk, rushed up to her, and chopped off her head. As her head tumbled onto the ground, the old woman flew into a temper and bellowed, "See yah now!"

The hilarity of this story—and the entire class was convulsed by it—is so idiomatic that only a native speaker of Jamaican patois would understand the subtle meaning of "See yah now!", the old woman's woeful lament, and enjoy it in this context as the classic understatement of comedy. Literally, the expression means, "Now look here!" or "See what's happened to me now," a rendering which robs it of the idiomatic associations that make it such a belly-laugh punchline in the story.

"See yah now!" is the cry of the beleaguered ramshackle dweller struggling against overwhelming forces of disarray, confusion, chaos, and squalor, to uphold and maintain the standards of high-church decency and manners in this sea of tropical disintegration in which she is adrift. In that cry of desperation the old woman is summoning a public chorus of the community to bear witness to the misery and wickedness all around her, to hear out her declamations against this flood tide of undeserved calamities that life can and does capriciously pour on the back of an innocent sufferer. Her indignation is crowned with innocence and righteousness: she is harmfully and wickedly wronged, and this is her call for vindication. But, of course, her head has been chopped off and is now rolling on the ground. Yet with "See yah now!" she vainly stands on ceremony as she seeks to empanel a grand jury of bystanders to hear out the litany of wrongs committed against her this day.

When the student told the story, I nearly fell off my chair from laughing so hard. It was a good unforced laugh, the kind that bubbles up straight from the heart and sweeps you along irresistibly with its power. The story struck me as so funny that for days afterwards I would be sitting in the staff room gazing out the window at the tangle of bushes and trees on the grounds and suddenly think of it and start laughing all over again.

I was home again, laughing among my own people. There was joy in my heart.

But there was no joy in Cathy. She was languishing before my very eyes. The house was too small to occupy her days and when I was away at school she sat alone and idle on the hilltop surrounded by the beauty and stillness of a land that was foreign to her. There was no telephone in the entire village so she couldn't spontaneously ring up a friend and talk. We lived too far in the bush for visitors and, besides, everyone else in the vicinity worked during the day.

But mainly she was suffering from the lonely isolation of the stranger. She did not understand the people she lived among, could scarcely fathom their ways, and was perplexed by their thinking. She had only a dim grasp of patois and had to listen carefully to understand what was said to her. Most of the time she could piece together the meaning of some chance remark directed at her by a student or teacher, but usually she understood only in the most syntactically narrow sense. Subtle meanings completely escaped her because they were invariably grounded in an idiomatic vocabulary and experience she did not share. The person she was talking with would see her perplexity and start speaking standard English, but the effect of this politeness would be one of unintended distancing, making Cathy even more painfully self-conscious of her standing in the community as a foreigner.

But what she found especially difficult was the obvious attention her white skin provoked everywhere she went. Nothing I had said could have prepared her for the stares of interest and curiosity she was met with in the countryside. Often the stares were resentful and hostile, but mainly they were inquisitive or probing, with the starer plainly wondering what a white woman was doing in such a backward place. To be white in a black country with a long English colonial history is to be a pariah, an ambiguous entity. It is to be simultaneously respected and despised, to arouse suspicion and curiosity, to evoke defiance, rudeness, envy, and condescension. It is to be separated from that inalienable birthright every white American enjoys in his own country: the expectation of being treated with indifference in a public place. When you are white in a black land like Jamaica, you are no longer merely a man, or a woman, or a child. For good or ill, you are also immediately transmogrified into a living symbol of a detested colonial past.

Bewildered and hurt, Cathy began to slowly withdraw inside herself.

The hardest thing about growing up white in a black country is the nagging feeling of not belonging. It is a persistent malaise

experienced in varying degrees by every white Jamaican I know
Jamaicans of all races who have lived abroad for any length of time
also suffer it after returning home, but for the white Jamaican the
feeling of not belonging is a cross he must bear even if he has never
set foot out of his own country.

One day on a visit to Montego Bay I was standing and gazing
nostalgically at the house in which I had spent most of my boyhood
years when a higgler woman and her young grandson who were
selling fruit nearby spoke to me. I walked over and we began to talk.
Her grandson looked up at me defiantly when I said that I had spent
much of my childhood in that house across the street.

"You saying you a Jamaican?" he asked suspiciously.

I said that I was.

His lips curled with contempt.

"You not a Jamaican," he said.

"I was born in Kingston Public Hospital," I said angrily. "I went
to Cornwall College right here in Montego Bay. I lived in that house
for seven years."

"You not a Jamaican," he repeated stubbornly. "You a white man."

This was too much to bear in front of the very house in which I
had spent so much of my childhood.

"I'm a rass claat Jamaican!" I snapped.

"Lawd Jesus God, sah," the old woman wailed, "Beg you! No
cuss no bad word in me old ear."

The boy was unmoved. "Any white man can learn bad word
from book," he said scornfully.

"De gentleman is a Jamaican!" the old lady scolded. "Me could
tell from me first set eye 'pon him. Hush up you mouth 'bout it."

But there was no convincing the boy. His grandmother lamented
that he was a youth, and like all the youth of today had no manners,
and she was sorry for his rudeness. It was a pinprick, and I no doubt
made too much of it. But I was so enraged that I could have strangled
the wretch with my bare hands and laughed about it afterwards.

White people do not usually fare well in Jamaica. In the early years of the island's history, yellow fever sent them by the thousands to an early grave. Then there was the everlasting sunshine all year round to which many of them, accustomed to long grey winters, could not adapt. Lady Nugent, who lived in Jamaica between 1801 and 1805 and whose husband was governor, lamented constantly in her diary about the sultry weather, about the sandflies and mosquitoes and the porcine ways of the rich planters who could sit down at midday in the broiling sun to gourmandize a five-course meal. She found them gluttonous and difficult to understand.

While the slaves thrived and flourished, the white population in Jamaica succumbed in vast numbers to the effects of heat, tropical parasites, and bad water. Those few whites who survived tended to· be the sturdiest and most hardened of men. And even after medicine had finally solved the riddle of the murderous anopheles mosquito, life in the island was still easier for the white man who had a callous eye and an unfeeling heart. The poverty was everywhere, the squalor in which most of the poor people passed their lives was a constant stench in the nose. In America one can live one's entire life in an enclave of wealth and cleanliness and never meet a beggar on the street or gaze into the scabrous face of a hungry child. In Jamaica these sights are all around you no matter where you live, no matter how circumscribed the daily path of your life.

To be a white man in Jamaica is to be constantly haunted with feelings of illegitimacy and dispossession. Against this the white Jamaican uses two stereotypical defences. If he is ignorant and callous enough, he revels in his whiteness and professes contempt towards the majority all around him to which he does not belong. That he is not one of them, that he is not really part of this poor country in which misfortune has marooned him, are two lies he wears around his neck like a placard. He takes care that his children do not marry into black or brown families and professes to treasure the sense of dispossession with which he lives.

Whether or not he feels this way in his heart of hearts is another matter. But many white people in Jamaica have consciously walled themselves in with this way of thinking. Most of my mother's family have used it. One result is that their children are reared with no sense of patriotism or love for the land in which they were born and migrate as soon as they become adults.

The second defence is not as common. The white man simply surrenders to the superior forces that surround him and marries into the family of his heart's love—whether black, brown or otherwise—his skin becoming an anomaly belied by every other fact of his life. He is accepted in his own community where the conditions of his life choice are known, but whenever he ventures into the outside world he must still suffer the ambiguous consequences that result from his whiteness.

Yet in Jamaica, black is not always black, nor is white always white. One cannot find, as is true of America, a polarization of cultural opposites along racial lines. Indeed, some black Jamaicans not only identify with the white cultural model—the one left over by the Englishman—but also suffer acutely from the same sense of alienation with which the white population is burdened. These Jamaicans, although they are black, stand as vehemently apart from the black majority as any white outcast. They have internalized the white man's sense of racial dispossession and are as pugnacious in practising his arrogant defence against it. Black in Jamaica is less a colour, and more like a way of being.

This topsy-turvy state of affairs has been driven home to me in many incidents on many different occasions, but two experiences stand out above the rest. The first occurred in Jamaica, the second in America.

Once when I was staying at a hotel in Montego Bay, I fell head-over-heels for its director of entertainment, a strikingly black Jamaican woman with voluptuously robust proportions. For days I followed her around the premises like a lovesick puppy until finally one night she consented to have dinner with me. After dinner, we danced for hours and, when the hotel band signed off, headed for a nearby disco. But we had no sooner poked our heads·into its dingy and smoky surroundings when she exclaimed loudly,

"What a lot of ole negar here tonight! Too much! Too much! Come, me can't stand it here!" and left in a huff.

For a moment, I was so offended by her remark that I very nearly blurted out that hers had been the blackest face in the house before my gonads got the better of me and I wisely shut my mouth and pantingly trailed after her. But it also occurred to me as I stood there for that milli-second of indecision, with the reggae music blasting and the acrid smell of sweat and smoke tingling my nose, that although my skin was white and hers was blue-black, these swaying hordes were my people, not hers. By a fluke of temperament and the muddle of our psycho-historical heritage, she had been born black but had internalized a white identity, while I, who had been born white, had internalized a black one.

She was not an isolated and foolishly confused woman. When it comes to colour, nothing is Jamaica is simple except the fairy tale often repeated that the island suffers only from class, but not from colour, prejudice. This lie ranks as high in the pantheon of Jamaican delusions as the myth of the innocent American does in America.

The second incident happened when I was a student in Glendora, California. A friend from Kingston wrote that he would like to come and visit me. Three weeks later he showed up, spent the night at my apartment, and the next day I took him on a tour of the college to which I had just been admitted. On our return we passed the apartment manager who, glowering fiercely at us from his doorway, beckoned for me to come over and talk to him.

"I don't allow niggers in my apartments," he growled when we were alone in his office.

"Niggers!" I blurted with astonishment. "What nigger?"

"Don't get cute with me. The one you just walked in with. I want him out of here!"

"But," I protested, "he's not black!"

In fact, my friend was brown. Not only was he brown, he had been my neighbour, his father was a prominent barrister in Kingston, and he himself was headed for law school in England. None of this meant "black" to the Jamaican way of thinking. It emphatically meant "white." The idea that my friend was black was so scholastically preposterous that I was eager to debate it with this stupid manager merely for the satisfaction of proving him ignorant.

I did not understand then how Americans think about race. Later, after I had lived there for a while and seen a white woman crowned Miss America who the press insisted was black, after I came to understand that on racial matters Americans are the world's most consummate casuists, it all became clearer to me. But that was only years later. When I had the confrontation with this manager I had been in America for only three months and my head was still in a whirl.

Americans see colour strictly as a consanguineous and physical quality: it is to them so much a matter of blood that a pint inherited from a great-great-great black ancestor is enough to classify anyone as black no matter how white he may look. Jamaicans, and West Indians as a whole, regard colour as inseparable from manners, behaviour, background, education, and culture—that whole constellation of traits the Englishman once labelled "breeding." This fundamental and deep-rooted difference between Americans and Jamaicans, and possibly all Caribbean peoples, may in part be responsible for the antagonism that some say exists between American blacks and blacks from the West Indies.

It is not difficult to understand how Jamaicans and West Indians came to think about race as they do. Simple mimicry of the English was to blame. When the Englishman was plundering the world during his colonialist binge, the standard he carried everywhere around with him was his precious English culture. Take the most uncouth English second son and plant him among black people on a distant shore, and overnight he became oppressively boorish and legalistic about his customs and manners. If he had dropped his "h's" like flies in London, he tacked them on again scrupulously while bawling for his slave in Jamaica. If he had never read a book in his life in Yorkshire, in Jamaica he acquired the airs of a pedant. Away from home, he was suddenly obsessed with preserving and practising English ideals and virtues with an unslaked passion.

Part of this pose was a defence against being engulfed by the preponderant black races among whom he had been posted. George Orwell, who was himself part of the colonial shock troops sent to subdue India, wrote that the Englishman abroad lived in terror of losing face. Death by pillorying was preferable to public embarrassment before the hordes of savages among whom he was supposed to spread enlightenment. Keeping a stout English face, putting on a good front, became the primal duty of the colonial.

This effort made the colonial Englishman a figure so clotted with distinctive mannerisms, ceremonies, and pretensions as to be ludicrously theatrical. The slaves witnessed this white man daily enacting his bizarre theatre of what it was like to be English and thought to themselves: so that's what it means to be white. As the more venturesome among them rose to positions of favouritism and prominence, they aped their masters with a vengeance; and colour became equated with a certain cast of mind and mannerisms of behaviour. The equation has persisted to this day in Jamaica.

There was no explaining all this to Cathy. In any event, explanations alone cannot condition you to live among the peculiar cultural worldview of a people. Only experience can truly teach about culture, and, now that she was living among my people, she would have to learn to grapple with their ways of thinking and behaving. It was plainly a difficult and painful experience for her, and in her struggle she reminded me of my paternal grandmother, who lives in my memory as the classic example of a maladjusted white foreigner.

Grandmother was a lissome and strikingly beautiful young American when she married Grandpop in New Jersey. There are pictures, aged in the sepia tones of the time, that show her as the pert and flirtatious ingenue coyly clinging to the arm of a young and strapping Grandpop on the deck of a ship bound for Jamaica. Her eyes are shining with excitement at the adventure of life abroad that lies ahead of her. She was no doubt the envy of all her New Jersey friends. She sent them back photographs of every trivial and inconsequential aspect of her Jamaican household, and on the backs of these shots she scrawled messages identifying this piece of furniture as her Jamaican vanity that stood in the corner of her bedroom, and this cluttered hat rack as the one that keeps watch in the drawing room. There was this view out the north window and that view of a mango tree out the south. There were snapshots of a uniformed maid standing at attention in a breezeway and of an aged gardener crouched at the stoop of what must have been the servants' quarters with his perplexed young son standing beside him ogling the foreign mistress behind the camera.

But soon the bitter times set in. Perhaps they were brought on by the failure of Grandpop's business and the ensuing bout with poverty that followed its collapse. Perhaps she had finally discovered that Grandpop, like most Jamaican men of his class, found the plentiful and willing pool of poor black women irresistible and had been sneaking at nights into the servants' quarters to sample the wares of successive maids. Whatever the reason, by the time I was born she had hardened into a querulous and cantankerous woman. She threw tantrums, ranted and raged over quibbles, and often gave vent to an implacably selfish nature.

One day when I was visiting with them, Grandpop and I made our way slowly through the gully to the bus stop and then downtown, where we rode the tramcar and ate Slim Jims in an ice cream parlour. Grandmother had asked Grandpop when we were leaving to bring her back some chocolate, but he became so engrossed in showing me the sights that he forgot and came home empty-handed. When Grandmother found out she flew into a towering rage. She stormed up and down the small wooden house screaming and crying and finally, in a fit of uncontrollable petulance, crawled under the bed from which dark burrow she shrieked at the top of her lungs. Grandpop crouched down beside the bed begging her to come out, but she stayed there sobbing and pummelling the floor with her fists. Finally, after a tempestuous hour, she grudgingly consented to come out only to find that she couldn't budge because her dress was snagged by the springs. Grandpop, on his hands and knees and huffing and puffing as he peeped under the bed, did his best to free her, but her rage had blown her up like a puffer fish and she was stuck. The only solution seemed to be to lift the bed off her.

Grandpop with his bad heart took one side of the bed, and I with my eight year old child's body grasped the other, and we tried to lift the four-poster brass ensemble off Grandmother, who was now screaming hysterically to be free. We strained and hoisted, but the bed would not budge. Finally, Grandpop sent me next door to fetch our sickly neighbour for help. The poor man had lately been released from the sanatorium where he had had a tubercular lung removed, but he willingly came anyway and was soon kneeling down beside the bed and peering under at trapped Grandmother with astonishment written all over his brown face.

"But good God, Missus Winkler!" he exclaimed. "How you get under dere?"

"I was cleaning out cobweb, Missah Stewart," Grandmother sobbed, "when I found I couldn't move."

"You crawl under bed to clean out cobweb from de bedspring?" Mr. Stewart asked, clearly impressed by the meticulous cleanliness of these white people who lived beside him.

"Yes, Missah Stewart," Grandmother replied piously, "because I'm a woman who can't stand a cobweb no matter where it might be."

"What a woman hate a cobweb so!" Mr. Stewart marvelled, standing up and gazing nonplussed at the enormous bed under which grandmother was pinned. We deployed ourselves onto three corners of the bed, each taking hold of the spring, and at a signal from Mr. Stewart, all simultaneously lifted. The bed wobbled an inch or so then settled back again squarely on Grandmother's belly, drawing an anguished squeal out of her.

"Lawd God," Mr. Stewart moaned at one point, "to think all dis trouble bring about by cobweb under a bedspring where eye can never see!"

Finally, however, after much sweating and grunting, we managed to hoist the bed high enough for Grandmother to squirt out from under it, and she stood up brushing her frock off with as much dignity as she could muster in front of Mr. Stewart, then retired with a regal and hygienic air that proclaimed to the world that this contretemps would certainly not deter her from the righteous business of ferreting out future cobwebs no matter where they might hide.

As Mr. Stewart made his way down the walkway towards his own house, I heard him mutter,

"If I live to be a hundred year old, I never goin' forget what me see here today: white woman crawl under bedspring to clean out cobweb! Boy, she good, sah! She good!"

Poor Grandmother suffered homesickness all her life. She longed to go back home and visit her brothers and sisters, but Grandpop could not afford to send her. She was always talking about America, about where she had grown up and what games she had played there, and to the end of her life she carried around with her a family tree, copied from ancient Bibles, that traced her ancestry back to one Edward Coburn who had landed in Boston in 1635 aboard the ship *Defence*. The document catalogued eleven generations of her family from that day, all of whom had lived and died in America until Grandmother broke the chain by marrying Grandpop and moving to Jamaica.

It must have been hard for Grandmother to spend her life in a land she did not love, among people she only dimly understood. It must have been harder still to age, grow feeble, and die in that faraway and foreign place among a race of strangers. When Grandpop died and abandoned her there alone, she turned her anger and grief on the last dream of his failed life and vengefully savaged his novel.

CHAPTER 9

Cathy needed a job for her peace of mind, but finding one would not be easy. We were surrounded by bushland and emptiness, and the only prospect for work lay in Ocho Rios, which was on the coast and half an hour's drive away via a tortuous country road.

Ocho Rios has always struck me as a positively ugly part of Jamaica. It is a seacoast town surrounded by mountains whose mangling over the years by bauxite mining has soiled the landscape with an unsightly red dust. Off the main road one of the bauxite companies has jabbed a hideous loading dock into the belly of the sea and it stands there, red and rusting and gnawed at by the waves, a crusted metallic teat giving suckle to a steady stream of aging, dishevelled ore freighters.

Yet the tourists flock to Ocho Rios in unending streams of floral bermuda shorts and peeling noses. Why they come there mystified me as a child, bewilders me still. There is a small crescent-shaped beach, a white pimple on a bleak and otherwise ironbound shoreline, and several enormous hotels rise up around it in a protective cluster. Scattered throughout the town are other hotel buildings daubed onto the rocky shore, and some of these have chiselled a tiny cove of sandy beach at their doorsteps where guests can seabathe. If Cathy was to find employment, it would be here among the hotels of Ocho Rios, where her American accent and ways would be valued.

One Sunday she saw an ad in the *Gleaner* for a secretary at one of these hotels, and she wrote off a hopeful letter. We heard nothing for a week, and then early one morning were roused by the cries of a telegraph delivery man who stood at the edge of our yard huffing and puffing from the exertion of pushing his bicycle up the rutted driveway that led to our house. It was from the hotel calling Cathy to an interview.

When she got to the hotel, there were some fifteen other

applicants waiting before her. She had just sat down when the manager poked his head outside his office, spotted her white face among the crowd of brown and black ones, and skipping over the others who had been there long before, took her into his office. He asked one or two cursory questions about her experience then offered her the job on the spot. She had the nerve to quibble over the salary which, after a quick consultation with someone else, he increased by a hundred dollars a month.

"It was very unfair," Cathy said later. "But he obviously wanted someone white in the front office. The other girls gave me dirty looks."

Under the Manley regime, Jamaica had taken a definite turn against the white and fair-skinned people who had enjoyed favoured status up to then. Manley himself spoke out against racial discrimination and frequently mentioned in his speeches the unfair fact of brown men having enjoyed preference over black men under the English rule, and of white men holding sway over everybody. In this observation he was historically right, although Jamaicans persisted in denying that racism had anything to do with either social advancement or the way they treated one another. Class was always touted as the determining factor, apparently on the belief that discrimination based on class was morally superior to that based on colour. The number of times I have heard aunts and uncles and magistrates and barristers solemnly tell this lie to a foreign listener, always with a certain smugness, are uncountable.

In the earliest days of slavery, Jamaican society was strictly a pyramid, with the white men occupying the apex and the black slaves the base. Between base and apex lay a great unfilled area, and here the children of miscegenation settled in a brown flood. By the time I came to consciousness as a Jamaican child, this racial hierarchy had been permanently imprinted on the entire nation. You saw it practised in banks, where the visible faces that peered out at you from the teller's cages were always white, Chinese, or brown, but as you burrowed into the grimy and sweaty backrooms, the skin took a decided turn towards a darker shade. This stacked deck was evident in all kinds of businesses except those that dealt with the lower end of society into which brown-skinned workers could be inveigled to go only if nothing else was available. My uncles, for example, whose stores were always smack in the nastiest parts of Kingston, invariably employed only very dark clerks.

Accompanying this continuum of colour was a widespread and endemic disdain for certain kinds of work. Plainly put, the Jamaican on his home soil dislikes physical labour. It is abhorrent to him not because he shirks hard work—Jamaicans are tireless workers in foreign societies that pay well and treat them fairly—but because over the centuries physical labour has come to be associated with blackness and lowly field-hand status. This idea was exported wholesale from the days of slavery and the plantation and is now practically etched in the genes of the nation. The white collar, even when it entails low pay and a stunted career, rules supreme by offering the blandishments of pen, unsoiled hands, and respect. Jamaicans are traditionally fussy about bookish learning, about calligraphy, about training their children in the niceties of clerkdom, because these attributes were so visibly paraded by English overseers during the plantation days that they have come to signify, like the ministerial collar, the intangible and mysterious aura of status. When I was a child I was struck repeatedly by the calligraphic flourishes of even the most humble clerk in some backwoods post office. To write a "good hand," to make one's letters legibly and stylishly, is something most Jamaican clerks do effortlessly. It is part of the expectation drummed into them from birth by disciplinarian grandmothers and cane-wielding pedagogues who, consciously or unconsciously, still bear racial memories of the occupying throngs of English clerks and overseers that had once ruled Jamaica with copperplate.

Given this state of affairs, one would expect the teacher to be among the most revered of professionals in Jamaica, and it is undeniably so. In the streets of the village through which I walked daily to school now that Cathy was working and needed the car, I would often pass streams of cultivators, herdsmen, or higglers going or coming from the surrounding bushlands and was always greeted with "Good morning, Teacher," or "Good afternoon, Teacher,' uttered with the hushed tones that Americans use to address ever quack physicians.

This kind of public display of esteem has the tendency to bring out the worst in anyone. It complicated my daily walk to school by saddling me with a public persona I felt obliged to live up to in the village. It also made it more difficult for me to cope with the bull.

The bull belonged to Mr. Jameson and was often let lasciviously loose with its harem of cows into the pasture through which the mar. driveway to our house ran. Jameson invariably rotated his grazing cattle through the pastures in a clockwise direction. If the bull had passed a week in the northeast pasture that abutted the land on which our house stood, he was certain to be moved into our pasture on the following Monday. With the car gone and the only way to the stree being the marl driveway scratched through the grazing pasture, I had to cross paths with the bull.

In the beginning, before the weight of being daily greeted as "Teacher Winkler" had put the burden of certain public expectation on me, I evaded the bull with shameless furtiveness. I would set out wearing soft-soled shoes an hour before my first class, make my way nervously down the grassy centre hump of the driveway which always seemed mysteriously clean of cow pats, one eye fixed on the enormous back of the beast grazing in a far corner, the other on the sanctuary of a leafy black mango tree, which I regarded as the half-way point of my skulk to the road. If the worst came to the worst and the bull spotted me, I assured myself repeatedly, I could always scurry up the tree and wait out the brute.

But then being the public figure of "Teacher Winkler" went to my head and I began to scorn furtiveness. One morning, after I had fallen victim to this narrow thinking, I started down the driveway as if I were parading through Trafalgar Square, hardly bothering to cast my eye over the pastures to search out the bull, and was well past the tree and vulnerably distant from the road when I looked into the unflinching stare of the beast peering up nastily at me from a tussock of grass no more than twenty yards away. Before he could give any sign of attack, I broke into an ignominious sprint and scampered like a mongoose onto the road, nearly barrelling into a knot of three or four villagers on their way to the market.

"Good morning, Teacher," they sang out almost in a chorus, deftly sidestepping my headlong charge.

I felt some explanation was called for.

"The bull," I stammered. "He's there."

They glanced at the beast which, having routed me, had resumed its kingly grazing.

"Yes, sah," one of the men said. "Bull."

"Big bull," another agreed.

"Jameson bull," commented a third, all without breaking stride.

Keeping up an idle antiphonal commentary about the bull, they left me stranded and breathless and feeling very much the village idiot at the mouth of the driveway while they trekked toward the market.

"One bull and fifty cow!"

They laughed merrily.

"What him do wid so much cow?"

"Is a wonder him no dead!"

"Bull is de boss."

Part of the reason for Manley's unpopularity among the managerial and middle classes in Jamaica was firmly rooted in the Jamaican thinking about race. In our national identity, blackness connotated not merely colour, but also a certain manner of thinking and behaviour linked in the popular mind with indiscipline, unculturedness, and general ill-mannerliness. This association had evolved intact into our cultural soul from the earliest slavery days when a black skin signified captivity and barbarism.

Indiscipline is the one word that most Jamaicans, on a free association test, would equate with blackness. Jamaicans of all walks of life seem to spend a lifetime bemoaning indiscipline. It is the most common lament heard from aunties, uncles, mothers, and grandmothers, and every generation seems to remember a time when national indiscipline was not nearly as rampant as it is alleged to be now.

And it was here, it seemed to me later, by his misreading of the national psyche that Manley stumbled. His administration, he declared often, was for the common man, which meant it was for the black man. But to be for the black man, in the Jamaican mind, is to be for ancient, abhorrent and unEnglish practices. It is to be for that *bête noire,* indiscipline, and as his term dragged on, Manley seemed to give tacit support to the middle-class criticism that he had sided with the beast.

Once, after a flurry of violence, the governor-general mounted his pulpit and gave a pompous speech against indiscipline, raging against it as the most odious trait in our national soul. It was the typical anglicised speech one would expect from a figurehead, filled with platitudes and high-flown bombast, and it excoriated our indiscipline in the tones of every indignant Jamaican grandmother. Since the speech gave utterance to primal and congenital fears about indiscipline that are rooted in the Jamaican mind, the *Gleaner* hailed it as a landmark oration and carried the full text on its front page. Manley was then asked what he thought about the governor-general's views.

It was, he said, true that a streak of indiscipline ran throughout our nature. But we had to ask ourselves, where does this streak come from? What was the basis of it? Its basis was injustice, he alleged, or the perception of injustice that is widespread among our youth. And so he went on, seeming to give aid and comfort to this most Luciferan of all traits.

I remember thinking at that time that if I had been Manley's speechwriter, I could have stopped at least fifty middle-class managers, in whom the speech surely cemented their determination to go, from migrating. I would have said about indiscipline what I have heard maids, garden boys, nannies, teachers, shopkeepers, say about it all my life. I would have denounced it with uncompromising damnation and hurled it into the blackest pit of odium.

America's Satan is communism, Jamaica's is indiscipline. Even the Ayatollah of Iran, buttressed by a fanatical religious and military apparatus, could not afford to speak equivocally about America, the national Satan of his own people.

Underestimating the deep-rooted and pernicious symbolism of race was one of the many fundamental miscalculations Manley seemed to me to have made in dealing with his own people. But still, it was also plain to me that his influence in instilling a feeling of pride and self-worth in Jamaicans had taken hold and with good effect.

At the school, for example, I was at first astonished to hear the teachers in the staff room freely talking in patois. When you think about it, this is as it should be, since patois is the language that all Jamaicans speak in the crib. But in the 1950s the Englishman still had Jamaica squarely in his grip, and many of the generation that reared us were convinced that patois was an infra-dig and ignorant tongue. Patois was the condescending language you might use on a servant or a menial, but it was unthinkable that two professional Jamaicans conversing in public should lapse into it. Yet under the Manley regime patois had gained widespread acceptance as the language of informal talk between Jamaicans, even as a symbolic badge of belonging, and in the daily exchanges between teachers in the staff room, the foreign staffers who could understand but not speak it seemed sorrily misplaced.

Manley's Jamaicanization also extended to matters of fashion. The idiotic tweeds and wools of the Englishman as well as the suffocating tie with which he daily garrotted himself in the streets of Jamaica began to give way to the Kareba, a loose-fitting outfit consisting of a short-sleeved jacket and matching pants. Manley himself seemed always to be dressed in one, as did many of his ministers. This garment was obviously a superior adaptation to the heat of the tropics than the Savile Row suit, but even this sensible change many Jamaicans could not accept.

One evening my brother took us to dinner at an elegant restaurant. We were in the bar waiting to be seated when the owner of the restaurant approached us with a grave air. He would let us in to dine this one time, he said solemnly, since we were already present and he did not wish to displease us. But he would like to make it clear that formal wear was expected of all guests.

My brother, who was dressed in a Kareba as I myself was, disputed the manager's contention that our dress was not properly formal. He pointed out that the men present had on Karebas, which Mr. Manley himself by wearing one to the opening of Parliament had decreed as formal wear. The manager scoffed. A black man, he was very elegantly dressed in a two-piece woollen suit and wore a grey tie stuck to his breastbone by a rhinestone pin.

"Mr. Manley didn't mean that," he said insistently. "He may have worn the Kareba that one day because of the heat, but he was not setting a precedent."

My brother, who loved to brandish his real and imagined connections, took offence.

"I know Manley and he meant to set a precedent, of course! Dis is Jamaica! How man can wear wool suit and tie in de Jamaican heat? Is a wonder you don't dead of a heart attack."

"Maybe this is Jamaica," the manager retorted with a thin smile. "But here we have standards to uphold. Standards are universal. We can't give in to whim and fad. That is our trouble today, we're always swept along by the latest. Proper dress for dinner is a necessity no matter where you go."

The debate raged between the white Jamaican clad in a Kareba and lapsing into Jamaicanisms and occasional patois, and the black Jamaican dressed and speaking like an Englishman.

We did not know who we were. We had been reared by a grand ancestor who had suddenly died leaving a rich legacy but no will. Now that he was gone we did not know how to dress. We did not know how to talk. We did not know how we should live. We did not know what we should believe. All we had to guide us was the memory of his example and the chequered history he had left behind, the epitaph scrawled on his tomb.

We did not know who we were.

In the 1950s to be white in Jamaica was a mixed blessing. It gained you access to places to which you could not otherwise go without feeling as though you didn't belong. It stereotyped you as a member of the ruling class, even if you were poor and utterly without influence. But then it also drew thieves to your house even if you had nothing worth stealing, made you conspicuous everywhere you went, and occasionally exposed you to random abuse in the streets.

On the plus side, if you were male, it made you an object of sexual attraction to poor black women who had rightly observed that the lighter the skin the higher one seemed to rise in Jamaica. If you were female, however, it shrunk your list of acceptable suitors to a pitiful few and made spinsterhood a strong possibility.

My own family had at least two instances of these unfair consequences. There was, for example, Grandfather Winkler who loved black women inordinately. Between him and Grandmother there was constant warfare over the presence of servant women in the house. Grandmother did her best to hire only the most repulsive servants she could find, but since she was herself a squeamishly neat woman, she could go only so far in selecting a maid loathsome enough to repel Grandpop.

One typical story comes down in the family. Grandmother had hired a stout black woman as a cook, certain that her coal-black skin and elephantine buttocks would prove unappealing to Grandpop. But here she had entirely misread the proclivities of Jamaican men, whose fondness for women with huge rumps matches in intensity the American male's love of big breasts. Instead of finding the woman ugly, Grandpop found her irresistible and was soon sneaking into the maid's quarters at night after grandmother was asleep. For her part, the maid seemed to have reciprocated and the two of them romped with abandon many a night in the back room under Grandmother's nose.

Then the inevitable happened: the maid got pregnant. Grandpop agreed to support the child if it looked like him and arranged for the maid to work elsewhere during her pregnancy. A few months later, she gave birth to a boy and Grandpop took the bus down to the tenement where the maid lived to inspect the child.

The infant was as black as the maid and showed not even the faintest trace of white ancestry. Grandpop stared at it with disbelief before blurting out,

"That child can't be mine! Look how black it is!"

But the maid had a ready explanation.

"Is de coal stove me cook on every day dat do it, sah," she said. "De smoke go up me all day long and turn de pickney black."

What answer Grandpop gave to this ingenious excuse I do not know. But he never supported the child and refused all the maid's claims of paternity.

The other example was a sadder one, involving one of my mother's sisters who died unmarried after an unhappy life spent searching vainly for a man.

Aunt Petulia was a gentle and bovine soul with a kindly heart and a simple, open disposition. But even with the bloom of youth on her cheeks, she had not been pretty. Her features were too thick and coarse, her limbs dwarfishly pudgy. Her face was rounded and blunt like a coconut, with an ugly tufted wart skewered to the middle of her chin by four wiry hairs. In her nubile years she had been imprisoned by the zealousness of her father whose God-given mission was to prevent any of his daughters from falling to a man of colour. She had gone to Rome as a young woman, waved to the Pope at a public appearance in the Vatican, and returning to Jamaica, bought and drove her own car in a burst of liberation.

She was working in one of the nasty rat-trap shops owned by her brothers and passing her days mainly in the company of labouring black men when the life force began grinding away at her sweet disposition with unrelenting hormonal warfare. She was starving for a man, for sexual affection, and although she spent countless hours among willing men of all temperaments, they were all black and utterly taboo to her. The idea of their ugly sister sleeping with a black man would have driven her protective brothers berserk even though most of them kept black mistresses on the side.

Whether from neglect or depression, poor Aunt Petulia went on eating binges and by the time I knew her had become morbidly obese, which made her even uglier. And then she went mad.

When I was a child it was an accepted fact of our family life that Aunt Petulia was mad. Aunts clucked sympathetically when they made this pronouncement, and uncles gruffly shook their balding heads in wonderment over what could have reduced her to this sorry fate. I used to see her occasionally when my mother took me to the house where Aunt Petulia lived alone with my maternal grandmother and would watch her carefully for signs of eccentricity. But she never ranted and raved the way every Jamaican has occasionally witnessed the mad do in the streets. Instead, she simply sat in a torpor of listlessness, answering any questions put to her in monosyllables, and staring around the yard in the dimwitted way of a nearsighted sheepdog. Every now and again, to some contrived stab of wit, her face would light up with a smile, but then it would immediately be smothered under the grey dullness of a blown light bulb.

She passed out of my childhood life, and then, as aunts and uncles are apt to do, came into it again when I became an adolescent.

After my father had suddenly dropped dead, we faced the terrifying prospect of being evicted into the street a week later when the rent was due. Then one of my aunts who had come rushing to our side remembered that my maternal grandfather's will had stipulated that his house should always be available to unmarried or widowed daughters in need. Since the five-bedroom house was then occupied only by my eccentric Aunt Petulia and her maid, it was the logical place for us to go. Here, some months later, I saw Aunt Petulia go through a bout of madness.

It hit her on a Monday. That morning, she got up and took a bath, which she sorely needed, for she was so fat that she always gave off the frowsy smell of an unaired cellar. But this Monday, she was ensconced in the bathtub and singing in a raucous voice as I got ready to go to work. When her maid, Edith, arrived and found her mistress in the bathtub singing, she threw her hands up into the air.

"She taking bath," she nodded to me meaningfully. "De madness hit her again."

"She needs a bath," I said, preoccupied with the *Gleaner*.

"Bath? What she need bath for? Me say is de madness 'pon her brain."

"It's madder not to bathe in dis heat," I retorted.

"Me calling Missah Henry," Edith declared. "De madness strike again."

Missah Henry was the oldest brother in my mother's family, a stingy and mean-witted old man with an insatiable appetite for the young bodies of his female sales clerks. Calling him would bring an invasion of busybody uncles down on our house.

"Mind your own business," I warned her. "Leave Miss Petulia alone."

"Me say, she mad! Me know how she go on when she mad, and she mad now."

From the bathroom came Aunt Petulia's falsetto voice, "Mona Lisa, Mona Lisa, child of my dreams."

Edith gave me a contemptuous look that said, "I told you so," and slunk back into her kitchen.

Aunt Petulia was still bawling out this song when I left for work.

I returned home that evening to find her perched on the wall of the veranda wearing a bright floral print and smelling overpoweringly of perfume. Her face was bedaubed with rouge and lipstick, and the wart on her chin had been ploughed under a furrow of pancake make-up through which, like the shoots of a spring bloom, the tips of the tufted hairs showed. Sitting beside her, his feet arrogantly perched on the wall, was a black man smirking with the boastful air of the conquering male. He was eating when I came up the driveway and paused to measure me with a careful stare and to wave airily at me after Aunt Petulia's introduction.

Inside, the whole family was in consternation. Mother was on the phone, trying vainly to track down her brothers. Edith was glowering triumphantly.

"Me know mad when me see mad!" she was exulting. "Tell me 'bout me don't know when de woman mad! Who see her go mad all

dese years? Me one! Me tell him dis morning dat she mad, and him
tell me 'bout me no know mad when me see mad. Nobody in dis
house know when dat woman go mad more dan me!"

"I can't get ahold of anybody!" my mother fumed, slamming
down the phone. "Tony, get that negar man off my veranda! She go
out into de street and pick up a perfect dirty stranger and bring into
my house and give him supper! Get him out of my house!"

"It's her house, too," I said.

"Me say me tell him dis morning dat she mad and him don't
believe. Come tell me 'bout me must mind me own business! Me
know mad when me see mad."

And so the argument raged while the phone calls were frantically
made and my sisters were banished into their rooms for the evening.
Meantime, Aunt Petulia and her new friend lolled on the veranda like
the lord and lady of the household.

Periodically, she would waddle into her bedroom, which adjoined
the veranda, call the man by name, and he would stand, hitch up his
pants, look around him with an air of self-importance, and follow
after her. Then they would come back out onto the veranda and Aunt
Petulia would serve him drinks or food.

As the evening wore on, however, the man began to get fidgety
and nervous, scraping to and from the bedroom with an increasingly
bedraggled air. At the fourth summons, he got up, looked longingly
at the walkway leading to the gate, then hung his head like one deep
in thought.

Aunt Petulia's voice rang out with an imperious edge.

"Me God!" I heard the man mutter heavily as he dragged himself
into the room. This time he did not come back out. But sometime
later I heard Aunt Petulia scolding,

"Come, man! Get up and me give you something to eat! Come
man, you can't sleep now! Get up! I going give you a Guinness
stout."

The man's muttered replies sounded like moans through the
French windows that closed off her bedroom from the veranda. Soon
after, with Aunt Petulia's voice taking on an angry edge, the doors

burst open and the man stalked off the veranda and down the walkway in a huff.

"No white woman going kill me dead tonight!" I heard him vow grimly as he trudged away into the darkness.

The next morning the uncles arrived in a righteous squad, roused Aunt Petulia out of her bed, and manhandled her into the back of their car for a trip to St. Joseph's hospital and shock treatments.

Two days later she came back her usual listless and dishevelled self and vanished into her room.

That was the pattern of my aunt's madness, which I saw repeated some five or six times over the years that we shared a house with her. But I always wondered what these uncles would have done if she had ever come back from the streets with a white English Presbyterian minister in tow.

Of course she never did. White Presbyterian ministers were scarce in Jamaica, and the few that were about simply wouldn't have her.

But all this was changed under the Manley years. With the new political awareness and pride sweeping the country the white man had been hurled headfirst off his throne. In his place we had the attitude personified by Daphne Dickson.

Daphne Dickson was a young Jamaican music teacher at the college. She was one of the new breed of professional and educated black Jamaicans staunchly loyal to Manley and his anti-colonial way of thinking. Her attitude towards the foreign tutors was one of formal politeness and distance. Towards me her manner was chilly, and once or twice in our conversations she made it plain that she regarded me, because of my white skin, as a bogus Jamaican. But towards Peter Matheson, the Englishman whose desk was next to hers, she was chattily friendly and coquettish.

One day with the bull loose, Daphne Dickson was driving past my house when I begged her for a lift. During the ride I tried to break the ice between us with a harmless joke about her and Peter Matheson. She nearly drove her Volkswagen off the road and into a ditch.

"Me and a white man!" she declared, her eyes blazing. "You mad, Winkler! Me and a white man! God would never put such a cross on me back! Never!"

"What's the matter with Peter Matheson?" I asked, taken aback. "I suppose he is an English bugger...."

"English, my foot! Him is a white man! Me is a black woman! God strike me down dead if I ever put white blood in the veins of my children! Kill me now before that happen, God! Hurl de thunderbolt."

Since it was a perfectly cloudless and sparkling day, her blasphemous wish for a thunderbolt went unanswered, but her vehemence startled me.

Some time later, I asked Elizabeth Robertson, a science teacher, about Daphne's attitude. Elizabeth was a voluptuous black Jamaican who walked about the grounds of the campus trailing a cobweb of languorous femininity after her, and we had lately become fast friends.

"I can understand how she feels," Elizabeth said. "If I married a white man, or had a child for one, I believe my friends would disown me. My father would probably kill me. My mother would never talk to me again."

By now I was feeling quite put out and aggrieved.

"But why? Wouldn't it matter who the man was?"

"Boy, Tony, you mind is in the past. This is 1975. Me want children of my own colour. My mother and father want grandchildren of their own colour. So Jamaica go today."

This change in thinking had taken place glacially in the scant thirteen years that had passed since our Independence. It was one reason for Manley's nationalistic (and therefore unavoidably racial) appeal to certain Jamaicans.

CHAPTER 10

Who was our brother, and what did we owe him? Where were w
going as a people walking through this valley of the living? These
questions were in the air with the coming of fall, which in th
mountains of Jamaica is marked by rain and a tangy coolness in th
evening breezes. They were questions implicitly raised by Manley i
his attempts to restructure our national life. So it was natural that th
tutors at the college should sit and debate them at the morning te
break, the lunch hour, the afternoon snack break, and at dinner
Between classes we debated them incessantly, weighing the lates
developments, haranguing over the wordings of Manley's mos
recent pronouncements, fussing over his legislative proposals an
programmes.

The schedule of the college was straightforward. It began every
morning with assembly in the hall for prayer, singing, and a sermor
the tutors took turns giving. When it became my turn I went to th
vice principal and told him that as a matter of principle I did not give
sermons. He replied frostily that I had to give one. I answered just a
stubbornly that I did not give sermons, that I would never have th
temerity to get up and give a religious sermon to anyone, and that n
one could make me do it. Say something inspirational, he urged
Forget about the religious content. Tell the students something t
uplift them. I could think of nothing to uplift anyone at that ungodl
hour of the morning, I countered. We parted with plain enmit
between us but also with the understanding that I would no
sermonize, ever.

After the assembly, the tutors returned to the staff room, gathered
their books and lesson plans and scattered to their classes. Those wh
had a free period sat around preparing their lessons or, as was more
likely, debating the latest sayings of Manley. At the morning snack
break, the tutors streamed from their classrooms and converged on
the dining room where we drank tea, ate sweet buns and cakes, and

talked Manley. More classes followed, then lunch, usually some gummy stew and invariably Manley for dessert. Then there were more classes, and by two o'clock, a distinct slackening of activities at the school marked by clumps of students meandering over the campus, the odd tutor or two chatting politics or the day's events in the staffroom, and athletic practice on the playing fields. Usually, by three o'clock I was done and ready to set out on my walk through the village and my furtive scurry up the driveway when the bull and his harem held office.

Democratic socialism was evidently intensely disliked by the Americans. From a practical point of view, I saw no difference between democratic socialism and any other political programme I had lived under in Jamaica. But politics is mainly a matter of symbols and this one stuck in the craw of the Eagle. The American press was continually filled with ominous reports about the gathering storm in Jamaica, and these articles, which matched the *Gleaner's* own dislike of Manley and his socialism, were liberally reprinted for the benefit of Jamaican readers.

Most of the apprehension in the local and foreign press seemed to centre on Manley's fondness for Castro, whom he was either constantly visiting or unconsciously aping in his pronouncements. Castro had dispatched some of his cadre to Jamaica, mainly construction or health workers, and they were openly regarded by some Jamaicans as the carriers of a sinister ideology. This fear struck me as fanciful and overdone, and I pressed this point whenever I participated in the mealtime debates with the tutors.

The plain fact is that Jamaicans have little in common with Cubans. Aside from being islands that are close together, the two nations are based on entirely different languages and cultures. The Jamaican is a made-over Englishman whose character incorporates the incipient disdain of the English for the hotblooded Latin. Jamaicans are wild about cricket and soccer, do not play baseball, and share none of the sickly brooding romanticism one stereotypically associates with the Spanish and their colonial offspring. Jamaicans have infinitely more in common with Barbadians, whose island is hundreds of miles distant, than they ever will with Cubans, who are camped only ninety-odd miles from their doorstep. Manley kept insisting that we should be neighbourly to all nations within our own narrow sphere, but in this judgement he seemed to have forgotten that history is strictly a temporal chronicle not a geographical one. Our hearts, minds, souls, and histories had been forged in the Englishman's fire; it is antagonistic to the Latin's.

One consequence of Manley's reaching out to the Caribbean was an influx of small islanders, especially from the Lesser Antilles, into Jamaica. Mainly because of the University of the West Indies, Jamaica had always drawn peoples from neighbouring small islands. We are comparatively large as these dots in the Caribbean go, and moving to Jamaica from, say, a mote like St. Kitts, must strike the traveller as nearly as momentous a step as a move to a continent would seem to a Jamaican. While I obviously did not know most of these small islanders who lived in Jamaica, the ones I did know seemed to me to stand squarely with Manley on almost every issue. They were vocal supporters of socialism, parroted his rhetoric of third world unity just as passionately, and were searching as determinedly for their roots in Africa, which most self-respecting Jamaicans of my generation would just as soon have forgotten.

One of them was on the faculty of our college. His name was Raymond Hunt, and he impressed everyone as a sincere although somewhat humourless socialist. His speech was vintage and lately minted Manley; his attitude was sympathetic towards the poor, hostile to the rich, wary of the foreign, and disdainful of whites. Encountering him and his rhetoric daily in the staff room made me feel like an outcast who had no homeland, identity, lineage, or history. Because I was white, he regarded me as an unauthentic Jamaican and several times insinuated that he thought I was aping an American accent. This was enough to drive me up a wall, but since I was becoming used to the neither-fish-nor-fowl syndrome that immigrants inevitably suffer in both their host and native countries, I endured his attitude with as much grace as I could muster.

Another time he explained that all the friendships and

acquaintances of my boyhood had been based on the wicked desire, congenital in the white man, to lord it over black and brown peoples. There was some sociological backing for this view, he contended, and he had the goods stashed away among his books at school (he had gone to the University of the West Indies). Melissa Richardson, the ugly Englishwoman, sat at her desk next to us during this conversation, listening intently. I was so astonished that I could only sputter about dear Mando, and dear Errol, and dear George, and dear Tom, Dick, and Harry with whom I had sweated and suffered at Cornwall College and played cricket and chased after footballs and swum to distant reefs (I did not have the nerve to mention dear Doris, who had given me my first piece, or dear Josephine, who had nearly killed me with pum-pum one rainy night when I was fifteen, for fear he see something sinister in a white boy debauching all these defenceless black women) while my hard-hearted socialist judge sat before me wearing a stony look of condemnation.

It was, however, as Thoreau is fond of tediously proclaiming in all his writings, the principle that matters, not the application. And Raymond struck me as representatively prejudiced and bitter towards white people as anyone from a similar sphere of experience and education. Part of his attitude no doubt was due to Manley's rhetoric with its constant harping on the sins of a colonial past. But much of it was in the bloodstream of the West Indian people and the inescapable consequence of our slave history.

Slavery is the mint in which an essential element of our souls was struck. When I was a boy, I regarded all the talk around me about the effects of history as nothing more than the stupid speculations of old men. By the time I was a teenager, I was convinced that Jamaicans are chronic liars about the past. I had heard so many extravagant stories told by my elders and had listened to so many dreamy romances about the years gone by that I had become cynical and suspicious about Jamaican reminiscing (especially when rum was flowing).

But when I went home to teach I soon saw that history, like

pollen, is constantly in the air. We breathe it in and out, it angers up our blood, it affects the way we live and think. Often unaware of its influence, we foolishly think that what we do we do because of personal preference or individual temperament, when the truth is that we are practising an ancient, invisible, and inherited pattern. A case in point was the Jamaican family.

One day in class we were discussing the morality of abortion when the question of illegitimate children came up. Parliament, at Manley's urging, was considering amending the legal definition of illegitimacy on the grounds that it had unfairly stigmatized a majority of poor Jamaicans. During the discussion I was surprised to learn that many of my students were mothers even though the vast majority of them were either still in their teens or early twenties and had never been married. Their children were invariably posted to the care of maternal grandparents while the mothers attended school. Not a one among them found the status of an unwed mother disconcerting or shameful. On the contrary, to a woman they were inordinately pleased with themselves and radiated obvious pride in their fertility.

This ravaging of the nuclear family, so evident among the Jamaican poorer classes, could be taken either as evidence of rampant promiscuity or the calculated practice of a tradition that has its roots in our deepest past. Historians tell us that it is the second. Slavemasters encouraged female slaves to bear as many children as they could, thus enlarging the available supply of labour, but simultaneously disallowed marriages and families. This tradition continued unchecked not only among my students, but also among a surprising number of the tutors. Men and women, many of them were married with children but did not live with their spouses for reasons either of economics or convenience. Raymond Hunt, for example, had a wife, but she lived in Nevis while he taught in Jamaica. The history tutor, whose name was Johnson, also had a wife, but she lived in Australia. Muschette, the head science teacher, had a wife and two sons but all lived in Washington, D.C. while he remained in Jamaica. And so it went.

Nor were these attachments ephemeral. Raymond's wife visited

Jamaica, became pregnant, and returned to her small island to have the child. Johnson went to Australia, got his wife pregnant, and several months later she brought the infant on a visit to Jamaica and Daddy. A month later she and the child returned to Australia. (Two years later Johnson visited Australia and got her pregnant again.) Muschette went to Washington every year where, if he were to be believed, his efforts to impregnate his wife were thwarted by her devious practice of American birth control. Though by monogamous standards these marriages may have seemed hollow, they produced children, fostered stable relationships, and endured. The only divorce to occur among the tutors during my tenure at Longstreet happened not to any of these separated spouses, but to a couple who shared a household in the village. They were miserable in each other's company, fought day and night, and finally had a nasty break-up. In contrast, the separated spouses seemed relatively happy, and during the infrequent visits by their other half, enjoyed ecstatic and contented reunions.

But it was the children whom I felt sorry for and on whom this long-standing arrangement appeared to take the greatest toll. Students of Jamaican history occasionally point an accusing finger at the overly harsh grandmother, who bears a disproportionate burden of the island's child rearing, as a prime contributor to the indiscipline and cruelty of the latest generation. Manley himself wrote about this convulsive violence sweeping the island:

> ...Robbery with rape had become the new curse. Perhaps too many ghetto youths had received too many blows from the grandmother who sought to keep order amongst half-a-dozen youths, deserted by their fathers and uncertain in their relationships with their mothers. *(Jamaica: Struggle In The Periphery* [Writers and Readers], p. 83.)

We had one graphic instance of the kind of harsh discipline for which Jamaican grandmothers are infamous. Our house stood on a knoll surrounded by a rim of encircling mountains and hills on whose slopes were scattered a handful of shacks and huts occupied by the villagers. All the tumultuous sounds and cries of life spent scrabbling on the slopes of a hard and stony mountainside rained down on our roof. On Sundays we could hear the raging of the preachers and sniff the fire and brimstone in their howls. Occasionally we could hear the crashes and screams of a domestic dispute. And sometimes we heard the demonic shrieks of beaten children.

One evening we were sitting with the Smiths on their veranda, enjoying a cooling breeze off the mountains, when somewhere on the slopes a child began a tormented shrieking from a beating. We could hear every slash of the strap and every shrill cry of agony that the blow drew. The child pleaded and begged its tormentor, but the blows rained down in an unabated fury punctuated by hoarse screams of rebuke from the parent. Derrick looked at me across the veranda.

"Beating," he said grimly.

For half an hour, the despairing wailing and sobbing echoed off the hills to the merciless gnawing of leather against flesh. Unable to bear it any longer, I went for a walk. But I couldn't help wondering about that child.

Twenty years from now with a gun in his hand and a victim impaled in its sights, what mercy would he show when his own pitiful pleas and grovelling had provoked only insensate anger and further blows?

The flesh heals quickly and forgets. But the heart sulks in its chamber, licks its wounds, and remembers.

The foreign tutors among us were a scattered and diverse lot, and I was especially interested in their reaction to Jamaica's present dishevelled state and in the reasons that had drawn them here during these days of turmoil.

Melissa, the Englishwoman who taught science, struck me as suffering the exile of spinsterhood that is unhappily the fate of some congenitally homely women. She was still a young woman, then only in her early thirties, but her body was as disproportionate and badly shaped as a frog's. An overpowering impression of homeliness, so evident in her ill-formed limbs, was worsened by a simian face complete with bulging brows and a massive jaw. Yet she had a sweet and even-tempered disposition, was quick to laugh, and her eyes shone with a bright intelligence that I took for an alluring sexual loveliness.

She had been with the school now for some six years, had stood firm throughout all the changes in educational and political fashion, and lived alone in a cottage by the sea in Runaway Bay, nearly an hour's drive away. Although I am sure she had suffered her share of racial abuse over the years, she seemed as impervious to insult as a cast-iron pot. She would not be baited into political exchanges, made no effort to shoptalk in patois, and generally went about teaching without altering her character or manner one whit to satisfy the winds of chauvinism that whooshed among us. The cannibals would have found her unchewable, unpalatable, indigestible, and in an earlier era she would have defied them behind an armament of teapot and china.

Adventure and the mirror, I thought, had brought her to Jamaica. One morning she'd gotten up out of bed, stared hard at her reflection, seen a future of empty beds and rainy English winters and said, Piss on it, then, I'm going where there's sun. And so she had come to Jamaica where she lived relatively content albeit loverless in her cottage by the sea. In return, Jamaica got a stalwart teacher who carried out her duties like a faithful nanny. She was a perennial favourite of the administration and especially of the vice principal since she never argued back over policy and took no stands on sheer principle.

Idealism was in her character, but it was the sunshine and the cottage by the beach that kept her back to the wheel. From talking with her I got the impression that she was sorry for the poor all around her, did what little she could to alleviate individual misery whenever she came across it (she might give a beggar a bob every now and again), but still saw no reason to not sleep soundly at nights. She brimmed over with sense and stability, and I speculated often to myself that one of these days a lucky man would tap into her heart and for the rest of his days be served nutritious dinners and pussy to his heart's content.

Peter Matheson, who was also English and walked about the campus trailing after him the murk of social science, was more difficult to fathom. Far from being ugly, he was handsome enough to arouse Daphne's interest in spite of her bigotry yet seemed curiously lackadaisical and indifferent to all the people and events that swirled around him. His one love was the piano, and every afternoon when he was done with his classes he retired to the assembly hall in which an old and stained piano sat in a corner and hammered out precise recitations of Beethoven's sonatas. I got so used to these afternoon concerts that I began to take them as an anthem of the day's end and a bellowing summons from my daily tormentor, the bull. He played with workmanlike dexterity and faithfully fingered every note with the touch of a skilful typist.

What was memorable about Peter was his fastidiousness. At first I put this down as an English trait—for example, I have never in my life heard an Englishman break wind, have never seen one pick his nose, and at one point in my boyhood could have been bullied into believing that the English were exempt from the tyranny of bowels (justification enough for their insufferable superiority)—but later I began to see that this fastidiousness was part of Peter's essential character. He was scrubbed and neat wherever you saw him and exuded the disciplined cleanliness of a hospital matron. Although he plainly preferred the company of men and had a succession of English male visitors during his term at the college, his manner was not prissy or effeminate. Peter had a secret that possessed him and made him guarded and polite. He kept to himself, did his job well, and the only time I attended assembly, gave a sermon characterized by such symmetry and balance that it reminded me of his piano playing. Its theme was, "If you fail to prepare, you prepare to fail," and the vice principal, a glutton for apothegm, was so impressed that later in the day I heard him clubbing some poor student over the head with it.

For the past eight or so years, Peter had spent his life going from one third world country to another, teaching. He had served in several Asian countries, had been recruited on a two-year contract to come to Jamaica, and planned to go to Chile when his term was up. As far as he was concerned, the classroom was his world, and it mattered not where it was planted, whether in Singapore or Jamaica. He was utterly apolitical and refused to side with any of the debating factions at mealtime. He tried hard to fit in with everyone, and even went so far as to speak in a strained Jamaican accent and to sprinkle his speech with local idioms. Like Melissa, he too lived in a cottage on the beach in Priory, nearly an hour's drive from the school.

Peter was in the tradition of the English second son who, denied his inheritance by an unlucky accident of birth, was obliged either to become a clergyman in his own country or go abroad and paw up the possessions of the colonies. Thousands of these second sons ended up in Jamaica during the early colonial years and nourished the soil with a steady supply of fertilizer through the predation of the yellow fever mosquito. The old graveyards of Port Royal are stuffed with the bones of these cast-off English sons. Their gravestones are so badly weathered and erased that you have to crane hard to read the inscription once crisply chiselled into the stone. One day my sisters and I took a Ouija board into one of these old graveyards and started playing with it. To our astonishment, an English parson immediately jumped up out of the grave to chat with us. "Why don't you go back where you came from?" I snarled at him and refused to work the board any longer. It was the only time in my adult years that I've ever stooped to that mean and chauvinistic insult, but I felt aggrieved that the English bugger still haunted Jamaica even after his foreign adventure had turned him into a ghost.

The other foreigners on our staff were Canadians. Evelyn Moon was one of these. Lately divorced, Evelyn had come to Jamaica as a volunteer under the Canadian equivalent of the Peace Corps. She had been subjected to months of rigorous training, had been shown films about Jamaican life and culture and steeled against the stench of poverty and tenements. She also brought her two children with her, whose custody she had won in a bitter divorce suit. Poor Evelyn's heart had been recently speared by an unfaithful husband, and the hilt of the weapon still protruded bloodily from her chest. She was over six feet three tall, had a comely and appealing shape, but a badly bruised ego. Her romantic wounds had also made her an impossible liar and exaggerator.

One afternoon she came visiting to our mountaintop. Derrick and I were discussing our plans to find a court someplace and play tennis. It turned out that only an unlucky knee injury had prevented Evelyn from playing at Wimbledon. Properly humbled, we adjourned from tennis to badminton. Evelyn volunteered that she had been the Canadian singles champion and had frequently used the current number one seed as her whipping boy during warm-ups. That career had been cruelly cut short by a balky elbow.

It was the same with every sport, every field into which we timidly ventured in our talk. She had played Cordelia in the Old Vic, had bench pressed two hundred pounds once before breakfast, had run a five-minute mile. Her son was Einstein's successor, her daughter had written an opera at three, composed her first aria in the crib between feedings. I knew that one head simply could not bear the weight of all these glories and was sorry that Evelyn thought it necessary to burden us with these fictions. Then the inevitable happened. One day after we had cleared the rubbish from a makeshift tennis court at the college, she was walking by when Derrick pressed her to come and hit the ball with us. After some protesting, she grudgingly came, swatted at the ball as though it were a pesky moth she was out to kill, and nearly broke her neck running down a lob. If she had ever before possessed a racket, it was one for which she could have been sent to prison. After bumbling about ineptly for a few minutes, she excused herself and practically ran with embarrassment to the restroom.

But Evelyn had a good heart and the courage of her convictions. She was fiercely religious and idealistic and believed strongly in hellfire and damnation, which endeared her to the vice principal, who was openly gleeful at the eternal broiling he trusted lay ahead for sinners. When Evelyn was assigned by the Ministry of Education to Longstreet, she was in a quandary: what to do with her own young school children. True, there was a primary school in Longstreet, but it was a humble and battered institution staffed by the graduates of our own college and hopelessly inadequate for teaching. It consisted of three narrow cinder block buildings whose dirty walls had been daubed over by the buggers of several student generations. The individual classes were held in an open room and separated from one another only by thin blackboards or by the arrangement of benches. On any given school day, the place was a bedlam of noise and confusion where thinking, let alone learning, was impossible. The playground surrounded the buildings like a muddy and half-drained pond, and during a heavy rain was transformed into a shallow and weedy lake.

The Jamaican tutors frankly told Evelyn that they themselves would not enrol their children in such a school. Not only was the place unhygienic and cramped, but its teachers were our own glorious students, many of whom had barely mastered arithmetic and could not even write a coherent sentence. We struggled with the sickly fruits of their labours every day in our own classes and shuddered to think what harm they might inflict on the minds of children.

Nevertheless, Evelyn enrolled her son and daughter in the local school and sent them off everyday to bleat and recite with the hordes of poor shoeless children from the village. Her children were the only white students in the school, but they seemed to suffer nothing more than the initial scrutiny of curiosity from the other students before they settled down with their own circle of friends. Perhaps the fact that they were foreigners, here only temporarily, made the difference. Perhaps it also helped that they attended a country school where the children, although from poor homes, are ruled with an iron discipline. For myself, as a white Jamaican attending a school with a majority of blacks, I know that there were only periodic and welcome interludes of relief when I was not made painfully aware of being clothed in a loathsome skin.

Idealism and the wounds of a broken marriage had brought Evelyn to us. She yearned to do good work, to make a difference, and she quickly assumed the role of the resident North American liberal who implicitly believes that government bureaucracy is the answer to the needs of the poor, not necessarily because it is efficient, but because it means well.

Then there was Mendoza, our other Canadian. Mendoza was the head of the math department, in her late thirties, and married to an Argentine whose eyes left a nasty sluglike trail up the legs of every woman he saw. She had come to Jamaica some six years before under a discontinued programme of Canadian foreign aid designed to attract the best and brightest to the teacher core. It paid Canadian salaries to its overseas teachers in Canadian currency and at Canadian scales. Since the exchange rate nervously and steadily shot up and up during Manley's gyrations, Mendoza soon became the wealthiest and most highly paid teacher among us. Her salary must have been twice the principal's. She drove an expensive car and lived in an opulent house built on the cliffs of Ocho Rios with a stairway carved out of the rock and winding down to a private beach. She could easily afford to support her ogling husband, who had had trouble getting a work permit, and he stayed at home and minded the baby while Mendoza journeyed to Longstreet every day and ran the math department. She was rumoured on campus to be a tireless and effective teacher. Students loved her and hoped for assignment to her classes (unlike the American system which gives students a choice, the class assignments at Longstreet were made by the department head).

Nothing seemed to faze Mendoza. Since her husband spoke faltering English, and since he was in charge of rearing their daughter, he had taught the child only Spanish, with the result that Mendoza, whose Spanish was worse than her husband's English, could barely converse with her own child. But that didn't seem to matter. When she was pregnant with her second child, she taught up until the day before her delivery, then calmly drove herself to Kingston, had the baby, and drove herself and the child back two days later (a Herculean feat, given the state of Jamaican hospitals and roads). Her dimwitted husband was of no help since he had no driver's licence. When the other math tutors, of whom there were two, disagreed with her on some fundamental issue, Mendoza invariably got her own way by being stubborn and tough-minded. She traipsed about the campus wearing stylish clothes,chic jewellery, arrived punctually for every class, never put in a minute of overtime, yet seemed to always get her work done. She socialized with none of the teachers—through her friendship with Cathy we were invited once to dinner at her sumptuous house on the cliffs but didn't go a second time because of her husband's sliming eyes—took part in no political discussions except to say that she detested Manley and what he stood for, and had nothing whatever to do with any extra-curricular programme at the school.

One afternoon, during a heated discussion about Manley and his programmes to help the poor, Mendoza put in a rare appearance in the staffroom, listened for a moment, and expressed a vehement political opinion. She was, she declared crisply, in Jamaica because she was being paid well and didn't give a damn about the poor. As far as she was concerned, life meant every man for himself, and she had her hands full trying to provide for a husband and two small children.

Everyone present was a little stunned by this defiant declaration, which butted smack against the prevailing winds of democratic socialism.

"Come, Mrs. Mendoza," Raymond Hunt teased. "You don't mean that. You not so hard-hearted as you sound."

"I mean it," Mendoza replied. "I mean every word of it. I'm not in the charity business. If they ever cut my pay, I'd leave in a second. I look after my family and that's it. None of this help-your-fellow-man rubbish for me."

Then she was gone, lopsidedly sagging under an armful of student papers, textbooks, and Ministry of Education notices.

The long silence in the staffroom was finally broken by Raymond, who said, almost in an admiring tone, "Mendoza is a hard woman, you know. She not easy, Mendoza."

For my own part, I saw nothing admirable in this selfish attitude and afterwards felt a deep antipathy for Mendoza that lasted throughout the entire school year.

CHAPTER 11

One of the nicest things about being home was that I once again lived among recognizable and familiar types of people. I do not know how character types are formed from one country to another, but I am certain that they exist and that they play an important part in our understanding and recognition of individual differences.

The first few years I lived in America, I suffocated in an ocean of individuals and was unable to tell personality from culture in the people I met. Everyone seemed so different, bizarre, and eccentric that my first line of defence was to think them all mad. For several years I went around with the idea in the back of my mind that I had to watch my Ps and Qs lest I say something to spark the maniacal fire in one of them. Many immigrants carry within them always a similar sense of disorientation, a gnawing sense of things not being quite right. I do not know if the sensitive immigrant ever really loses this and suspect that he eventually accepts it as the penalty of dislocation from his native culture.

Jamaicans do not see the world the way Americans do. Culture is in the person, and the person is an embodiment of the culture and the lessons it teaches. Only the mad share the same dark and undivided continent. The sane are marooned in lonely archipelagoes of experience and culture.

The Jamaican and American, for example, have distinctly different attitudes towards economic roles. The American nation is essentially a confederation of economic tribes known as businesses and corporations, each with its own totemic history, identity and, if large enough, personal pantheon and mythology. When you work for an American corporation it defines you, moulds you, instills in you a sense of belonging and membership, and eventually changes your values and perceptions. It provides for you not only by furnishing you with the necessities of living but also by encasing you in an economic and occupational role that becomes part of your formal identity. "What do you do?" is one of the first questions Americans ask strangers, not from idle curiosity, but because the answer is necessary for social appraisal and understanding.

Americans are reared with the expectation that a large part of their personal identity will eventually be defined in adulthood by an economic role. One becomes what one does. "What do you want to become?" Americans ask their children as if without this commitment to a career the child is doomed to be a perpetually stunted pupa.

One night I had two fathers over to dinner, one a Jamaican whose son was attending Oxford, the other an American whose son was at Yale. The question came up after dinner about what the son of each aspired to do. The American said that his son intended "to be an engineer." The Jamaican said that his son was "doing medicine at Oxford." The American was puzzled at first by the answer of the Jamaican father, but then after it was repeated, he said in a burst of understanding, "Oh, your boy is going to become a doctor."

Yes, replied the Jamaican. That was the ambition of his son.

But that was not what he had meant. Jamaicans *do* their careers, their occupational pursuits; Americans *become* them. The Jamaican's sentence had been no mere slip of grammar or syntax but neatly summed up an essential difference between the two cultures in their outlook about work.

In Elizabethan times one could tell the profession of a stranger by the way he dressed. Distinctive garb went hand in hand with different professions. But the American took this a step further, internalized the clothing, and made it psychological. And so occupational tests are used to predict what one will become based on one's temperament and preferences. Such tests would be impossible if norms did not exist that specify temperamental differences among the professions. But whether these differences are being inbred into America's children or whether they are inborn propensities of certain professional types, no one can say. All I can say is that in America, "You are not what you eat, but what you do (for a living)."

This wedding of personality and occupation is a most peculiar trait for Jamaicans to comprehend mainly because they have inherited from their own cultural experience a deep-seated dislike for ready-made economic roles. Jamaicans revel in the expression of an idiosyncratic self and reject any occupational role that brings with it blanket expectations of the self. Why this is so no doubt goes back to our experience with slavery when we waged an endless war of passive resistance against the slavemaster's desires and struggled hard to repudiate what he wanted us to become.

Because of this basic difference in the two cultures, much of American economic role-playing invariably strikes Jamaicans as adult tomfoolery. One of the earliest and most bizarre experiences I had with an American company came when I applied for a job as an insurance clerk. The job paid three hundred dollars a month and was a menial entry-level position that required nothing more than the ability to read and write and do basic math. For the money, one got to be another pair of hands grubbily pawing over policies in an clerical assembly line.

After being tested to death I was shuttled through a series of progressively larger offices and finally brought face to face with the manager whose final approval was necessary. He was a middle-aged man behind an impressive desk in an enormous office, and I was ushered into his presence by an unctuous secretary who deposited my application file before him. While I stood and nervously waited, he opened my file, glanced at its contents, then settled back in his chair and stared at me with an appraising wrinkle on his forehead. Not a word had yet passed between us. Still looking hard at me, he put his feet upon his desk (I remember being struck by the unworn leather soles of his shoes) and waved me into a nearby chair.

I sat and waited, his eyes boring rudely into my face.

"Well, Tony," he finally said, "what can you do for me?"

I was taken aback and for a moment did not know what to say.

"I need a job. I've always worked hard at whatever I do."

An uneasy pause settled in the room.

"But what can you do for me?" he asked, staring impatiently.

It struck me then that I was being asked to play a part, and I had read enough of American literature to have had a glimpse of my script. What I was supposed to do was to fulminate about how I would become the best damned clerk he'd ever had, how I would work my fingers to the bone, how I would devote my lifeblood to the company, and blah blah. But I simply couldn't. I desperately needed the job and without it there was a good chance that I would have to return home and lose my chance of going to college. Even so, I couldn't. Truckling to this idiot's theatrical demands would have been too demeaning to bear.

"I give a hard day's work for my pay," I said with as much dignity and as sincerity as I could, knowing even as I uttered them that my words were damning.

He jumped up and signalled for me to wait outside with a wave of his hand. The secretary was summoned and emerged a few minutes later with my partially crumpled file dangling from her fingers.

I was not hired.

The Jamaican's aversion to occupational roles is so intense and deep-seated that much of the power in the island's business and institutional life seems capriciously exercised, with the office often being subject to its holder's full range of personal idiosyncrasies. Examples of this over-personalizing of power can be seen in virtually every walk of life throughout the country, from the butcher who will sell you a better cut of meat if you give him the idea that doing so makes you personally indebted to him for life, to the postal clerk who will check for your mail if you put the request in a wheedling tone. The patois expression "Do!", pronounced "Du!" and used to beg on these occasions, has no English equivalent. It does not mean "Do," as in the command, "Do this or do that." Rather, it means "Beg you," and is often accompanied by endearing phrases such as "Me darling," "Me love," that would strike Americans as eccentrically inappropriate to address a customs official, a post office clerk, a butcher, a cabinet maker, or even the receptionist in a government office.

When I first came home I fell victim almost immediately to this peculiar streak in the Jamaican character, even though I understood it to the core. As a returning Jamaican I was entitled to bring in my car at a minimal duty so long as I could prove ownership of three years or more. I had all the necessary documents and went down to the appropriate government office hoping to get an import licence. But it was not that easy.

On my first visit I ran into a low-level official who recognized my family name and claimed to have been a school chum of my father's. We struck up a friendly conversation and he bustled about with me in tow doing his best to expedite the paperwork. Then we ran into a roadblock. An approving signature was required of an obese Indian lady, but she arbitrarily refused to give it. The papers were not in order, she said sullenly. I tried patiently to get out of her what was wrong with them. Her replies were vague, surly, and threatening. Finally she barked with sarcasm, "Get your friend Mr. Williams to help you," and tossed my application back at me.

And then it hit me. She resented the attention I had been paying to Williams and intended to teach me a lesson about her own importance. If anyone's bottom was to be kissed for this licence, her unspoken manner said, it bloody well should have been hers, not Williams's, and I was going to pay for smooching at the wrong rear end.

I have a stubborn streak in my make-up, and years of battering about on the lower rungs of the American social ladder have made me scrappy and hardened against begging anyone to do what he or she is being paid to do. Moreover, there is a part of me that is fond of gratifying institutional punctilios, even unreasonable ones. So instead of grovelling before this woman, I steeled my jaw and demanded that she tell me what I had not done and I would do it. This attitude, which she took as an insulting unwillingness to kiss the right bottom just because it happened to be hers, threw her into an even greater fury. She hit me with form after form, clouted me over the head with regulation after regulation, until finally I gave up. By then matters had soured so much between this official and me that it was too late to start all over—a hundred years of brown-nosing would not have appeased her.

One day I mentioned to my aunt the trouble I was having bringing my car into the country and dropped the name of the contentious official who was holding up my application. My aunt brightened visibly.

"But that's me good friend!" she said. "I tell you what. Come over next week Saturday afternoon for tea and I'll fix it for you."

So the next Saturday afternoon I showed up at my aunt's for tea and there in a wicker chair sagged my obstructing official in an enormous puddle of brown flesh. She raised her eyebrows slightly as I was introduced and muttered sarcastically that "we had met." But one or two tell-tale and triumphant sniffs hinted that she knew what this tea was really about and was, in the presence of my aunt her friend, finally prepared to accept the smooching that had been unjustly withheld from her bottom. For the next hour I answered all her inane questions about what America was like and what books I had written and smiled and simpered so much that I made myself sick.

As she prepared to waddle away, she said offhandedly, "Come and see me next week and I'll see what I can do for you."

And the next Monday I got my import licence.

The run-in with this stubborn official was not my worst encounter with the idiosyncratic abuse of power that is epidemic in the island. An even worse example occurred at the school, but this time I triumphed by "going on bad." This expression has a peculiar meaning to the Jamaican and no known equivalent in America. To "go on bad" is to employ the behaviour of the lower class in a sphere of life where it is outlandishly inappropriate. One cannot "go on bad" in a true democracy like America but only in a society that separates people into classes by a strictly prescribed code of manners. Under the Englishman's colonial blueprint, the ragged brute in the streets is expected to rant and rave over grievances and raise his voice in profanity, but not the tuxedoed gentleman at a formal dinner. And should the gentleman so behave for whatever reason other than rare excusable drunkenness, he is said to have "gone on bad." His sin is not so much bad behaviour as it is a degenerate hybridization of manners—bringing the lower-class brute into the drawing room—and the penalty is social expulsion. He simply will never be invited back.

The cause of my "going on bad" was the school's bursar. She was a rakishly lean young woman whose unblinking stare was an asp bite, and she had a terrible habit of paying the tutors only when she pleased. We were then living on my salary of two hundred and eighty nine dollars per month and having a difficult time making it stretch. At the end of every month, after we had forked over one hundred dollars for rent, the rest was quickly gobbled up by food and gas. So it was provoking not to be paid on time.

On this particular month our pay was three days late and all the tutors were grumbling about it. Our rent was overdue and we had no food in the house. One tutor had apologetically approached the bursar and had gotten pricked in the face by her serpent stare. I decided to take matters into my own hands and walked over to the bursar's office.

Our conversation went something like this.

"Yes, Mr. Winkler," the bursar said when she saw me standing in the doorway. "Can I help you?"

"Miss Mason, I was wondering when we would be paid."

"When I'm not so busy."

"Do you know that it's three days into the month? I have to pay my bills."

"Mr. Winkler, I said I will pay the tutors when I'm not so busy."

"What am I supposed to tell my landlord, Miss Mason?"

"I don't care what you tell your landlord, Mr. Winkler. I will pay the tutors when I'm ready."

"What could be more important than paying the tutors, Miss Mason?"

"Mr. Winkler, if you don't mind, I have work to do."

And then I began to go on bad.

"Miss Mason, I want my rass pay."

It was as if I had exploded a thunderbolt under her nose. Her head snapped back with a jerk and her face swayed grim and hooded like a cobra's above the clutter of papers on her desk. She uncoiled into a standing position and raised her right hand with ceremonious indignation to cup her ear.

"What did you say?" she asked dangerously.

This chilling act almost broke my resolution, but I had committed myself and the only course left was to revel in my gutter tactics and "go on bad."

"I said, I want my rass pay. I'm not leaving this rass office until I'm paid."

"You dare use such a word to me, sir!" the bursar said menacingly. "You dare!"

"Words, Miss Mason? You don't hear words yet! You want to hear some bad words? You know how many bad words I know?"

"No, sir, I don't want to hear. I'm sure you know them all."

"I do, Miss Mason. So help me God, I do. And I'm going to cuss every striking one of them if I don't get paid today. You hear me, Miss Mason? You going to hear bad words you never dreamt of in your life before if I don't get paid today."

"Mr. Winkler, you are a tutor at this school...."

"Tutor my backside! I want my blasted pay!"

And for the next half an hour I posted myself outside her door scowling and muttering bad words. But then I had a class so I poked my head into the room and told her with a sprinkling of "rasses" and other patois bad words that when I got back if my pay cheque wasn't ready I was going to raise a stink she would remember on her deathbed.

After class I trudged back to the staff room to find the faces of the tutors wreathed in glee and the banter of Christmas on every tongue. We had been paid.

But I was forever after in the bursar's bad books, and whenever we passed on the campus she treated me with the chillingly formal manner Jamaican spinsters use on incorrigibly hardened brutes.

Aside from the venality of officials, the constant shortages were most irritating and difficult to get used to now that I was home again. There was a shortage of everything imaginable: goods, books, food, gasoline, and expertise. This last shortage was the worst of them all because it threw the hapless citizen on the mercies of improvising amateurs. You wanted your car fixed, but there was no one who really thoroughly understood how it worked. There was a little man who knew electrical systems and could do a makeshift job of patching here and there, but he was stumped by the knock in the engine. You wanted your propane stove fixed but there was no one who really understood how this brand worked. You wanted a radio fixed but the man in town understood only English radios and yours was Japanese. It seemed as if every little breakdown of an appliance was the occasion for a full-blown emergency. Every fly speck became a mountain of tiresome inconvenience.

Derrick Smith, our neighbour on the hill, fell victim to the general shortage of expert help. One day I was leisurely walking home from school when I found him and his car stranded in the driveway. His car, an aging Fiat, had broken down and a collection of self-proclaimed experts summoned from the village were noisily digging into its open hood. Opinions and diagnoses flew thick in the air accompanied by derisive laughter and much vainglorious squabbling. From the hubbub one man emerged victorious and the others dwindled into kibitzing spectators while he had an unhindered go at the engine.

He proceeded to bang and claw and unscrew and dismantle, yelling occasionally over his shoulders for tools while passing wordy opinion on the design of the engine, and as the evening wore on its parts spilled out onto the guinea grass like the intestines of a frightened sea cucumber. Derrick displayed stoic patience during the early hours of this operation, but as the sun began to set and darkness settled in lengthening shadows over the fields, he began to lose his temper. The excuses offered by the mechanic were glib and familiar: this tool was not right for the job, this distributor cap had been incorrectly placed by the Italians, this wire was one he had never seen before in all his born days in an engine, and God knew he had

seen many engines in his time. By the time the twilight had
thickened around us like cold gravy, we knew the truth: the car
would not be fixed tonight. But there was always the hope of the next
day, and the mechanic was voluble in emphasizing that once he had
gotten hold of the right tool, the right wire, the right this and that, the
engine would be as good as new. Derrick and I trudged up the hill to
our respective houses with the man's promises ringing in our ears.

The next afternoon the mechanic reappeared and, fired up with
renewed vigour, made another scrabbling run at the engine. He had
gotten the right tool but the wrong wire but he thought he could make
it work on sheer ingenuity or his name wasn't Sam. So he banged and
poked and clanked and the pastures sounded like the inside of a body
shop. Night began to settle again, and still he wasn't finished, but the
wrong wire had been made right, and the right tool had done the job
so there only remained reassembling the engine, whose parts were
now so strewn over the grass that the scene wanted only blood to
resemble a gory dismemberment. After we had been reduced to
holding flashlights and lighting matches for the officious
mechanic—who was now exhibiting the megalomania of the expert—we
finally had to face the unpleasant truth that the car wouldn't be ready
this evening. The next day it would be fixed, was the mechanic's
parting shot, so help him God, or he would crawl into the grave beside
his dead mother.

And so he had another violent whack at the engine the next
afternoon. Derrick and I arrived early, ready to help the mechanic in
any way we could, and he lit into the engine with a fresh burst of
energy. But somewhere in the afternoon, in broad daylight and at
about the same time, the horrible truth began to dawn on me and
Derrick: the mechanic could not reassemble the engine. Perhaps it
was the way he stared at each new part with a puzzled expression, or
perhaps it was his constant scurrying back and forth from the car to
the parts scattered over the pasture, fetching a different one and
eyeing it with momentary mystification before plunging again under
the open hood in an orgy of banging and cursing. But I don't think
so. I think what finally tipped us off was how his swearing and

cursing became progressively more directed against Italians. He swore that this part had come from that hole, but the &*%$## Italians had made it so that once you took it out it would never fit back in. He knew that this ring belonged around this tube, but the &^%$$#@!* Italians had booby-trapped it so that once extracted, the ring could never be reseated. The stupid %$#$&**^%$ Italians had deliberately made this part the twin of that one just to confuse the public, and he didn't know whatever made the &$#@*+* jackasses think they were good for making anything other than pizza and spaghetti. The final straw was when the mechanic exploded in a flurry of bellowing and cursing and flung an unfittable part into the pastures where, as luck would have it, the piece buried itself right into the squishy core of a cow pat. Chagrined, the mechanic retrieved the part, only to find one of its microscopic holes, which had to remain open, plugged by a wad of shit. So from banging and clanging on the engine he was reduced to plucking away with a straw at a tiny and essential hole which the Italians knowingly had put into this part just so it could be stopped up by cow shit. Another sunset found us stranded in the pasture, wandering in a daze among the strewn parts of the dismantled engine.

The next day, when the mechanic did not show up, the truth was confirmed. He could not reassemble the engine. His ministrations had reduced the Fiat from a solid object to a collection of pieces that we gathered into brown bags and stored in the trunk and the back seat. Then, with the car bundled up into itself and marooned on the only driveway leading to the pasture, Derrick went into Kingston to hire a tow truck. Two weeks later one arrived and towed the car away.

In a fury, Derrick got a lawyer in Kingston to write the inept mechanic a letter threatening to sue for damages. The mechanic sent back a message that he would kill himself if Derrick.went through with the lawsuit. Derrick wrathfully replied that suicide was the least the mechanic could do. The messenger trudged down to the village and returned the next day to say that the mechanic meant his threat and wasn't joking and that Derrick could take the body. If he got hold of the body, Derrick raged at the messenger, he intended to bury it upside down in lime the way murderers fresh from the gallows were buried. And so the messages of lawsuit and suicide flew back and forth between our hill and the village for a good month.

But nothing came of the exchange. Derrick did not sue and the mechanic did not kill himself. As for the Fiat, the garage in Kingston said that they had to send away to Italy for a certain part and the car couldn't be fixed until it arrived. Three months later the part arrived, but it was for the wrong model Fiat. Six months later the new part arrived, but it was for the wrong year Fiat.

Eighteen months after the gathering of pseudo-experts in the driveway of our pastures, the dismembered Fiat still languished in the garage in Kingston, unassembled and unfixed.

CHAPTER 12

During the first term I discovered among my students one who stood head and shoulders above the others. Her name was Mavis Prince and she was a lissome black woman of twenty with a sinewy figure and waspish personality. She was one of the two students whose candidacy as student representative the vice-principal had rejected, sparking the silence strike. All of my other students were grappling with the unfamiliar medium of the written word in their papers, except Mavis. She was wrestling with ideas and expressing them in glittering images and sophisticated allegory.

The first essay that drew her to my attention was a suggestive allegory about a white cock penned in a cage for protection against a black mongoose that prowled hungrily outside contriving a way to breach the wire. There was no neat ending to the tale, merely a menacing envoi which promised that sooner or later black mongoose would get in and devour doomed white cock. I do not remember what the assigned topic was, but this allegory coupled with other unmistakable hints Mavis had thrown out made it plain to me who was white cock and who was black mongoose. Under different circumstances, white cock would have clawed through the wire and blissfully sacrificed himself on the jaws of ravenous black mongoose, but not this time. I was deeply in love with Cathy and had made up my mind to avoid all other romantic entanglements, which struck me as the only sensible decision for any young man teaching in a school of 385 female and 15 male students.

One day Mavis was waiting for me outside my classroom with another girl. The two of them came to the point: they wanted to sit for the A level examination in English literature but no one at Longstreet was willing to tutor them. Without an A level pass, they said, they would not even be considered for admission to the University of the West Indies where they both hoped to go after they were done at Longstreet. Would I help them? I said I would look into it and let them know.

My department head was against the project from the start. She reminded me that in exchange for their free education and board, the students at this school were bound to future service with the government as teachers. They were destined for the classroom of some rural school, not for the university, and to encourage them to think otherwise would be a mistake. The other tutors to whom I mentioned it were of the opinion that A level was decidedly beyond any Longstreet student, and that for one to even attempt the examination was sheer folly.

I do not know what convinced me to tutor these students, but I think it was the whiff of the colonial Englishman's gospel about minding one's place in these admonitions. Jamaicans as a whole tend to be quite taken with the English belief in inheritance and hierarchy and, like the Englishman himself, frequently mistake ambition for bumptiousness. When I asked myself what on earth was wrong with tutoring ambitious students who wanted to take the A level exam in English literature, I could find no good answer. If the students were willing to devote their evenings to the extra study required, what was wrong with trying?

On my next visit to Kingston I went to the University library looking for past A level examinations, found several, and spent an afternoon reading them. They consisted of the sorts of imponderable questions about the works of dead writers that juniors in American universities have to grapple with.

There is something inevitably legalistic about literary papers. One is not quite as caught up in the cant of citing precedents as the lawyer, but one is every bit as argumentative about abstract (and frequently meaningless) issues, and almost always what one says counts as much as how one says it. Next to saying things well, saying imaginative things about the writer's work also counts a great deal—whether they are demonstrably true or not. I remember that for my own Master's comprehensive examination I undertook to prove the absurd argument that a certain poem I liked was just as alive as a landlady I despised, and I must have been convincing because I earned a pass.

Could these two students take A level literature and pass? Mavis definitely had a chance. My days in graduate school had taught me that the stolid burgher you would gladly have as a next-door neighbour usually did literary criticism badly, while the born assassin who but for want of a cause and a victim has never struck a fatal blow, often did it well. It needed a mind not overly impressed with the premises of reality nor particularly bounded by its truths, and Mavis struck me as having these nihilistic traits in just the right combination. She had a poisonous tongue and often tried to slip some nasty gossip about my fellow tutors into her conversations with me—usually some wicked rumour of sexual perversion or wife-beating—and burned with a fiery resentment of authority. Given the opportunity, she definitely had the mind for tunnelling through the carapace of some abstract poem and wriggling out with its symbolic heart between her jaws.

As for her friend, whose name was Jeanie, I had my doubts. Although she was not nearly as quick as Mavis, her writing showed a flair for getting to the point and hammering it home with economy. Yet she seemed altogether too awed by the written word to criticize it effectively, but there was hope that close contact with Mavis over the year would change that.

I could be of no help to Mavis and Jeanie unless the syllabus for the upcoming examination contained the works of authors I felt qualified to teach, and after locating it, I still wasn't sure. The assigned works included Shakespeare's *Hamlet* and *Love's Labours Lost;* several books from Swift's *Gulliver's Travels;* Pope's *The Rape of the Lock;* the "Prologue" and "The Wife of Bath's Tale" from Chaucer's *Canterbury Tales;* a selection of verse from Dryden and Donne, and the "Don Juan in Hell" excerpt from Shaw's *Man and Superman.* I felt competent to teach *Hamlet*, Swift, Chaucer, all of which I had written lengthy papers on during my Master's seminars; uncertain of Pope; tottering on Shaw; and hopeless with Donne and Dryden. *Love's Labours Lost* was a complete blank to me because I had never formally studied it or seen it performed.

Having got hold of a specimen passing A level paper, I made copies of it and met with the two girls at the school one night. I told them that I would tutor them but I wasn't certain that I had the time or even the necessary books to get them through. We would have to meet every evening for at least two hours, and they would have to cram like they had never crammed before in their lives. I showed them the passing paper and sat quietly while they read it.

They were downcast when they had finished. Did I think they had a chance? they asked. I was a great believer in chances, I answered. Where there's life there's hope. Two or three more such platitudes and Mavis sourly demanded to know what chance I thought they had of passing under the circumstances.

"Honestly?" I asked.

"Of course!"

"Maybe twenty percent."

"Twenty out of a hundred," she murmured.

"Two out of ten," Jeanie said without hope.

They both looked crestfallen.

"I will do it, if you girls want to try," I said. "But I want to be realistic with you. None of the other tutors think you have even a ghost of a chance."

Mavis looked angry.

"I want to try," she said with determination.

"I suppose I'll try, too," Jeanie added faintheartedly.

"Good!" I said. "So we need to get started right away on Chaucer. We meet tomorrow evening at eight. We'll work until ten. That's our schedule from now on. Five classes a week, from eight to ten."

I got up to leave. The two of them hadn't moved.

"Mr. Winkler," Jeanie said softly, her eyes on the floor, "we don't have any books."

"You don't have a copy of Chaucer?"

"No."

"Let's go to the library and see if there's one."

So we went to the library and found a volume of collected British poetry containing the Chaucer works, but since it was on the reserve shelf, the librarian wouldn't let us check it out.

Outside the library, standing on a walkway lit with the glow from the dormitory's lights and stippled with the quivering shadows of windblown trees, we had to face the fact that without books we couldn't even begin. The whole enterprise suddenly seemed utterly hopeless to me. I promised to get them some volumes of Chaucer on my next visit to Kingston, and we agreed that next week we would begin our study.

That weekend I located two school editions of Chaucer and delivered them to the girls. The following Monday night, in the middle of a torrential thunderstorm, we began our cramming.

It is a truism of village life that unknown numbers of destinies palpably intersect, often with immediate and profound consequences. For if a city is an enormous concrete switchyard through which every life is a trolley shuttling on its own private track, a village is a tipsy ferry boat which can be upset by anyone with a wilful eccentricity.

A case in point was the bus driver who ruined the mornings of the entire community. He drove a bus that ran from Kingston, stopped off in Longstreet, and then disappeared up a winding road that squiggled past our house and climbed the dark face of a distant mountain.

Early in the morning with the larval earth still wrapped in a cocoon of fog and amniotic dimness, this madman's bus swooped down on the village with a horrendous honking. It honked with the wild and frenzied trumpeting of a mad goose. And it honked on the loneliest and emptiest of roads, one so lightly trafficked that you could have catnapped daily on it and still lived out your allotted years. At six o'clock sharp every morning, the honking would begin. Rain or shine, fog or clear sky, the bus would blow into the village like some tormented beast, then make its way down the empty mountain road, snarling and coughing and honking.

The villagers complained to the police, and a constable was said to have gotten up early one morning and rebuked the driver. But rumour also winded through the village that the driver had replied that he loved the sound of his horn in the fog, and it was only in Longstreet that he ran through such a deliciously echoing patch of it. So he honked and honked and honked, and although several of the villagers swore that one morning they intended to set up a roadblock, ambush the bus and hack out its horn, they could do nothing but endure the nuisance.

"Maybe he'll catch sick and die," a villager muttered to me hopefully one day about the bus driver.

He might have done so in a Hollywood movie. But in real life he continued to grow stronger and heartier, and every blessed morning before even the gurgling cries of the canaries splashing in our outdoor tank, several blasts from his air horn shattered the stillness of the fog-shrouded land and rudely roused all but the very dead.

Then there were the soldiers whose camp was just on the outskirts of the village. Ordinarily we heard nothing at all from them and if their tents and barracks had not been visible from the main road we might not even have known where they were bivouacked. But occasionally a soldier would take a fancy to bird shooting and come sauntering down our country lane in hunt of prey. One day I was setting out for my class when I heard the clatter of automatic weapon fire. The sound rattled through the pastures and drum-rolled off the face of the mountains in a murderous tattoo. A few minutes later I came across two stony-faced soldiers tramping down the road with M-16s slung over their shoulders. Between the fingers of one of them dangled a dead sparrow with a gaping red hole punched in its side.

We were nearly abreast when they spotted another bird in the limbs of a tree. One soldier pointed excitedly, the other unslung his weapon, and opened up with an ear-splitting fusillade. Startled out of its wits, the poor sparrow appeared to madly dance and duck like a cartoon bird dodging whizzing bullets. Then, inexplicably, it crumpled and plunged to the earth like a rockstone. I watched the soldiers trample into the bush and retrieve it. They stood by the roadside poring over the limp body and marvelling out loud that they could find no bullet wound. I was tempted to yell at them that the poor bird had obviously dropped dead of sheer terror. Life in the bush-country had not prepared it for military assault by soldiers of the Jamaica Defence Force armed with American made M-16s.

"Come shoot little bird with machine gun," an old woman muttered with disgust as she scratched past with a basket of yams swaying on her head. "Out of order!"

Then there was the madman in the village. He was a middle-aged black man with the perfectly tonsured head of a medieval monk and a comical rounded body that looked roly-poly from too much baby fat. But he was completely mad and occasionally would even become stark and raving about it. When his madness struck, he would sit on an embankment and shriek or stagger in the middle of the road, cursing the heavens in a ranting gibberish. People would scurry out of his path, but once they were satisfied that he was drifting away safely in another direction, pause to observe him keenly.

As far as mad behaviour went—howling and prancing and that sort of thing—his repertoire was no wilder than the antics of seasoned lunatics I had seen in Kingston. But he was our madman, our own village lunatic, and when he even mildly erupted every villager within earshot would stop and watch him with the fondness of a geologist doting over a local volcano. Once or twice on my way home from the school I would hear him blowing off steam and see the crowds attending his fulminations in a discreet circle. But I never paused to join them, reasoning that the sight of a gawking white man might really cause the poor fellow to run amok. To be white in a black country is to be conspicuous enough; to be the only white man watching a black man go mad in the streets is asking for trouble.

But the sharpest tremor in our small boat was set off by an ugly rumour. Two motorcyclists were said to have stopped off at the village gas station, taken a disgruntled turn around the pump, and then made the menacing remark before leaving that "dis place too quiet, man! Saturday, we goin' come back and liven it up." What that mischievous remark intended we did not know, but many villagers took it to mean that a horde of Kingston gunmen would invade Longstreet that weekend.

It is common to see country people carrying machetes, but that Saturday the profusion of sharpened blades in the hands of men slouching against the stained walls of dilapidated buildings or placing bets in the off-course horse racing shop seemed especially sinister. Some of them got drunk, as they usually did, and the talk was wild and loose about the upcoming invasion.

Fortunately, none occurred. No bloodthirsty gunmen charged down our narrow main street and butchered the garrison of flies guarding the smelly entrance to Mrs. Simpson's rickety country shop. Manley gave a speech and Mrs. Simpson's radio carried it live over the loudspeaker nailed to the transom of her shop's doorway. A few passersby listened with faint interest, and a dog fight broke out among the mangy mongrels over whose turn it was to snooze in the middle of the road and goad the stupid human drivers into an indignant honking. And at seven o'clock sharp, the grey door of the tiny police station was tacked shut with a padlock as one constable drifted off into the foggy countryside on his bicycle while another was swallowed up by the smoking mouth of a rum shop.

Our village been been spared.

Whenever I saw our local madman stomping down the back lanes, he brought to mind my father and the curious relationship he had developed over the years with his mad sister-in-law, my other mad aunt.

When he was sober Father was not unpleasant to be around so long as he was not engaged in carpentry work or trying to repair a machine. Then he would bellow oaths and curses at appliances and machines and tools as if he could hear them taunting him in return. Everything inanimate became fair game for his rage when he was in this temper. He kicked doors, punched windows, bucked walls, bit tables, and gouged chairs. Unjustly attacked, the physical world replied with equal virulence. A tree broke his back; a window pane lashed his face; an overstuffed chair snapped his leg bone. Casings skinned his knuckles, wrenches bit him on the fingers, springs raked his forearms, and doorways spitefully reached out and clouted him on the head as he innocently walked past.

But when he was not on a mechanical mission, Father could be a model of tolerance and equanimity. And he was especially so with my mad aunt.

This particular aunt was the same who had been married off at sixteen by my bigoted maternal grandfather to a Lebanese gentleman from the country thirty years her senior. The philosophy of this old gentleman was that a young wife should be ruled by the strap, and he proceeded to practice this wickedness on poor Aunt Sophia. By the time I was old enough to know her, Aunt Sophia had hardened into a battle-axe fifty pounds heavier than her despotic husband, who had withered with the passing years into a frail old man. Several times I had seen her bare her teeth at the enfeebled tyrant and watched him slink off mumbling helplessly. Once she had even boxed him in my presence for answering her impertinently, and not knowing of his former cruelties, I had felt sorry for him.

Yet it was obvious to all who knew her that Aunt Sophia was mad. She was tormented by an obsession that had become the grounds of a lawsuit against one of her brothers-in-law and an embarrassment to the whole family. As Aunt Sophia told it the story was garbled beyond comprehension, but it hinged on a visit she had made at Christmas to one of her sisters during which, she proclaimed wildly, the sister's husband had tried to murder her with an injection. Suffering imaginary infirmities and pains, Aunt Sophia had gone into Kingston seeking compensation for her injuries and fallen into the clutches of an unscrupulous lawyer who encouraged her madness by filing a lawsuit against the bewildered brother-in-law. Like the chancery suit in Dickens's *Bleak House,* the case had been pending now for several years and required only periodic transfusions of a fresh fee to keep it alive.

This lawsuit was all Aunt Sophia talked about. She lived and breathed and ate and dreamed her lawsuit. She babbled and

masticated constantly on it. She told of her injuries, she muttere
about memory loss and weaknesses, she affected to walk with a limp
Constipation, diarrhoea, headache, changes in the weather, slumps i
business—all were laid squarely on her attempted murder b
injection. She regaled everyone who came within earshot with detail
about her case, with the lawyer's latest letter, with fresh aches an
pains in her bones caused by her poisoning.

And Father listened. At least he pretended to listen. I saw ther
together many times, especially at lunch, because whenever we wer
in her parish, it was to Aunt Sophia's house that Father went for
home-cooked meal. And Aunt Sophia happily served it in exchang
for the chance to bring Father up to date on her case.

The thing went this way between them. Lunch would be served
Father had a wonderful appetite and a trencherman's gut, and Aun
Sophia was a superb cook. Father would read the *Gleaner* and chev
on a dumpling, and Aunt Sophia would sit beside him and chat in
monologue about her imaginary injuries.

"De doctor said he never see such arthritis in his born days. H
say only poisoned people have arthritis so bad as I have it. He say
someone poison you. Who would do a wicked thing like that?"

"Brute people, dem," Father muttered.

"Last night de whole night I suffer one beast of a headache.
take five aspirin and it don't help. Even today, me head still painin;
me. Is de poison coming back out of me liver. It circulate into m
liver and stop dere for a while, but den it come right back again. I
like underground river, you know, dat how poison work. It sink dowi
and don't trouble you for a while, den it come back up again and
pain you all over."

"Wicked people, dem," Father editorialized, turning the page o
the *Gleaner* and attacking a slab of mackerel laid out on the plate in a
vitreous puddle of onions, peppers and grease.

"Imagine, dis, eh? I go visit me own sister, me own flesh and
blood, and her damn husband come give me poison injection as me
sleep as a guest under dem own roof. You ever hear of such
wickedness in you life?"

"Wretch!" Father said, stuffing mackerel down his mouth.

After I had watched them together on a number of occasions, I began to realize that Father had a round of only three remarks to make and that he always delivered them in the same sequence no matter what Aunt Sophia said. If he said, "Brute people, dem," or its simple variation of "Brutes," he always followed this up with a phrase about "wickedness." From wickedness he journeyed to "wretches," and from wretches sallied back to "brute." If his mouth was too stuffed for him to say anything, he would shake his head sorrowfully without interrupting a chew.

For her part Aunt Sophia said everything in a monotone, whether it had to do with the cresting of the river of poison in her liver, the latest twinges in her joints, or the poisoned injection by the wicked brother-in-law. Discussing either murder or dumpling, her tone never changed: it was always flat and droning like the Hail-Marys of bored children.

I was then fifteen, keen on psychology, and positively eager to help Auntie get over her obsession. I had spent considerable time and trouble thinking about her problem and believed I had hit upon the answer. That the crime had been attempted in bed at night with Aunt Sophia flat on her back made it elementary to my mind that the imagined assault was a juicy textbook case of tabooed sexuality. In brief my theory went this way, although I worked it out with endless refinements: Aunt Sophia had had the hots for her brother-in-law and, unable to admit it, had projected her illicit passion into the demented fantasy of assault by a symbolic phallus (the phantom injection). To insulate herself from this unbearable truth, she had filed her famous lawsuit.

I am not sure what outcome I expected from my decision to reveal my theory to Aunt Sophia; but I suspect that in my adolescent innocence and naivete, I would not have been surprised if, after an enlightened gasp and pause, she had said,

"Yes! Yes! I see it now! You're quite right! Me God, it's so clear! All along it was Clarence's cock I was after, but I couldn't bring myself to admit it. I've done the family wrong. I'll call the lawyer and cancel the suit right away! Thank you, Tony, for bringing this to my attention!"

Whereupon I would reply modestly, "It's nothing, Auntie." And then mutter a lie about her being my favourite aunt. Freud would have done no less.

I had worked this out on the mental drawing board and pored over it innumerable times when my chance finally came. We had stopped at Auntie's house for lunch, Father's nose was buried in the *Gleaner,* and Auntie was mouthing her usual monologue as she served the meal.

"Imagine dat, eh," she said to me as she dished up a helping of plantains, "you go and visit you own sister and her husband creep into your bedroom and give you injection in you sleep!"

"Aunt Sophia," I asked in a tone I hoped did not sound too scheming, "where did he give you the injection?"

I held my breath, fearful that she might blurt out, "In my pussy," and ruin the brilliant denouement I had carefully prepared.

She stopped dead in her tracks and peered down suspiciously at me.

"In me arm. Right in de fleshy part of me arm."

"Which arm?"

"What you mean, which arm? Me right arm, of course. What you mean, which arm?"

"Was it dark in the room?"

"Dark in de room? Of course, it was dark in de room. Is nighttime, it must be dark in de room."

"How big was the needle?"

("Eight inches" was the answer I was hoping for.)

"How big was de needle? What you mean how big was de needle? It big enough to hold poison. How you mean how big was de needle?"

"Did you fondle de needle?"

"Fondle de needle? How you mean? De needle stick me! Me never fondle de needle! Me was sleeping! How me can fondle de needle and me sound asleep!"

It was getting a little unnerving having her repeat all my questions. What's more, her voice had jumped an octave with each reply and was now menacingly shrill.

"Did the needle feel metallic or, er, fleshy?"

"Did de needle feel metallic or, er, fleshy? What you mean, did de needle feel metallic or, er, fleshy? It feel like poison needle, dat's what it feel like. Him stick de needle in me arm and inject de poison. How you expect it to feel? When doctor stick needle in you arm, how t feel? It no feel like a needle?"

Up to now I had been trying to be nonchalant in my questioning and had affected to be absently engrossed in lunch. But Aunt Sophia was bellowing in such an angry voice that feigned indifference was no longer possible. I glanced up and grasped with sudden insight that she was an enormous heifer of a woman and that in her rage she now towered several biblical cubits above my chair, her fists clenched and within striking distance of my unhelmeted head.

Her old husband, who had been dozing in the drawing room during this exchange, awoke at her angry tone and slunk away after a furtive glance over his shoulder. Father was glaring at me over the edge of the *Gleaner*. But it was the murderous, insensate look in Auntie's eyes that riveted my attention. I cleared my throat and pretended to take another nibble of plantain.

"Why you ask me dese damn fool-fool question?" Auntie shrieked in the voice of the madhouse. "De man come jab needle in me arm when me dead asleep under him roof! Him poison me and now de poison circulate like underground river in me liver. Him creep into de room where me sleeping and give me injection! Now me can't sleep because every joint pain me at night!"

There was a sinister pause while she calculated whether to do me in with a butcher knife or a machete. I thought quickly, my head in a whirl. Finally, with my mouth nearly filled with plantain, I muttered,

"What a brute!"

Auntie gave an unappeased snort.

"De lawyer say him hear case like dis all de time, when brother-in-law try and poison sister-in-law with injection. Up to last night me

head pain me so bad me walk de floor all night. All for what? Wha
me do dis man? Why him do this to me?"

Another probing pause.

"Wicked people, dem," I said ignominiously, tamping the bod
of Freud deeper into the garbage can.

"Dem wicked of course! Only a wicked man would d(
something like dis to him sister-in-law who is a guest under hin
roof. Who else would do something like dat to him own family?"

"Wretch!" I said with feeling.

I had lost my appetite. I pushed away my plate of uneaten food.

Auntie became solicitous.

"What happen? You don't like your lunch?" she asked, her wrath
completely gone.

"I'm not hungry," I said faintly.

Father snorted.

Years later, after Father had dropped dead from a heart attack,
saw Aunt Sophia at his funeral. This was to be our last meeting. She
drew me aside in the cemetery, patted me consolingly on the
shoulder, and said, "You father was a good man. I going miss him."

Through my tears, I thanked her.

"Me case come up next week," she added triumphantly. "I'm
sorry you father won't be here to see me collect from the murdering
brute."

And those were the last words I heard her say.

Her case came up the following week and was instantly thrown
out by the court. Why, the magistrate demanded of the lawyer, was
this obviously troubled woman and her demented fantasies
encouraged to be the basis of a lawsuit? Why was she not, instead,
referred to professional help, which she obviously needed? The
attorney's reply was not printed in the *Gleaner* story and the only
reference to Aunt Sophia in it reported that she "behaved oddly"
during this scolding.

Three years later Aunt Sophia died, still raving about her case,
and was laid to her rest beside Father.

CHAPTER 13

Every night our cottage was besieged by an army of bugs. Wave after wave of them nightly scaled the window screens and clawed at the netting. As soon as we turned on the lights at dusk the green mesh came alive with the pestilential swarms, mandibles grinding, feelers gingerly probing the interstices, hairy legs tapping impatiently.

The first wave consisted of a type of ungainly green bug that walked with a drunken roll. It had two barbed pinchers which it fastened around the pores of the screen, emitting a tiny screeching like a distant off-key violin. Once it had hooked its pinchers through a pore, it remained in place for hours, motionless and inert like a leech.

Later came a wave of fidgety bugs with a splash of red across their armoured brows and piercing, needlelike feelers which they used to puncture the mesh as if to suck out the marrow of warmth and light from our house. I took a warped pleasure, once they had driven their feelers through the screen and were twisting and turning like a probing blade, in flicking these bugs off to drown in the ocean of darkness below.

Then came the love bugs, their rounded red backs splattered with ink drops, scampering with the rough and tumble air of rugby players. If I were starving in a desolate place, these were the ones I would eat, for they seemed as if they would crunch deliciously between the teeth like an overcooked kernel of corn.

Sometimes a praying mantis would goose-step ceremoniously onto the screen, seize a bug dreaming there, roughly bite its head off and slowly chew while the decapitated body exploded in agony between its daintily upraised paws. The mantis would peer around like a bishop leisurely at breakfast, nibble on the lower half of the bug, crack off a twitching leg, or tear out a chunk of the soft underbelly and shiver with sensual delight as if it had just bitten into the sweetest spot.

Our nights were vast and hollow, the skies splattered with a million stars, but because of the bugs they were never still. Always in the background resonated a sound like the quivering string of a cello as the night air hummed with the vibrations of insomniac bug gossip. Add to this the raspy hawking of the croaking lizards in the woodlands, the sopranino shrieks of tree frogs, the buzz of crickets and cicadas, the whirring of bat wings, and it was little wonder that on our first night away in a peaceful Chicago suburb bathed in the soothing yellow of mercury vapour street lights and pelted by a gentle snowfall, Cathy sat up in bed and could not sleep. She was unnerved by the silence.

Then there were the rats. One night I sprang out of bed and grabbed my machete, certain that a thief was battering down our front door. But in the glare of the outside lights only the gloom of the darkened pastures and distant mountains was visible. We padded nervously into the next bedroom and also found it starkly empty. Then we heard the noise again, a loud banging in the ceiling, but this time it was followed by an arpeggio scampering overhead—the unmistakable footfalls of rats.

The next day when we complained that he had rented us a rat-infested house, Jameson was amused. All Jamaican country houses, he said airily, have rats. Why, one night they had made such a clatter in *his* ceiling that he had gotten his gun and flashlight and gone stalking for an intruder. We would simply have to learn to make friends with the vermin.

But making friends with rats struck us as a desperate last resort. Murdering them seemed the more civilized thing to do. On our next trip to Miami, I bought several packages of D-Con rat poison, and as soon as we got back to our house, I pried open an overhead ceiling panel and laid out the lethal banquet. That night, we heard the rats scurrying and squeaking excitedly and smugly assumed that they were at their last supper. But they were noisily back the following night, and the next, and when I climbed into the ceiling to see if they had eaten the poison, I found it devoured to the last crumb.

American poison does not work on Jamaican rats, Jameson sighed patiently when we told him what had happened. It only fattens them up.

My sister proposed a solution: she would give us a cat. It was a hardened ratter, took sadistic delight in tormenting all kinds of rodents, and would make short shrift of ours. When the cat arrived it looked so bad-tempered from being locked in a box during the long drive from Kingston that I immediately shoved it into the ceiling, expecting to hear the vengeful snarls of feline carnage. But instead, it mewed pitifully, crept through the eaves and out onto the roof, leaped on an overhanging limb, and scaled down a tree.

Several times after that when I tried to coax it into the ceiling it howled as if the devil himself lived up there. "Be a cat!" I would admonish it, using that stern tone of voice American women reserve for scolding sissified husbands.

Occasionally I would lose my patience and fling it bodily through the open panel, but it would race out on the roof, jump onto the overhanging limb, scamper down the tree trunk, and flee into the pastures. Only when it was safely distant would it turn and stare at me with distaste before slinking moodily away.

So there was nothing left but to make friends with the rats, which meant indulging their nocturnal football games, their irregular thumpings in the darkest hour of the night, their capricious wind sprints right above our bed, their games of leapfrog, tenpin bowling, and tumble-over. One particular rat, as fat and sleek as a squirrel, even took the initiative and came calling.

I was writing *The Painted Canoe,* a novel about a Jamaican fisherman, and had fallen into the habit of working late at my desk which was in the spare bedroom and right under a window. One night I was tapping away at the typewriter when the rat came promenading solemnly down the screen and peered in captiously at me like a critic. I waved my hand and it scurried away.

But after that it became a regular visitor and nearly impossible to shoo. It seemed drawn by the sounds of my typing and would

brazenly stop and stare at the sheet in the typewriter. I finally began
reading it aloud the passage I had been working on, with mixed
results. Sometimes it would hurry off as if it couldn't stand to hear
another word. Other times it would linger with what I took to be faint
approval. But more often than not it would listen with one ear
cocked, lick its feet, sniff the air, and then disappear broodingly into
the night as if to say that in its opinion there was too much bloody
fiction being written nowadays.

As accustomed as we became to the nocturnal roughhousing of
the rats, our occasional guests never could. One morning a friend
from Southern California who was staying with us came wearily to
the breakfast table, her eyes red from sleeplessness.

"Do all Jamaicans stable horses in their ceilings?" she asked
squinting blurrily at the bright sunlight flooding through the louvred
windows.

"Actually," I began, "what you heard were....."

"Don't tell me!" she shrieked, holding her hands up as if to fend
off something disgusting. "I can't stand it. What I heard had to be
horses. Lilliputian horses. Like in *Gulliver's Travels*."

She sipped her coffee morosely.

"I wish I could stay longer," she said after a thoughtful pause
"but I really should be getting back."

That very afternoon she departed, never to return.

Then there were the mosquitoes, the cow ticks, the sandflies, and
the fleas. The twilight hour was a thin gruel thickened by the
mosquito millions. You could see clumps of them hovering like an
artist's lead-pencil smudge over every creature in the pastures.
Stealthiness was beneath them. They brazenly perched on any
unoccupied spot of flesh, skewered it without ado, and began to sip
blood. We sprayed ourselves from head to toe with repellant we had
bought in Miami, and this seemed to lessen their attacks. But every
inch of bare skin had to be covered with the oily paste, making us
reek of insecticide in the evenings.

Even the lovely pastures and fields that surrounded our house concealed a canker—a particularly nasty tick that would sneak up and bite you so guilefully that you wouldn't feel a thing. But a few days later you'd suddenly notice a teardrop, turgid and purple like an overripe grape, dripping out of your flesh. It was the tick, its abdomen engorged with your blood, its head dunked deep into your bloodstream. If you grabbed it and yanked, it would pop like a balloon between your fingers, splattering you with your own blood, and the decapitated head would fester into an infection. Instead, you had to coax the glutton out by swabbing its upraised rump gently with alcohol, which would bring it slowly backing out of its bloody burrow.

Once out it was at your mercy, for in its glutted condition it could barely waddle. You could then sadistically grasp it with tweezers and torment it with a pin, burn it with a cigarette, scald it with household cleanser, or pluck its bandy legs off one by one, exacting from nature a thoroughly satisfying human revenge.

The sandflies were Cathy's nemesis. Every bite produced a welted water blister that itched mercilessly. When she scratched, the blisters would pop and a milky fluid suppurate over her skin, driving her mad with itching. Goaded beyond endurance, she would finally give in and scratch violently, stippling her arms and legs with rake marks from her fingernails.

One weekend we stayed at a northcoast hotel that was offering a bargain rate for locals. Cathy spent the entire day napping in the sun, rousing herself for an occasional dip or to apply more oil.

"This used to be a swamp," I told her uneasily, surveying the powdery sand of the bay. "I remember shooting ducks here with my father years ago."

"Well," she sighed with contentment, "it's a beach now."

That night she awoke itching furiously. Every square inch of her skin was dotted with blisters, nearly driving her out of her mind with a tormenting itch. Nothing helped—not soaking in a warm tub, not rubbing herself over with lotion, not standing naked on the balcony in the cooling night breezes. We checked out early the next morning and drove into Kingston, where we got some pills from my cousin the doctor. Weeks later her body still bore the mottled scab marks of the broken blisters.

"And to think I never even knew they were biting me!" she often wailed despairingly as if she could not imagine a nastier, more low-down trick.

Cathy had a job, had taken up cross-stitching, embroidery, diary keeping, and compulsive reading, but still she was miserable with inactivity and boredom. She started going to bed earlier and earlier. Sometimes when I left for school at seven-thirty to tutor my students she would already be asleep. When I got back, she would still be sleeping. She left for work at seven and was gone until nearly five. Two hours after coming home she would crawl into bed, pull the covers over her head, and go to sleep. She began to complain of persistent stomach pains. She was stultified and miserable.

What made Cathy especially unhappy was that we had still not gotten married, although everyone at the school addressed her as Mrs. Winkler. Because of our living arrangement, she was estranged from her family, and her mother had made it plain that we were both unwelcome in her home. Before meeting me, she had lived alone with a cat in an apartment stocked with favourite possessions and had led the carefree social life of a single woman. Now she was isolated from the only world she knew, with only a few letters dribbling in from her married girlfriends in Chicago, all of whom gushed with envy at the exotic life they imagined her enjoying in the mountains of Jamaica, which, in fact, she was finding unbearable.

One night we sat down and had a long talk. It came out that she wanted to get married very badly, for she desperately wished to be reconciled with her family and to spend Christmas with them. Yet her mother, a staunch Catholic, would never accept her if she continued to live with me out of wedlock.

"All right," I said. "Let's get married."

The next day we put on our dressiest clothes and drove into Ocho Rios intending to enquire at the police station for some official in town who could marry us.

"Marry?" A big-bellied sergeant replied with amazement when he encountered us on the steps of the police station. "You want to get married?"

"Yes," I said. "Do you know anyone who can marry us?"

He scratched his head doubtfully, then turned and bellowed through an open door,

"Johnson! Wha' de name of dat man dat marry people?"

"Marry people?" drifted Johnson's bemused reply from inside the concrete station house.

"Yes, man! De man down de road dat marry people."

"You want marry, Sarge?"

"Me, sah? No, sah!" Sarge scoffed contemptuously at the very idea. "Dem two people out here want marry. What de man name?"

"Who want marry?"

His curiosity getting the better of him, Johnson came out of the station, carrying a fountain pen with which he had no doubt just been recording some public wickedness on the police blotter.

"Oh," he said when he had laid eyes on us. He scratched his head with the tip of the pen.

"What de man name, again?" he wondered aloud, scratching furiously.

"It on de tip o' me tongue," growled the sergeant with exasperation.

Johnson turned and bellowed back through the doorway.

"Stegbert! What de name o' de marrying man down de road?"

From inside the cavernous station came a faint reply.

"Which man, dat?"

"De man dat marry people. Where him live?"

Silence.

"Who want marry?"

"What de name o' de man, man? Just tell me what de man name?"

"Who want marry?" came the stubborn query again, followed shortly after by Stegbert, who had come to see for himself.

After Stegbert, a similar antiphonal recital was winded back and forth at Corporal George, then at Constable Lindsey, each of whom trooped out of the station to view the bride and groom quizzically. Finally someone remembered a name and directions and we went on our way.

The place to which they had directed us turned out to be a school, and the man to whom we had been sent, its headmaster. We entered his office just as he was putting a cane away and a tearful schoolboy was departing through a side door rubbing his rump.

Yes, he did indeed marry people, he told us gruffly, but only members of his congregation and only after the bans had been read and a period of enforced waiting observed. What we wanted was a marriage officer, someone paid by the government to marry anyone, and he told us how to get to the house of the only one in the vicinity.

So we drove back into the mountains, looking for the house of the marriage officer, which we found after stopping repeatedly to ask directions from pedestrians.

It turned out that the marriage officer lived in a country manse on a breezy hill that overlooked a spanking vista of the ocean. We waited nervously on the veranda, whose eaves were festooned with an elaborate rind of gingerbread moulding and coloured with flowering vines of bougainvillea, while a maid went inside to fetch him.

A few minutes later a little man, officious and dapper, clad in a clerical collar and black gabardine suit and carrying himself with an air of ominous self-importance, came out to greet us. He listened to our request with evident suspicion, then herded us into his office.

"Marriage is a serious step, you know," he said gravely once we were seated before him and he had installed himself with appropriate ceremony behind a mahogany desk.

We said we appreciated that it was a serious step.

"Counselling is what you need before marrying," he said, with a sniff. "Nobody should marry without counselling."

Behind his desk rows of shelves bulged with dog-eared tomes by Freud, Adler, Jung, Fromm, Skinner—the whole distempered pantheon of twentieth century psychological writers and thinkers. Obviously our official had laboriously ingested the collective wisdom of these latter-day gurus and now hungered to swat someone on the side of the head with a pennyweight of his learning. But how often did anyone who would submit to counselling descend on his manse asking to be married? Jamaican country people were notoriously prone to concubinage—common-law relationships—and even if the odd backwoods farmer should choose to formalize his relationship with his mistress, not for a minute would he would put up with the minister's bookishness. Freud was so out of place in these rustic and crude surroundings that to our marriage officer we must have seemed as miraculous and heaven-sent as the goat to Abraham in the biblical fable.

Just as I was speculating in this vein, a real goat roamed up to the edge of the veranda, munching lazily on one rose bush after another, gobbling down clumps of hibiscus, and occasionally peering up at us with undisguised ruminant curiosity.

I insisted that we knew what we wanted and didn't need counselling.

"People who think they don't need counselling are in the greatest need of counselling," he replied with an ironic smile. "It's people who think they do need counselling that usually don't need it." We squirmed in the face of this paradox. The goat clambered onto the veranda, made its way around a wicker chair, and chomped into another flowering bush with a vengeance.

"I'm sure you're right," I said thinly. "And I'm sure we could use counselling. But first we want to get married."

He rebuffed my nuptial impetuosity with a finger of reproof.

"Counselling, first. Marriage after. Marriage is a perilous step. Everywhere you look is a quicksand. Counselling gives you de map that show you how to negotiate around the traps. Think of marriage as a safari into darkest Africa. There's a jungle out there with man-eating animals...."

"Could we at least fill out the forms?"

"I suppose so," he said with a severe frown, handing the forms to us reluctantly.

We filled them in, gave them back to him, and waited.

After a long pause during which the official read every line of our application, he raised his eyes and peered at me.

"Well," he said, as if to gloat that this proved his very point about counselling, "you're both divorced. Do you have your divorce certificates with you?"

I said I'd left them at home.

"I can't marry you without the certificates," he said, putting the forms down on his desk.

"If we get them and bring them back, will you marry us then?"

"Without counselling?"

"We just want to get married. We don't want to be counselled. We know our own minds."

"People who think they know their own minds...."

"We only want to be married, not counselled."

"I'm a marriage officer," he shrugged, glowering at me with evident dislike.

"So if the papers are right, you'll marry us?"

"The government pays me to perform marriages."

"Good! We'll get the papers and come right back."

"Not today," he said, standing. "I have a service to conduct this afternoon. A husband dropped dead. That's another peril of marriage people don't consider, that sometimes a spouse drop dead for no reason. All that enter into counselling. Come back another time."

Cathy drooped with disappointment.

We thanked him and left.

We gathered up our divorce certificates and drove back to the manse the next day. The marriage officer was out, the maid said, and wouldn't be back until late that night.

On the way back to our house, Cathy started to cry.

"Don't worry," I assured her through gritted teeth. "We'll get married, if it kills us."

We drove again that weekend to the house of the marriage officer. He came shuffling out to greet us, escorted us into his office, and pored over the divorce certificates.

"Everything seems to be in order," he announced.

"Good!" I exclaimed. "So you can marry us?"

"No," he said curtly. "Today is Sunday. A preaching day. I don't marry on preaching days."

"What kind of sh....." I began before Cathy stopped me with a hard jab in the ribs.

"We'll be back again," she mumbled, practically yanking me out of his office.

We returned again three days later, on a Wednesday.

This time he didn't even bother ushering us into his sanctum. He just took one blank look around at the empty veranda and asked,

"Where are your witnesses?"

"Witnesses? What witnesses?"

"The law requires you to furnish two witnesses."

"Why didn't you tell us that?" I demanded through clenched teeth.

"I assumed you know the law," he replied, smirking vindictively. "You're a man who knows your own mind. You don't need counselling, or so you say. So I assume you know the law, too."

"We'll get witnesses," I threatened, glaring at him. "And we'll be back."

The next Saturday my two sisters drove over from Kingston to be our witnesses, and we caravaned over to the manse on the flowery hilltop.

After leaving us stewing on the veranda for nearly half an hour, the marriage officer finally appeared.

"I can't marry you," he said, glancing at my sisters with scarcely disguised triumph. "The law says one witness must be male, and one female."

"What?" I roared.

From the dim interior of the manse a voice suddenly roared with startling power and authority,

"Hector!"

We turned and saw a burly woman, who outweighed the official by at least a hundred pounds, beckoning at him from a doorway with an air of palpable menace.

"Come here!" she said curtly.

Hector glanced nervously from us to her and then hurried inside.

We could hear their muffled voices arguing behind the bedroom door.

"Why you have de damn people dem coming and going like fool for?" the woman scolded. "Marry de people dem, man! You have dem coming and going when all dem want do is get married."

"But dey need counselling!" Hector protested feebly.

"Counselling you backside!" she cracked. "You want counsel somebody, go to de madhouse and find a madman to counsel! Leave decent people alone, wid you damn counselling. Come tormen decent people wid all you damn foreign book 'bout counselling."

"Marriage without counselling...." Hector sputtered.

"Is counselling you want? You want counselling? Go marry de people dem or I goin' give you counselling you never forget!"

A few moments of strained silence later, Hector emerged from the bedroom, closed the door behind him, and marched towards u with chilling dignity.

"I decide to marry you," he muttered savagely. "Since you are ignorant of de law, I will get a male witness to sign de paper."

And so at last we were married in a simple ceremony in the presence of my sisters and a phantom witness whose name appear on our marriage certificate.

As we were heading for our car, the marriage officer's wife appeared on the veranda beside her little husband, dwarfing him with her imposing bulk.

"God bless you," she waved cheerfully.

We drove away leaving them on the veranda, the wife beaming at us with benevolence and goodwill, her husband standing sulkily beside her, his face wreathed in an unforgiving scowl.

Among ordinary people life does not offer many plain examples of defiance against unjust authority that turns out for the ultimate good. There are the puffed-up lessons usually preached by the fates of overblown historical figures, used in schoolbooks to torment innocent children. But there are like examples in the lives of ordinary men and women, and one such is offered by my Aunt Josette, the only one of my maternal grandfather's six daughters who refused to wed the man the tyrant had hand-picked for her.

One evening in 1927 when Aunt Josette was a nubile sixteen-year-old, this grandfather came trudging home huffing and puffing with paterfamilias authority and dragging in tow a portly middle-aged man whose breath stank of garlic and uncooked meat. He was a man of wealth, corpulence, and respectable connections—my grandfather's brother-in-law on his wife's side. Grandfather ordered Aunt Josette to come and meet her future husband.

Aunt Josette ventured out of her room, took one look at the middle-aged tub who stood in the doorway beaming with contentment from an overfull belly, and cried that she would rather die than marry him.

Grandfather bellowed with rage, tore off his belt, and lunged for her. Aunt Josette fled into her bedroom and locked the door. The entire apparatus of patriarchal discipline then set up siege outside her room, blowing salvos of threats and recriminations through the keyhole. Her mother wept that she could have borne such a wilful and ungrateful daughter. One by one the strapping brothers came home from work, learned of their sister's defiance, and banged on the door demanding that she open up and yield to Papa. Finally the wife of Grandfather's brother—who had proposed the match in the first place—was sent for and arrived in an indignant swish.

"Josette!" the matchmaking sister-in-law shouted, banging on the door. "Come out at once! Come out and talk to Tufty!"

"I dead first!" Josette replied.

"Honour thy father and thy mother!" the sister-in-law shrieked piously.

"If he was the last man on earth, I wouldn't marry him."

"What's wrong with my brother Tufty? You tell me, what's wrong with poor Tufty? Poor Tufty never trouble a fly!"

"He's old and fat! His breath stinks!"

"That's because he just had dinner! He had cabbage for supper. Didn't you have cabbage, Tufty?"

But Tufty had fallen asleep, in spite of the commotion, and couldn't reply.

Grandfather bellowed with fury and hurled himself at the door.

"Old and fat!" he roared. "You dare to call the husband I pick for you old and fat?"

The door held firm.

"You like him so much, Papa, you marry him!"

This taunt goaded the old man into a fiery blast of Lebanese imprecations and curses.

"I marry him? I already marry! I can't marry a man!"

"Josette, why you so rude to Papa?" came Grandmother's heartrending wail. "Poor Tufty! He don't trouble a soul! He only want a wife!"

Tufty seconded this sentiment with a bilious snore.

But Josette would not give an inch. The quarrel waged back and forth through the keyhole. When it became clear that nothing but physical force would budge her, Grandfather summoned his sons and shouted that he would break down the door and beat his disobedient daughter within an inch of her life. Tufty was roused to add his two hundred and fifty pounds of dead weight to the human battering ram, the sister-in-law deployed in the garden to prevent the quarry from escaping through the window, and at a command from Grandfather, the three sons and frustrated suitor hurled their united corpulence against the door. The whole house shuddered from the blow as the door buckled with an ominous creak.

Aunt Josette pocketed the key to the front door, threw open the window, and jumped out into the garden below right into the waiting arms of the suitor's vengeful sister.

"I have her!" the sister screamed, at which Aunt Josette kicked her hard in her crotch, felling her with a thud into a bed of hibiscus before bolting into the night and disappearing into a vacant overgrown lot next door.

Lanterns were lit and an angry search made of the woody lot. But

Aunt Josette was a little woman and she cowered deep behind a dark thicket. Two hours later the search was called off with the men screaming at the darkness that sooner or later she would come home, and when she did, God help her.

She stayed hidden until the house was dark and quiet, then she crept up onto the veranda, her heart pounding, let herself into the front door, and skulked into her empty bedroom. Once there she bolted the door, threw herself on the bed, and fell asleep.

She lived the next few days like a thief in her own home, evading punishment only because her father and brothers lived by strictly regimented habits. She would remain locked inside the room until they had all left for work, then she would slink into the bathroom, wash for the day, put on her clothes and leave for her own job. Her mother would reluctantly serve her breakfast along with a litany of laments and reproaches. Nevertheless, Auntie remained unmoved. She would only marry a man of her own choosing.

Aunt Josette survived furtively in this uneasy stand-off for two weeks. Then one night she was betrayed by a swinish brother who coaxed her into unlocking her barricaded door by swearing an oath that Papa was still at work. Auntie stepped timidly out of the room and into the clutches of waiting Grandfather.

For the next hour, the old man brutally mauled her with his fists until he couldn't strike another blow from sheer exhaustion. When his savagery was finally spent, Auntie's lip was split, her eyes were puffy and black with contusions, and her menstrual period gushing from repeated thumps in the stomach. She crawled into her bedroom, gasping for breath, packed her few things in a battered suitcase, and limped out of the house into the darkness.

Some compassionate nuns took her in at a nearby convent and gave her a bed for the night.

A few months later, on her own, Auntie met an English soldier and married him. She bore him a daughter but divorced him three years later because of his alcoholism, setting off another furious family scandal and a round of triumphant crowing from her despotic father over her bad choice.

Then she met and married my Uncle Eric for whom she bore two children.

Many years later, on the celebration of her fiftieth wedding anniversary when she was in her mid-seventies, Aunt Josette complained ruefully to a company of well-wishing friends and relatives that whenever Uncle Eric was home she had to resort to undressing in the dark of the closet with the door closed because even a glimpse of her nakedness made him want to make love to her immediately. Although her tone dripped with wifely indignation that a woman of her age should still have to put up with such tomfoolery from a man after fifty years of marriage, the gruff note of pride in her voice and tinge of red in her cheeks betrayed her true feelings.

CHAPTER 14

I do not know if there really are categories into which personalities can be conveniently divided. The textbooks say so, and much of psychological myth-making rigidly takes this to be a truth. But if such divisions are possible, certainly the crudest and most widespread would separate those souls who live in the world from those who live chiefly in their imagination. Going home to teach made me sorrily aware that I belonged temperamentally to this second lot.

Cathy, on the other hand, lived wholly in the external world and was healthily adapted to it like a camel to the desert. No doubt when she slept or daydreamed she made occasional trips within, but they were the briefest excursions from which she always happily returned as from a dutiful visit to a boring old relative. Hers struck me as the better way to live and I often envied her ability to brighten herself up merely by reordering her slice of the external world. If she were gloomy, cleaning the house made her instantly happier. If she were downcast, visiting a friend, writing a letter, basking on the beach, revived her spirits. If she were pained, it meant that there was a prickle in her foot or a grain of sand in her eye. Extract the prickle, wash out the grain, and she felt instantly better.

It was not so with me. Alien assassins occasionally infiltrate my world and go stalking. What childhood haunts they come from I cannot say, but I deploy the loyal palace guard against them and a fierce guerrilla warfare ensues. Washing out the sand grain, or extracting the prickle, does not affect the outcome of this skirmishing. Sunning on the beach does not send the enemy running for the trenches.

But there is one consolation for those of us whose real lives are within. It does not matter to us that our village butcher shop stinks or that it houses slabs of raw beef hanging from hooks under a quivering coat of flies. It does not matter that rats rumble in the ceiling or that the bats dive-bomb us in the evenings or that we live socially isolated on a friendless hilltop with only a portable radio for company. What matters is whether there is peace within, whether the latest invader has been hurled back from its beachhead and sent scrambling to the no-man's land of quiescence.

But practical sights, events, things, mattered to Cathy. The village butcher shop with its marbled slabs of smelly beef bothered her. She was affected by the bugs, the rats, the loneliness of our life. She was troubled by the poverty around us, by the shoeless urchins, by the nicks and dents of scarcity and inconvenience. Our clothes smelled perpetually of mildew. Her leather belt acquired a green patina of mould. The salt would not shake freely from the cellar. There was no telephone to ring, no television to watch, no friendly neighbour to chat with over the fence. Although we shared our hilltop compound with Derrick and Heather, we had not become friends.

Most of all Cathy was troubled by the occasional racial insult in the streets. She could not understand or cope with the daggers of hate sporadically hurled at her.

There was, for example, a ragged urchin who sat always on the same stretch of wall on her way to work and yelled "Pork!" as she drove past. He was there early in the morning when the fog still lay curdled on the ground, and he was there in the evening when the egrets were sailing in formation towards their nighttime roosts. "Pork!" he would screech as she drove past. Once she pointed him out to me as we cruised past his usual perch, but that day he stared stonily at us and said nothing.

But what if he had screamed "pork" just then? In a democratic country with egalitarian institutions an insult is wonderfully personal and can be answered by a fist in the mouth. But in Jamaica with its miasmic colonial past, with its lingering ill-will of racial and class prejudice, with inequality ingrained in the body politic, the urchin who screams "pork" at a passing white man or woman is crudely about the business of redressing old sins, and if you repay his vigilance with a fist in the mouth, you will probably spark a riot.

It struck me as a curious epithet. I often wondered, "Why pork? Wherefore pork?" Daphne Dickson would know. Hers was the blackest skin among the tutors and her rancour against whites the deepest. I asked her outright one day in the staff room. Why pork, Daphne?

Since there was no love lost between us, she was glad to explain the insult.

When you sliced the rind off roast pork, she said with obvious relish, the underlying fat is ghastly and rheumy like congealed egg white. This was what a white skin looked like in the public imagination. Hence "pork."

I thanked her for explaining it to me.

"Not at all, Winkler," she replied coolly.

People hated us because we were white. You sensed it in the streets, in public places. You saw the resentment smouldering in the thick curled lips, the eyes that pricked at your person. You sniffed the dislike in banks, in the stores, in the post office. It was blind, rabid, seething—this hate—and if you were smart you took great care when you ventured out in public to do or say nothing to make it worse. You averted your eyes or you pretended to be deaf or you feigned abstraction in some private worry that blinded and deafened you to the hostile stares or surly muttering on the sidewalks.

Personal hatred was a relief, a blessing, compared to this. It was, at least, answerable by words—harsh or soft—or just as cleanly by a club or a brick. But this widespread resentment was too collective, too deeply symbolic to be placated by any personal word or gesture. You felt helpless and muddled when you encountered it.

And we met it often.

We were at the races, sitting in the enclosed first-class pavilion watching the horses run. Below us, separated by plate glass, was the general admission section where the poorer players milled about in a rowdy throng. Usually a white person under these circumstances will never look directly into the eyes of someone sitting in the "penny section." But I looked. I did it out of envy, for I have always longed for a face that would be nothing more than another inconspicuous smudge in a dark crowd.

A young man sitting directly beneath us met my stare. His lips curling with rage and contempt, he stood up and glared menacingly at me. I read the challenge on his lips, for it was impossible to hear him over the roar of the crowd,

"What're you looking at, pork?"

If I had looked away that would have been that. But instead, I smiled and nodded, and that enraged him even more. He sprang at the glass with doubled fist, his face a twitching mask of hatred.

"No!" Cathy screamed. "What're you doing?"

Of course, he could not hear her, for the crowd was screaming at the horses thundering towards the finishing line, and a partition of thick plate glass separated us. But there was no mistaking the implacable hate, the ugly rage that disfigured his features. While the deafening roar of the crowd shook the pavilion as people stomped and screamed at their horses, he stared at me with the soundless animal longing of a beast barred from its primordial prey. Then, in a sinister pantomime, he drew his finger slowly and evilly across his throat.

One day we went into Claremont to shop. I left Cathy in the car while I ran into the open-air market to buy some fruit. She was pale and shaking when I returned.

"What's the matter?" I asked.

"Nothing," she said through clenched teeth. "Let's go home."

"But what happened?"

"Nothing. Please, let's go home."

On the way home, she started to cry.

It turned out that a man had come up to the car while I was inside the market and screamed abuse at her, telling the "pork bitch" to go back where she had come from.

You could not argue with such mindless hate. You could only ignore it, endure it with a show of brave public stoicism. During his colonial reign, this was what the Englishman did.

When I was a boy in Montego Bay, I witnessed a scene between an Englishwoman and a boisterous black man. The woman was shopping in the thickest and smelliest part of the market where white people generally did not venture. She was poking among the wares of the higglers scattered on the dirty sidewalk when she drew the attention of a ragged and brutish-looking man who stank of sweat and whose clothes flapped from his limbs like the tattered feathers of a half-plucked bird. He began trailing the woman through the throng, hurling racial jibes at her. Her head held high, the Englishwoman paid him no mind whatsoever but continued imperturbably through the market, stooping to make an occasional purchase. Soon the man was shrieking at her elbow, his spittle sailing past her face or stinging her cheeks, while the woman elbowed her way through the jabbering mob pretending for all the world that he was not there. Occasionally, one of the higglers would bawl something scolding to the man like, "Shame on you! Leave de woman alone!" but for the most part, his antics drew only looks of amusement.

This went on for at least half an hour until the woman finally picked up her bag of purchases and made her way shakily to her car with the shrieking hooligan still dogging her heels. Then she was gone, driving off into the traffic leaving her tormentor howling and gesturing on the sidewalk after her.

For reasons which I did not then understand, I had the distinct feeling that the Englishwoman had scored a victory, and that it was her tormentor who had been made to look and feel the fool. Later, I witnessed similar acts of stoicism from other English people taunted in the streets, and in every case I was also left with the odd impression that the abuser had been repelled.

But however a white person reacted to street harassment, it was evident in these troubled times to even the densest Jamaican that the prevailing anti-white mood was a calamity for a country whose livelihood depended on the patronage of white tourists. And under democratic socialism, the tourist industry suffered one jolt after another. Bookings fell every season, and hotels began closing one by one to be taken over by surly government workers. The country was getting such bad press overseas that one day Manley addressed the racial problem in a speech.

What he said boiled down to this: It was wrong for us to discriminate against anyone because that was not the way of democratic socialism. All men were equal under democratic socialism, whether white, brown, or black. So this pointless hatred, this xenophobia directed against white tourists had to stop since it was contrary to our most cherished ideals.

It was then, after I had listened to this dimwitted speech, that I finally grasped what was idiotically flawed about Manley and his programme: it was all too doltishly theoretical. Being nasty to white people in the streets violated a punctilio of the party and therefore we shouldn't do it—such specious reasoning by the prime minister of a nation whose economic well-being hinged on white tourism would make even a lunatic blink!

No doubt every hothead and firebrand on the street corner, every illiterate, pauperized and aggrieved Jamaican who had reason enough—personal or historical—to resent white people, would be struck dead in his tracks by this tepid blast of ministerial logic.

It was a knife in my heart, this hatred I felt from my own people. The feeling of inauthenticity, of being a bogus Jamaican that had haunted me as a child, grew in force and intensity. I longed to say in public: Look! I am one of you. My heart is your heart. Your blood is my blood. Look at me, here I am, one of you. It is only the skin that's wrong, that's different. But I am of you.

It was a childish impulse. Once I almost gave into it, but prudence restrained me at the last minute and probably saved my life.

I was driving slowly from St. Ann's Bay down a lonely stretch of road that ran through shimmering cane fields when I spotted a ragged black man trudging on the shoulder of the road, carrying a crocus bag and a machete. He must have been one of the many homeless madmen that roam Jamaica because, glancing over his shoulder and seeing me approach, he suddenly began to scurry along the embankment in a crouch, wildly casting about for stones to throw. I

ped up and was safely past when, struck by a sudden impulse, I
tepped on the brakes.

Overcome by a feeling of reckless benevolence I meant to get out of
he car and reason with his hatred, which I rashly assumed was
prompted by my race rather than by his madness. In my momentary
dementia, I even had a mad vision of tearing off my bogus white
skin—like Clark Kent shedding his mortality in a phone booth—and
revealing to the lunatic's speechless astonishment that we were brother
Jamaicans. We would embrace and be reconciled on the roadside, and he
would see the folly of his mindless hate.

Luckily an engrained bourgeois caution stopped me, for I could
see in the rear-view mirror that the fellow was rampaging towards
he car with an unrelenting scowl of wickedness, and that the hand
clenching the machete was gleefully flailing in anticipation of
severing a jugular. He was nearly upon the car when I jammed hard
on the accelerator and screeched away, leaving him jumping up and
down in the middle of the road with wild-eyed fury.

That was how I was feeling about myself these first few months
of being home again: muddled and stupid and confused.

But it was the land itself that I loved, and even if my own people
despised me on sight, nothing they said or did could lessen this raw
blood love, this passion I felt for my homeland. Now and then the
stillness of a valley creamy with morning mists, the sullen beauty of
a gorge licked open by the tongue of a green river, moved me to such
inexpressible wonder that tears came to my eyes, and I longed to
stand naked and newborn before the land and voice the childlike and
innocent love it awoke in my heart.

I felt it often, this overpowering welling up of love for my
homeland, but to my credit I never succumbed to it with tawdry
show. I never stopped my car and clambered down a green hillside to
strip naked beside a river. I never did it, though I often felt like doing
it, because I knew what would happen.

Some peasant girl or boy would peep out of a thicket of bamboo,
espy me, and gasp at her unseen throng of friends and neighbours,
'Coo yah! (Look here!) One naked white man!"

"Me God! White man stand naked 'pon river bank!"

"Send for Massah Jim!"

"Is so white man scrawny without clothes?"

"Come! Come look 'pon naked white man!"

"Rass! What him doing here?"

"Pork in de raw! Come, yah! Look!"

"Me never see nothing like dis in all me born days! Pork standing naked by riverside! Lawd God, look what pork come to now!"

As a people Jamaicans are hobbled by a streak of self-hatred and suspicion against their own. This poisoned self-concept was what Manley struggled against in his idealistic homilies about democratic socialism. But an engrained sense of self-worthlessness acquired in a demeaning colonial history dies slowly, and in the Jamaica of democratic socialism, black still regarded its own kind with suspicion and an ambivalence that was at best, indulgence, at worst, undisguised contempt. Over and over again I saw the uglier face of my people exposed in wanton acts of petty vanity and cruelty.

The chairwoman of my department, for example, a half-Chinese lady who was fond of name-dropping about her spotless pedigree, occasionally drove onto the campus with an old black woman, who turned out to be her maid, crouched in the backseat of the car. It struck me as an odd arrangement—the mistress driving all by herself in the front seat, the maid bundled servilely in the back. Why did she do it? One day I asked her.

She looked at me as if I were dense.

"She's not my equal," she said caustically. "Why should she sit in the front beside me?"

"But it looks like you're her chauffeur," I pointed out.

"I don't care how it looks," she replied tartly. "She sits in the back because she's not my equal. She's my employee."

So whenever they travelled together by car, the mistress signalled to the world the inequality of their relationship by chauffeuring the maid.

A mathematics teacher at our school was involved in a terrible car accident and was rushed to the hospital with grave injuries. He was a strikingly black man with an unkempt Afro hair-do, and at the time of the accident had been on his way to harvest his hillside farm and was therefore dressed in crude labouring clothes. Lingering on the brink of death, he lay for days in the public ward of a Kingston hospital where many of the tutors went to visit him. After several weeks of convalescing, he was discharged. One day he lifted his shirt and showed me an ugly, crooked ridge of cream-coloured flesh across his back—the remains of a neglected bedsore.

"This is what nearly killed me," he said indignantly. "And you know what saved my life?"

I said I had no idea.

"The visits from the faculty. One of the nurses suddenly started paying attention to me. She said, 'Oh, I didn't know you was anybody until I see all dese respectable people come visit you. Den I say to meself, "But wait? Dis is an important man."' So she start turning me over and giving me medicine. Otherwise, they'd have left me there to dead."

Noonday at an isolated countryside school where I had travelled to observe a student teach.

It was a typical country school, two stained cinder-block buildings driven into the scuffed and grassless hollow of an open field. At lunchtime the students burst out of the airless buildings with an abandoned shriek of pure joy and scattered wildly over the cricket pitch. I was settling under a tree with a bag lunch when my student, whom I was there to observe, came over and stood nearby, obviously troubled.

When I asked her what was the matter, she hesitated then blurted out the story.

One of the children in her class was being denied lunch every day because he did not have the ten cents the government programme required him to contribute.

"Does the headmistress know?" I asked.

The student glared at the ground with anger.

"Is she doing it, sah," she mumbled.

She pointed out the boy to me—a scrawny, underfed child who sat against a tree trunk on the far side of the grounds listlessly watching the other children romping on the playground.

This was none of my business. My role was to supervise my own student's teaching, not interfere in the running of the school. But I decided to ask the headmistress for an explanation.

The headmistress heard me out with evident distrust and impatience, then brusquely shrugged off my concern.

"You don't know these children like I know them, Mr. Winkler," she said curtly. "Dey parents give dem de ten cent for de lunch programme, but they prefer to buy sweetie with it rather than spend it on lunch. He must learn a lesson."

"But I hear he hasn't eaten lunch for the whole week!" I protested.

"Den dat's his business!" she snapped. "He must give de money dat his parents give him for lunch, and not buy sweetie with it."

"But how do you know he has the money to give? Maybe his parents can't afford ten cents a day."

She stared at me as if she were at a loss to answer such stupidity.

"Mr. Winkler, I know these people the way you don't, the way you will never know dem! I know how their brain work! Dese people born to thief and tell lie! He has de money! He buy sweetie wid it rather than pay for lunch like de programme require! Dey would rather thief de government and starve dan pay de ten cent dem supposed to."

I was so livid at her sanctimonious unreasonableness that I had to fight for self-control.

"All right, Mrs. Anderson," I said as calmly as I could, reaching for my wallet. "I'm going to give you a twenty-dollar bill. That will cover his lunch for the next two hundred days, until the school year ends. Is that all right?"

"If you want to throw 'way you money dat way, dat's your

business, Mr. Winkler," she snapped, taking the money and disappearing into a makeshift warren of an office created by the arrangement of blackboards in the open classroom.

Then I explained to my student what I had done and asked her to make sure that the boy was fed every day.

When the lunch bell rang, my student went over and talked to the boy, pointing to the children standing in line at the kitchen. With awkward embarrassment he joined the line and waited his turn for a pannikin of government fare—a muddy gruel of red peas soup in which small oblong flour dumplings floated on their sides like dead minnows.

I was in a Kingston patty shop at lunchtime when two men standing in line behind me began an angry squabbling. One man accused the other of hogging two parking places; the other scoffed that the first was a bad driver. The argument was heating up with every exchange, the men drawing menacingly closer and more threatening.

"Dat is de trouble wid dis country," one man snarled. "De damn negar man have no discipline! Him have no home training! Him don't have no sense of decency. Him don't have no pride. Him don't even know how to conduct himself in a decent establishment."

"Who you calling negar man?" the other demanded with a scowl. He rolled up the sleeves of his shirt and bared a brown and hairless forearm. "Look 'pon my skin. My skin fairer dan yours. Who you calling negar man?"

"Fairer, what?" the other practically spat, extending his own forearm beside the other's. "Look 'pon my complexion and tell me dat your own fairer. Is blind you blind?"

There was a sinister pause in the quarrel while they glared at their naked forearms extended side by side. Then both of them looked as one in my direction.

"Ask de white man who have de fairer complexion," one of them suggested.

"Whose complexion fairer, sah?" the other growled.

A sudden and deathly stillness had fallen over the line of onlookers. Every eye in the shop was now raking me over with open curiosity.

I gulped.

"Nicht spreche English," I managed to say.

"Wha' dat him say?"

"Him is a foreigner," the other spat with disgust.

"So solly," I added, forgetting that I was supposed to be a German, not a Chinaman.

"Him no speak English, man," one of the disputants snapped.

They turned to the man in line behind them.

"Who have de fairer skin, sah?"

"Me no business wid dis argument, sah," the man said hastily. "Leave me out of it."

When it was my turn to order, I momentarily forgot my bogus persona and said to the woman behind the counter,

"Two patty and a cola champagne."

The men, who had by now settled down to pelting each other with grim looks and muttered insults, glared at me. Then both suddenly laughed.

"Dat's why de white man own de world," one of them chuckled. "Him tricky like mongoose."

"When negar man thief, him thief a dollar. When white man thief, him thief de bank."

I skulked out of the shop with my patty and drink, feeling oddly vainglorious about myself, like a master swindler among lowly pickpockets.

If you were white in Jamaica during these days of democratic socialism, no matter where you were or among whom, your skin still provoked ambivalent reactions.

By now I had made several friends on the faculty, and our get togethers during the morning snack break and at lunch were filled with lighthearted banter. We teased each other and flirted shamelessly, and there was a constant clink of chatter and laughter in the air.

My favourite among the Jamaican women tutors was Elizabeth Robertson. Elizabeth did not walk; she flowed like a silted brown river, and when she came to a rest, she seemed to collect in a quivering puddle.

One day she looked me dead in the eye and declared sweetly,

"My pum-pum is so soft and juicy, Winkler, that if you were ever lucky enough to get into it, you'd move up and down twice at the most and then grunt and be done."

I believed her, though my endurance was never put to the test. But if ever a woman was born to shame men with premature ejaculation, it was Elizabeth.

If Elizabeth was a sinuous brown river, Fay Murphy, the physical education tutor, was unabashedly a bone—knobby and tough like an old femur. She was tall and lean and sinewy with a fiery manner and the disciplinarian's edginess. She was always crying the equivalent of "Off with their heads!" about the students—as she had done during the students' strike. At snacktime Fay usually had an indignant story to tell about some new student rudeness she had lately encountered and beaten off. She would regale us deliciously with the impertinence, reflect the wide-eyed horror she had shown in facing it, and then explode in a jittery and long-winded rebuke that must surely have caused the upstart one to cringe. Then she was gone, bounding across campus like a skittish ibex, and it would not have surprised me to see her hurdle a stump in her path for the sheer joy of it.

Missie was also among us, the home economics tutor, a kindly and gentle soul who was reluctantly slipping into spinsterhood with an air of good humour and quiet despair. She longed to practise her art of happy homemaking on a family of her own, but the years had brought no willing suitor. In her late thirties, she was now struggling with the hard fact that a lonely life of sterile classroom theory about happy home management lay bleakly ahead.

The Jamaican tutors who knew me assumed that my heart was in the right place and that my love of homeland was sincere, and even Raymond, the fiery socialist, had come to grudgingly concede as much. But they were also troubled by my white skin. On this particular morning the discussion centred on my run-in with the bursar over her habit of paying us late, and the tutors were having a laugh at my expense.

How it came up I do not know, for our snacktime talks were often desultory and fitful, but someone mentioned facetiously that for a white man I was certainly peculiar.

Fay jumped to my defence as if I had been attacked.

"White?" She glowered fiercely at every face at the table. "Who say Tony white?"

Elizabeth chimed in.

"There isn't a white bone in Tony's body," she declared silkenly.

Missie agreed. "Tony not white."

Raymond chuckled.

"Him only look white," he said. "But him definitely not white."

"I know lots of families in Kingston much whiter than Tony," Missie said. "You not white, Tony. "

"White, my foot!" Fay scowled. "Tony, white? What a stupid idea."

Grandfather Winkler would have known all about the ambiguity of growing up white in a black country. One experience that occurred to him at the outbreak of World War II left him especially indignant, for years later he told me about it in a voice dripping with outrage.

At the outbreak of war Grandfather was in his middle years, had ventured abroad on only a few occasions, and knew no other home than Jamaica.

With the declaration of war the whole island became jittery as wild rumours about spies and German saboteurs swept the country. Jamaicans were urged on the radio to turn in any German nationals to the authorities for internment.

One day during the height of this anti-German feeling Grandfather was walking down King Street, in the very heart of the city, when he was suddenly accosted by two men. One of them blocked his path and pointed to him suspiciously.

"You no a German?" he growled.

"German, you back foot!" Grandfather snapped, trying to walk around the man. "I'm a Jamaican just like you!"

"Jamaican, what? You a German. Him is a German."

The other man blocked his way and chimed in,

"See how him eye blue! See how him skin white!"

"Move outta me way!" Grandfather growled. "I'm going about me business in peace. I not troubling anybody."

"Him talk like a Jamaican," the first man said dubiously.

But a bystander who had overheard the exchange so far had a plausible explanation for Grandfather's accent.

"Because him is a spy, that's why him talk like a Jamaican! You don't see? If dem send a spy here, dem goin' train him to talk like a Jamaican!"

The force of this logic swept the other two off their feet.

"Where you come from?" one of them demanded of Grandfather.

"From Kingston, you damn fool! Where you think I come from?"

"See wha' I mean!" the bystander interjected triumphantly. "Him talk just like a Jamaican. Him is a spy, man! Dis is a spy!"

A crowd gathered and began pressing hard and tight around Grandfather.

"Me hear dem offering a reward for German," one man said.

"Reward? Dem offering reward? How much reward?"

"Five pound for a German. You have to carry him to de soldier camp."

"Five pound for a German! Rass!"

"Is me find him!"

"Leggo me rass arm," Grandfather roared, trying to shake himself loose from the closing ring of gawkers and capturers.

"See what I mean! Dem even teach him Jamaica bad word! Is a spy man!"

"Is me find him, you know, sah! Is me to get de reward!"

"Is not you one find him, you know. Me find him too!"

"Is me prove him is a spy!"

"Hey, Joshua!" one of the men shouted at someone across the street. "Dem catch a German spy!"

The man came running to look, trailed by several others.

The two men who had first stopped him now had Grandfather firmly by the arm, while the one who had deductively demonstrated that he was a spy had hooked his hand possessively around a loop in Grandfather's trousers. One of the original men tried to pry loose the interloper's grip on the quarry's pants.

"Is we catch him!" he snarled. "Leggo de man pants. Is we spy dis. We getting de reward."

But the hand tenaciously clung to Grandfather's waist.

"But is me prove him is a spy!"

"Me say, leggo de spy! Is fi we spy dis!"

Grandfather began struggling and swearing at the top of his lungs during this debate, but it did no good. The men pinned him between them while they squabbled over splitting the reward.

A policeman elbowed his way into the centre of the throng, where Grandfather vainly wriggled and argument raged.

"Mr. Winkler?" the policeman said. "What happen, sah?"

Grandfather was so furious he could hardly talk.

"De damn fool dem won't let me go! Dem think I'm a German!"

"Is Mr. Winkler, dat!" the policeman said. "Leggo de man! Him is a Jamaican! Him own de music business down de street!"

"What you talking 'bout! Is fi we German, dis! Is we capture him! Is we goin' get de reward!"

"Me say, me know de gentleman," the policeman rasped, shoving the men away from Grandfather. "Me know him since me was a little boy! Is Mr. Winkler."

"Den if him not a German spy, how come him know how to cuss Jamaican bad word?" the logician stabbed the air with a challenging finger.

"Because him is a Jamaican like you!" snapped the policeman.

"What kind of fool-fool argument dat?" rebutted the doubting one.

But it was evident from his lame tone that disappointment and truth had begun their cruel work.

The policeman prevailed. Grandfather was released from human encirclement and allowed to catch his tram.

"But if I was you, Mr. Winkler," the policeman advised as Grandfather boarded the tram, "I wouldn't walk de street by meself. Me would always walk wid a black man for me passport."

When Grandfather told me this story, I was a small boy and he was reflecting on an episode that had happened at least ten years earlier.

"So for de next year, whenever I went out," he said, "I walk wid a negar man everywhere. My passport."

He shook his head slowly and with bitter puzzlement.

"And I born and grow nowhere else but here in Jamaica!"

CHAPTER 15

The Christmas holidays came and we flew to Cathy's hometown of Cicero, a suburb of Chicago. A few days before we left, my students trooped up the hill through the darkened pastures and serenaded us with carols. They stood in the seine of light shining through the burglar-barred windows of our cottage and chorused in the dimness. Then they came inside and we sang and celebrated with an early Christmas party.

In Cathy's hometown of Cicero, which had been settled mainly by Eastern Europeans, everywhere I looked—in the restaurants, the malls, on the streets—I saw an ocean of white skin, Slavic cheekbones, enormous skulls, and simian limbs. The houses are squat and ugly like abandoned bunkers, stained with the colour of dried egg yoke, and crowned by a ridiculous facade of crenellated roofs. They stand side by side in gnomically gloomy rows, as indistinguishable as toadstools, each fondling a ribbon of sidewalk with a grimy stoop. Driven like a spike between each house is a narrow cement gangway where old ladies can be glimpsed peeping out suspiciously at the world from tiny backyard gardens. The entire town seemed crushed under a brutal ugliness.

But it was a relief to be nothing more than another inconspicuous white face in the crowd. And it was exhilarating to see the shelves of stores bursting with goods. Democratic socialism had so impoverished Jamaica that it was common to walk into a Kingston grocery and face aisle after aisle of naked shelving and ugly rivets. But here the shelves of grocers groaned under sacks of rice, sugar, flour; display windows twinkled gaily with Christmas lights; shops and stores and malls overflowed with consumer goods.

It took our breath away at first—the sheer, dazzling, breathless opulence of America. We had forgotten its richness, its variety, its sprightliness and energy. Plenty was all around us: conspicuous, shameless, intoxicating Plenty that goaded us to wallow and revel and joyously spend. This is what an immigrant first sniffs in the American breeze. It was the scent that had made me light-headed when I first stepped off the plane in Miami some thirteen years ago: Plenty, wafting on the air like the dizzying scent of spring after a gloomy winter.

In Manley's Jamaica a longing for Plenty made you feel like a masturbating schoolboy, made you want to skulk as if you concealed a secret sin. You had fallen prey to a debased craving, a sick appetite. Poverty was upright and holy and when it died would go straight to heaven like a righteous nanny. But Plenty was a painted whore and if you kept her company you stood naked and with your exposed nasty erection before choiring multitudes in a cathedral.

But I found myself asking: what was wrong with Plenty? What deranged theology was this, that made Human Want seem righteous, but Plenty wicked? Manley never came right out and said so, but this equation was implicit in every scolding utterance of democratic socialism that had lately made life in Jamaica insufferably straitlaced. It was as if the humourless Franciscan nuns at Mount Alvernia Academy, where I had gone to school in Montego Bay, now held sway over the country with their merciless Latin conjugations and smugly triumphant virginity.

It was a refreshing interlude for us—those three weeks in Cicero. We bought. We spent. We splurged without remorse. My attitude was, Piss on Socialism: here was a land where rice could be plucked with an indifferent hand off the shelf of any corner grocer, where flour, soap and cooking oil did not have to be hoarded or purchased with furtive premeditation. American money was all you needed to go on a spending binge, and we had twenty thousand dollars of it piled up in banks from textbook royalties. Cathy shopped for gifts and clothes. I bought books for my A level students. We revelled and danced practically every night.

A long time ago my father had visited America, and it had struck him then very much the same way that I was now affected.

When I was a boy I overheard Father and some uncles on the veranda drinking rum and talking about America. An uncle asked Father what he remembered most about his visit there.

Drunk as usual, Father screwed up his face and thought.

"They had a toilet that flushed on the floor," he said finally. "Step on a pedal, and the toilet flushed."

"A pedal on the floor! Like a brake pedal in a car?" asked an incredulous uncle.

Yes! Damnedest thing you ever saw. Step on the pedal on the floor and you flush the toilet. You never have to touch a lever with your hand."

"On the floor?"

"Right on de floor!"

"But what a damn inventive people, eh?" gushed the uncle. "Imagine dat. Flush the toilet on the floor!"

"I couldn't get over it," slurred Father. "I must have flushed da damn toilet fifty times. Dey came looking for me, for I was supposed to be in class. Dey thought I was dying of diarrhoea—there I am sitting in de stall and flushing de damn toilet over and over again."

The uncles laughed.

"If it was me, I would've flushed it a hundred times over," said one marvelling uncle.

"You can't beat de American man for ingenuity!" commented another. "You just can't beat him."

"When you think about it, dat is just where de damn toilet flusher belongs—on de floor, where a man can squash it like a bug. But you know why de Englishman will never put it dere? Because of tradition. Because when Henry VIII took a shit over two hundred year ago, he flushed wid his hand, dat's why. So from now till kingdom come, every blessed English man, woman, and child in de world is doomed to flush toilet wid him hand, rather dan wid him foot. But in America! Dey put it on de floor! You mash de bug wid you foot, and de toilet flush, and human palm never touch metal. God Bless America."

So toasted an uncle.

The assembled men silently drank to America.

Not ideology, not fatuous jingles about purple mountains or fruited plains lure us immigrants to cower at the bullying hemline of the Statue of Liberty with her haughty stare and megalomanic crown of thorns. What draw us there is the glitter, the allure, the shameless enticement of Plenty and her various relations—such as the novel toilet whose flusher was on the floor.

Yet I began to grasp on this visit that it was all too easy to become holier-than-thou about socialism and poverty, for I often caught myself displaying just such an ugly streak of gloating self-righteousness.

Immigrants invariably think of native Americans as a whining people who carp endlessly about trivialities, and on this visit we too were struck by this overwhelming impression. I was tempted to say to the querulous native: I'm living in a country where rice is impossible to find on the grocery shelf, and you're complaining about the neighbour's cat shitting in your daughter's sandbox? I can't walk de streets without people giving me murderous looks like they'd love to shoot me just for de fun of it, and you're griping about de bus driver who doesn't smile at the regular passengers on his morning route? I have to drive fifteen miles to use de telephone, and you're popping off about some operator who talked rudely to you last month? And I'm supposed to feel sorry for you?

The idea that misery can somehow be ranked is hard to refute on paper, but it is speciously wrong when applied to real life. In the closed universe of the self where all suffering is silently done and miseries privately counted, your neighbour's fatal brain tumour is simply no match for your very own hangnail. And although I had always believed that to dismiss someone's lesser evil because you happen to endure or know of a greater one is among Christianity's more hateful corollaries, yet that was exactly what I now found myself doing.

We went to dinner one night with a young couple, friends from my college days. In his early thirties, the husband stood on the threshold of inheriting great wealth—some fifty million dollars—and was barred from it only by the stubborn longevity of an uncle in his late eighties. Signs were promising, however, that any day now the uncle would kick the bucket and the millions would come raining down on the husband's head, with the run-off also drenching the wife.

I don't know why, but that night I was telling endless anecdotes about the Jamaican country children who walked the streets without shoes, whose pants often fluttered in shreds around them, whose bellies were swollen with the distention of persistent hunger, and I was deriving something like a born-again Baptist glee from doing it.

Soon the husband could stand no more.

"I know what it's like," he said gruffly. "I've paid my dues. I know exactly what you're talking about."

"Really? How do you know?" I asked.

He sighed heavily, like one who had seen and endured a mountain of ills.

"I've been on safari in Africa. Four times. I saw it with my own eyes. In Kenya. The Kalahari. The Congo. It was awful."

I said, "Oh," and nodded as though we were both suffering fellow travellers.

Without a doubt, socialism brought out my most loathsome side.

Cathy had wept at O'Hare airport in Chicago. The immigration official who checked her passport had merely murmured in a friendly voice, "Welcome home," and she was reduced to tears.

She wept, too, when we got back to our cottage in the hills of Jamaica. During our absence the rats had invaded our house. Rat shit was everywhere—on the beds, the tables, the floor. It was on my desk, my chair, my typewriter cover. Every turd was identically shaped like a dolly crescent roll and dropped with geometric neatness as if the rats had been fussily laying eggs instead of merely shitting. One turd to every square inch: no mushy scat indicating occasional diarrhoea, either. Our rats all had healthy stools and regular constitutions from the wholesome diet of American poison we had been feeding them.

We shook the pellets of shit off the sheets and swept them off the furniture onto the floor, where they bounced and rolled like BBs. Late into the night we swept, scrubbed, washed. It was nearly dawn before we finally collapsed into bed.

What had been especially wonderful to witness in America was the lavish availability of competent technical help. There talent grows prodigally wild on trees. Your television breaks down, so you call someone up and he comes and fixes it. That is that. Your car makes a funny sound, so you drive into a garage and a mechanic tells you exactly what's wrong. Getting things fixed or serviced is generally such a simple and straightforward matter that Americans take it so impiously for granted that they do not urge their children to bless the plumber in their nightly prayers.

But in Jamaica, nothing technical is ever that simple. There is a labyrinthine complexity to virtually every chore. One trail leads to another. You start here and end up there, and wonder how you got there when all you set out to do was to get your radio fixed. And in the seventies matters had been made even worse by Manley's fiery sermonizing about socialism which had sent specialists, fixers and technicians fleeing in droves to foreign lands.

I began to glimpse with oriental clarity that at the core of my native land, at its very heart, was not parliament, not the governor-general, not a pale, dewlapped English queen, not even the prime minister and his incessant homilies: but one indispensable little man planted by a mischievous providence in a far-flung place and endowed with exactly the missing part you desperately needed. No matter where you started from or on what technical errand, sooner or later its successful outcome brought you pleading at the feet of this unlikely goblin.

You want your car fixed. It blows its horn every time you turn the steering wheel, and since you customarily travel on serpentine roads, you are quickly becoming a laughing stock and neighbourhood nuisance. So you drive into Kingston and take the car to a shop. After keeping you waiting in the hot sun for a tiresome

interval, the shop mechanic finally pokes under its hood and report
that the car needs a certain part which is very scarce. But he know
where one can be had "down de road" and if you want to run an
fetch it he can fix the problem in a minute.

In your innocence you are gulled by this story, so you ge
directions and set out "down de road" to find the shop that has th
necessary part. Fifteen miles later "down de road," you learn from .
clerk that the shop indeed has the part, but it is kept in a locked safe
and only the manager has the key. But he's down de road at a ba
having a drink, and if you'd only drive there and tell him what yo
want, he'd come and get it for you.

So you drive down de blasted road again and find the bar an
poke your head through the smoky doorway of a dingy rum hole
where the barmaid points out the man you want sitting on a stool an
drinking in a dirty corner.

He does have the part you need, but unhappily he doesn't hav
on him the key to the room where the parts are stored, for he's give
his key ring to a boy and sent him down de road to fetch him a clea
shirt from his closet—this morning he had an accident that made hi
clothes smell like an old oil drum. He doesn't know why the bo
hasn't gotten back yet, but if I am in a hurry, I could drive down de
road to de house and tell the maid there to send the boy back with the
key and I'll get the part I need.

Well.

You set out for the house. But it turns out not to be just "down de
road," but up on the edge of a vertiginous cliff tethered to the eart
by a winding and perilous marl trail which requires you to use firs
gear and hug the hillside as you crawl at a snail's pace. To your left
the abyss yawns hungrily for you as you inch your way up the
mountain; to your right, pulpy outcropping spurs of the cliff threaten
to claw the paint off your car. You begin to wonder how you go
here, what had started this whole quest, then you remember as you
negotiate a tortuous curve and your horn blares.

The maid appears in the doorway, looking dishevelled and
breathless, and you glimpse the miscreant boy timidly peeping over

her shoulder as you explain why you are here. A few minutes later the boy shyly appears on the veranda with his fly half-open and babbling nervously that he doesn't have the key on him because he lent it to a man who lives "down de road" and who needed the pocketknife attached to the key ring to take a nail out of the foot of a donkey. Rather than pry the knife off the ring to lend it to the man, the boy has given him the whole set of keys. But the man will be back in a moment, or if you are in a hurry, you could drive down de road and tell him to give you the keys and keep the pocketknife.

All right, then, where's the man?

Down de road. About two chains down de road. Follow de road to the fork, go left, until you come to a house on de side of de road. The man is there. His name is Massah Ezekiah.

Come wid me, you tell the boy, but the maid appears menacingly on the veranda to say tartly dat de boy has unfinished work to do and couldn't be gallivanting all over de place just now. She has fire in her eye and glares from you to the boy, who is quailing behind her in the doorway.

All right. You'll go down de road again, even though by now you understand that down de road is never down de road but is either down de gully or up de mountain or through de swamp or around de bog but it is never ever just down de road and finally this is beginning to dawn feverishly on you as your car lurches and sways and rattles down a rutted and stumpy goat path that could be called a road only in a moment of malarial delirium.

But you soon come to the only house by the side of the road, and its appearance is so exact and expected that your spirits soar and you finally feel that you're getting someplace. A bad dog comes out to greet you, baring its teeth wickedly and snarling, so you remain in the car until a toothless woman comes clopping out of the house wearing ill-fitting slippers.

Yes, Massah Ezekiah was just here, but he has gone into de bush for a minute to do a thing. If you just follow dat footpath over dere, you'll soon find him down de road in a clearing.

Would you please hold de dog while I get Massah Ezekiah? you beg the woman, who exposes her naked gums in a ghastly smile and assures you that the dog won't bite, him just love to show stranger him pretty teeth. Nevertheless, you get a little fussy about it and insist and she reluctantly grabs the dog by the scruff of the neck and holds him while you clamber out of the car and set out to follow the trail into the bush.

So you follow the trail and it leads through a tropical jungle where the thicket snags you as you pass, macca bush pricks at your shoes and socks, and an occasional mongoose scurries across the path and burrows into the undergrowth.

Massah Ezekiah! You bawl forlornly, looking often over your shoulder to be sure that the Hound of the Baskervilles isn't hurtling murderously after you.

Massah Ezekiah, sah!

Who dat call me?

Thank God! A voice.

Massah Ezekiah, sah!

Who dat?

Is me, sah, Missah Winkler. Missah Brown send me for him boy who have him key. But de boy say him lend you de key chain because it have a pocketknife.

Oh, you need de key?

Yes, sah. We need de key to buy a part to carry to me mechanic to fix me car so de horn won't blow when me turn a corner.

Oh, is so it go? I see. Well, I soon done wid de key. Me just have to take this macca outta me donkey foot. See how de macca stick him inna him hoof. Me trying fe dig it out wid de knife. Hold up, dere, Rupert! Stand still!

Oh, you donkey name Rupert?

Yes, sah. Him name dat since de day him born. Me name all me animal dem. Just like Adam and Eve do inna de Bible. Me soon done. Sit down in de shade and catch you breath, den we go back to de house.

Lawd, sah, me glad me find you, for me 'fraid of you bad dog.

Him bad fe true. Him bite a man last month and nearly eat off im foot.

True, sah? But how come de woman say him don't bite?

She just jealous 'cause him have teeth and she don't have none. You never notice dat when a woman only have gum in her mouth she always love keep dog dat have plenty teeth?

No, sah, me never notice dat.

But so it go, me son.

I see, sah.

You laugh, but this is no joke. So you sit in de shade near the man with de donkey in the bush, the one on whom all technical mercies in Jamaica depend, the indispensable one to whom all roads eventually lead, and you wait while he works at digging a macca stick out of Rupert's hoof with the pocketknife that is fastened to the bunch of keys that you need to get the part the mechanic wants to fix your horn so it won't blow when you take a corner.

I myself have taken many such quixotic and inscrutable journeys, feeling very much as if a pesky providence had nothing better to do with its time than to spend a day cuffing me on the ear and conniving to stab my weary body deeper and deeper into the bush. Once it was to have a radio fixed. Another time I was chasing after the man who refills the natural gas cylinders. In both cases I ended up pleading with a stranger in the bushland who had nothing to do with my quest when it began but who, through a series of chained events and unlikely referrals, had become the key player in the makeshift drama that followed. His face was unfamiliar and he used a different alias each time, which only proves the depth of his wickedness, for I remain obdurately convinced that he is the same wilful duppy to whom all Jamaicans who want anything fixed must eventually go bawling.

It is not because Jamaicans are unindustrious or incompetent that this omniscient phantom wields such power. Scarcity is the real explanation. Jamaicans are masterful at adapting to want, at making do with little or nothing. But inevitably this want, this desperate lack of talent, tools, and parts lends a nuisance theatricality to even little chores.

As I became more and more hardened to this intricate pattern an
its foreordained destination, my forays into the bushland becam
fewer and fewer for I would stubbornly say "no" to an
blandishment to venture "down de road" in the hunt for anything, n
matter how speciously reasonable the journey seemed. It is a stric
policy I have followed ever since I went home to teach, and my hard
hearted practice of it has often bewildered my naive family, who ar
easily duped by a Jamaican invitation to go "down de road."

For example, many years later Cathy and I landed in Monteg
Bay for a holiday with our two children, only to be greeted at th
airport by a guileful representative of the local car rental office fron
which we had ordered a car.

Where was our car?

It was down de road, all gassed and serviced and ready for us.

Why wasn't it here at the airport where it was supposed to be?

Because the lady behind the counter had a bad running stomacl
and de driver had only my reserved car to drive her home. To get it
all we had to do was pile into the company van and go "down de
road." Everything was there and waiting for us, the keys to the car
the papers, our maps.

I was immediately on to his ruse.

"I'm not going chasing after that man in de bush wid de donkey,"
I told the driver sternly.

"Man in bush wid donkey? Wha' you mean, sah? Which man ir
bush wid donkey?"

"De one who is de key to dis whole business, dat's who. I know
he's there waiting for me to come and beg him again. But I'm no
going to give him de chance."

"Wha' you talking 'bout, sah? All me have to do is carry you
down de road in de van and get de car dat de driver carry de lady wic
de sick belly home wid. Dat's all."

"Oh, is that all? So why didn't de driver bring de car back after
he dropped de sick lady home, den? You answer me dat!"

"Because he live dere, too, sah. In de same district. So rather dan
come back and drop off de car and have to walk home or take a bus,

him just decide to keep de car dere and wait for me to bring you."

"A likely story. I know who's behind dis, and he's not going to get me into de damn bush wid him and his stinking donkey again. Not dis time."

"What man dat, sah? What bush? What donkey? What you talking 'bout, sah? All we have to do is go down de road and pick up de car and sign de paper."

"No! No bush. No donkey."

"What dis man talking 'bout, eh? What bush? What donkey? See me crosses here, now! Me ready to carry de man and him family to get de car dem reserve, and all him talk 'bout is bush and donkey."

"No. I'll rent from Hertz. I'll walk if I have to."

Shrieking in the hysterical voice with which aggrieved Jamaicans empanel a streetside jury to hear out their differences, the man began bellowing about how unreasonable I was and how I had wasted his time by making him futilely wait two hours for my plane.

"All him have to do is drive down de road wid me in de van. See de van park over dere! And him get him car. Den him come tell me 'bout me carrying him inna bushland to meet man wid donkey! Which man dat? Which donkey?"

A judgmental chorus of workers and hanger-ons gathered in a lupine ring and listened in damning silence.

"Is so foreign living madden up de brain of Jamaica man, you know," one of the silent ones eventually said.

"So white man go on sometimes," echoed another.

I herded my bewildered family into the terminal towards the Hertz desk while the disgruntled man bellowed his grievance behind us on the sidewalk.

My daughter tugged my arm.

"Daddy, what man and donkey did that man want to take us to?"

"You wouldn't understand," I told her gruffly. "You were born in Nevada."

"If any man came to me with a donkey, I'd give them both a karate kick," my son said truculently.

Then he karate-kicked the Hertz counter, causing the lady sitting behind on a stool to jump with fright.

"Why you kick de counter, little boy?" she asked with strained sweetness, peering sternly down at him. "Don't kick de counter."

"That's for the man and his donkey," he said fiercely.

"You want to kick a donkey, kick a donkey, little boy. But don't kick de counter dat I'm writing on, please."

The lady continued to write, occasionally glancing peevishly at my son, who continued to smite the imaginary donkey with deadly and vengeful karate kicks. My daughter grumbled that she still didn't see the link between the man with the donkey and our rented car and she didn't understand why I was unwilling to explain it to her.

"Is it because I'm only eight?" she asked querulously, pouting and tugging at my arm. "Is that it again?"

The driver on the sidewalk was blaring to his assembled chorus,

"Who say anything 'bout bush? Who say anything 'bout donkey? All we have to do is drive down de road and get de rass car!"

Culture shock can affect those suffering from it in the oddest ways.

CHAPTER 16

Dr. Levy was back from sabbatical, murder was rampant in Kingston, and there was a duppy loose in one of the girls' dormitories: That was the state of affairs in Jamaica in January, 1976, a bad month for socialism. Overnight the police had become targets for assassination. On January 7 six gunmen invaded a construction site in Kingston and brutally murdered two constables on guard duty there, causing a strike in the police barracks where the dead men had been posted. Manley went to the barracks and addressed the disgruntled constables, vowing a hard line against crime. That very evening two more policemen on duty at the US Embassy were shot.

But in our small corner of the countryside, the reappearance of Dr. Levy and the visitation by the duppy were the hot topics. With Dr. Levy's return, the vice principal was relegated to his duties of nagging maids and tormenting secretaries, and it was with relief that I saw him deposed from the headmaster's office. He practised a mean streak of punitive Christianity and we had come to despise each other heartily. The sect to which he belonged mercilessly squashed every ordinary human function on Sundays except those practised by stubbornly unchristian bowels and stomachs. They wrapped their heads with turbans and congregated into small wooden churches rooted on hillsides where they howled and moaned the whole livelong day.

Nevertheless, Dr. Levy was back and prowling the pathways of the campus with the dignified stride of a migrating elephant. But his return, which I welcomed, was not viewed in the same light by the students. Mavis explained why, grinning wickedly throughout the telling. Dr. Levy loved a big-bottom woman. He gave private interviews to female applicants to the school. And he especially loved a woman with a big bottom.

"How you know that, Mavis?"

She grinned without mirth.

She knew, she declared brazenly.

Jeanie, her eyes modestly on the floor, occasionally snickered.

"You don't know these Jamaican people like I know dem, yo
know Mr. Winkler," Mavis said with the devil's glint in her eyes
"You don't know how dem go on, how dem think."

Jeanie, who was more temperate in her opinions, shuffled an
drew a deep breath.

We had books now, and we were plunging ahead into th
syllabus for the A level exams, studying night after night. We ha
ploughed through Chaucer, tramped through Shaw, and wer
presently hacking our way through a Shakespearean thicket.

"What are you trying to say, Mavis?"

"I say, Mr. Winkler, dat you don't know de way dese peopl
think like I know dem. Dr. Levy love a big-batty woman. I know dat
And I know, too, dat now him come back, we might not get to tak
we A level exam."

A pause that was rightly pregnant.

"Why not?"

"Because Dr. Levy going try to stop us."

"Why on earth would he do that?"

"Because him jealous."

"Why? Jealous of what?"

"Jealous dat you giving us de chance to take de A level exam
Him going try to stop us."

This was stupid beyond comprehension. Why would Dr. Levy
who had a Ph.D. from Cornell, try to stop two of his own student
from taking an A level examination that might help them get into th
university?

"Mavis, you're quite mad."

"You wait and see, Mr. Winkler."

"Jeanie, do you feel that way, too?"

Jeanie hung her head and stared hard at the floor.

"Jeanie?"

"Sometime people get jealous, Mr. Winkler," she whispered.

"I can assure you that Dr. Levy has no reason to be jealous of you two. You probably won't even pass."

"If we even get a chance to take de exam."

"All right, Mavis. Enough of dat."

I could not grasp such a virulent distrust and suspiciousness of authority that Mavis, and even placid Jeanie, seemed to harbour within them. Yet it is a commonplace belief among black Jamaicans that their own kind are not gladdened by a neighbour's triumph but would, instead, move heaven and earth to thwart it. I have heard this sentiment uttered all my life. It is implicit in our folklore, the common saws of our culture. It may be the most poisonous axiom in our national theorems: Jamaicans would rather hinder than help their own kind.

It is not difficult to trace the root of this wicked belief, even though one does get a little weary of trotting back to slavery days with every national idiosyncrasy. But this one definitely came off that dirty shelf. There was only so much room in the manor house for liveried servants and their soft jobs, and those slaves who broke their backs in the fields vied mightily for the few cushy places. This struggle pitted slave against slave in a blood rivalry whose outcome immeasurably improved life and whose harsh memory lingers in the deep-seated suspiciousness of Mavis and Jeanie. And since the war to catch the master's favoured eye was waged by slaves with only two possible weapons, sexual attractiveness or intelligence, it is understandable that Jamaicans should tend to view these two characteristics in their fellows with envy.

So here was Dr. Levy planted squarely in the doorway of an educational institution and having a fondness, as Mavis put it, for girls with big bottoms.

There were hundreds and hundreds of nothing but big-bottomed women in our school.

Plainly if I didn't stop listening to Mavis, I would become a stark, raving paranoiac.

If he had been a white man Dr. Levy would have had a rubicund and florid face, for he was a seasoned rum-pot with an unquenchable fondness for drink that was legendary in the village. Hardened cultivators accustomed to drinking the worst rotgut white rum could not hold their own against him. He spent his days strolling the campus casting a critical eye on the lawns and gardens and his nights in the one or two village bars holding forth to any fellow binger who had the stomach to keep pace with him drink for drink. But because he was a very black man, his face did not give off the sickly red glow of the alcoholic, but merely looked soft and puffy like an over-ripe onion.

It was his eyes that gave him away. They were filled with the broken crockery of tiny red veins and afloat in a yellowish rheum. He was exceptionally tall, and his height combined with his pedantic insistence on correct enunciation made him a formidable scold of underlings. He was particularly keen that the campus grounds be kept in immaculate condition and was always beckoning to cringing garden boys to come and hack away at some particularly overgrown plot or dig at an unweeded bed. The ocean of wild underbrush in which the surrounding parish was awash lapped only feebly at the shoreline of our campus. Our lawns were always cut and manicured by boys slaving in the blistering sun with swishing machetes, and even the lower playing fields, which throughout most of the year were abandoned to the mercies of the villagers' stray animals, came under the critical scrutiny of the doctor and the grinning blades of his gardeners.

Shortly after his return, with the warnings of Mavis and Jeanie ringing in my ears, I went to see the doctor in his office.

Did Dr. Levy know I was tutoring two A level students on my own time in the evenings?

He knew, and he approved. It was good of me to do this to help our students.

Benignity, the ghastly yellow of a freshly beaten egg, frothed up in his bulging eyes.

Would there be any problems with the students taking their A level exam?

None that he could foresee.

Even if the exam conflicted with our own end-of-term exams?

Definitely not. We can adjust to that as necessary.

Good. I was relieved to hear that. My students were worried that after working for a whole year, they might not be allowed to sit for their exams.

That was foolishness.

Of course.

A formal pause intruded between us as though our exchange had just been ceremonially paragraphed. Dr. Levy coughed and moved on to the next topic.

He understood that I had had difficulties with the bursar.

Indeed, I had. I explained them.

He also understood that I had had difficulties with the vice principal.

We just despised each other, that was all.

He stared at me gravely for a long moment, and then chuckled ¨onorously and with genuine humour.

Well, at least I was honest.

At least.

The vice principal, he said carefully, had strong religious views. But he had a good heart and meant well.

I was certain of that, too.

I could not help liking the man—he seemed such a classic example of the patchwork personality one finds in the colonies and in Jamaica. The American grows organically into his nationality, his occupation, like an egg becoming a chicken, a fingerling a trout. But the Jamaican personality often seems like a quilt sewn together by a klatch of tipsy seamstresses. You see where this particular patch or that one has been crudely tacked on and beginning to peel, and ever so often you get a glimpse of the real Jamaican child—the one reared on backyard cricket, patois, and Mumma's switch—peeping out cautiously behind the ruffles and seams of the costume.

When I left the interview there was a young lady waiting demurely for the doctor outside his door. She bore the fretful look of a hopeful supplicant, clutched a bundle of testimonial letters from village elders in her lap, and smiled coquettishly as I came out. She had a luscious, succulently engorged bottom, and as soon as she disappeared behind the doctor's door with a seductive frou-frou, I heard the distinct metallic click of a latch.

The duppy put in a fitful appearance one night, scared the girls in the haunted dormitory half out of their wits, and promptly became the rage of campus gossip for the next few days. Only one girl had actually seen the duppy, and she was graphically lurid in describing it. Since she was in one of my classes I got to question her closely about the incident and came away unconvinced that she had glimpsed the supernatural. She was a frail, asthmatic girl named Gloria who had thrown a fit or two in my classes during exam time and once I had even had to send her to the clinic for a particularly severe attack. She struck me as a chronic malingerer and complainer and her virulent Christian beliefs and background seemed to me as likely an explanation of her asthma as any medical condition.

Opinion on campus split rather quickly into pro-duppy and anti-duppy factions. Most Jamaicans fervently believe in ghosts—or duppies as they are called on the island—and are usually willing to grant undisputed credence to anyone claiming to have seen a supernatural presence. Even those who didn't believe that this particular girl had really seen a duppy would have conceded that such creatures do exist.

Of all members of the anti-duppy faction, Fay Murphy was especially vocal in heaping scorn on what Gloria had seen.

"Is man she want see," was Fay's terse explanation. "De only duppy she see is man."

The tutors who knew Gloria and her tendency for hysterical outbursts were convulsed by Fay's explanation. One or two chimed in with additional details about what Gloria had wanted to see and what she might have seen, and soon everyone was rolling in the staffroom at the implication, wittily and collectively limned, of a ghostly penis hovering above Gloria's fevered bed.

For my own part I was rather glad for the appearance of the ghost and listened eagerly to every detail about it. I have been brought up on ghosts and, like most Jamaicans, believe rather keenly in them. Coming home from America on a visit, stepping for the first time off the plane onto the tarmac at Kingston or Montego Bay, I used to immediately put my nose into the air and sniff for the smell of the ocean, the pungency of burning garbage, and the whiff of brimstone. And when darkness fell on that first night back home, it always brought back that delicious primordial childhood dread of night when you clutched at the hem of your parent's pyjamas or groped for the reassuring hand of your teddy bear.

The American night is an ocean of fluorescence, meaningless and sudden death from heart attack, loveless insomniac dialogues with a sated stranger beside you in a motel bed. But the Jamaican night is a crack in the heavens through which the sleepless dead can peep, and with the fall of darkness comes the same slinking sense of predatory evil that primitive man must often have heard scraping outside the yawning mouth of his dimly lit cave.

Jamaicans are always seeing omens, are forever looking for signs of the approaching evil in daily events. If you do not understand how Jamaicans think, you might regard some admonition to take care as harmlessly intended. But let anything happen and that same casual remark will be recalled and trumpeted about with a wild and frenzied clamouring and much regretful keening that you didn't follow it. The attitude of Jamaicans to omens is a very literary one, much like foreshadowing in a play or short story where an author tries to show, at the very outset and when it is not needed, the range of equipment that will be used in the outcome of his plot. So if a gentleman in a play during the first act is about to head for the office and his wife pointedly advises him to carry an umbrella, you may be certain that the umbrella will play some critical part in the events of his commute.

At the heart of the Jamaican attitude towards the supernatural is the island's capricious and unjust history, where abduction and lifelong captivity in slavery might have resulted from something so simple as the wrong path taken in the forest and where free will was rendered powerless by brutal captors. If you cannot control your own destiny through rational means, the intelligent next step is to try to propitiate the forces behind it. Jamaicans therefore tend to be superstitious and alchemical in their thinking, perpetually alert to omens and warnings, even half-believing that they can influence the course of reality with talismans and magic.

If you are sensitive to this omen-mongering, as I tend to be, it will invariably make you indecisive. You cannot help sniffing about for a sign from the heavens or perpetually wondering about the meaning of some trivial event that perhaps has none. Indecisiveness is assuredly a trait in the Jamaican character, and the degree to which this individual or that one is afflicted with it varies with the particular experience and personality.

Because of this appetite for omen-mongering, innocent conversations between Jamaicans can take on sinister undercurrents that a foreigner might entirely overlook, especially when they concern a clear fork in the road ahead.

Once, for example, I went to the Air Jamaica New Kingston office to confirm my booking on a flight that was to depart the next morning at the crack of dawn. The clerk behind the desk and I became engaged in a friendly conversation made warmer by the discovery of many mutual acquaintances and friends. She was having difficulty confirming my booking on the computer and strongly suggested that I postpone my trip for a day later when there was a more convenient flight.

I said no, I wanted to go on my original flight.

Suddenly we were at a fork in the road. Last week there had been a disastrous plane crash and the fumes were still in the air. Without warning the conversation took on a theatrical heaviness with untold omens and consequences.

"Lawd, Missah Winkler," she said plaintively, "why you don't just wait and go anodder day, eh? Better late dan never!"

"I don't want to."

She laid on the foreshadowing thickly with a crude stroke. "I just have a strong feeling you should stay the extra day, you know,

Missah Winkler."

I thought that she was prepping me shamelessly with omens. If I insisted, caught my original plane, and it crashed, she would be a triumphant prophet while I would be sorrily wrong and very dead. I could hear her lamentations now. "If only he had listened to me. I begged him not to go. I had a feeling in me bones. Why didn't he just listen!" And on and on to her acquaintances, friends, neighbours, family, to every bloody one who would hear, and since this was Jamaica, every bloody one would listen to her and nod sagaciously in return, and I would not only be dead, I would look the heedless, incomprehending, witless fool. For the rest of her life she would be able to lord it over me that I was in my grave only because I'd been stupid enough not to mind her.

Her insistence put me in a creepy, paralytic mood, but I shook it off adamantly. I wanted to go on my original flight, and I didn't care if that meant her slaving for two hours behind the computer terminal.

"All right," she sighed gloomily, sitting down as to a grim toil. "If you insist."

"I insist," I croaked, not at all sure that I insisted.

The plane thankfully didn't crash and it became just another case of wasting words on a sunny day about a needless umbrella.

Yet once in a while coincidence will explode among the gimcrackery of the drawing room like a blast of thunder, leaving eternity ringing in your ears. Such an event was the death of my father.

In the sixteen years of life I shared with my father under the same roof I do not remember ever once seeing him ill. I had seen him injured many times, usually because of something rash that he did while he was drunk, and I had even seen him in a wheelchair nursing a broken leg he suffered after kicking a solid mahogany door behind which my mother was hiding to escape his drunken rage. But I had never seen him sick.

But then one Wednesday in an otherwise uneventful week, an enormous green limb of a tree in the backyard of our house suddenly

fell to the earth with a thunderous crack. The maids flew into th
backyard, took one look at the fallen limb, and began to babb
hysterically that someone in the house was going to die. Mothe
heard the hubbub and ran to see what was the matter, and all of u
children likewise gathered sombrely around the splintered limb.

It showed no sign of rot, disease, or insect damage. Its leave
were green and shiny, and it was not laden with overripe fruit th
might have explained its fall. On a cloudless day, the limb had bee
severed cleanly where it had joined the bough as though sheared o
by lightning.

Father dismissed the incident with a scornful laugh.

Although he claimed not to be at all superstitious, when he wa
drunk he took a devilish delight in scaring the wits out of th
servants. Once he took a dislike to a certain maid and drove her fro
our household by skulking outside her room in the dead of night an
smearing a handprint covered with catsup on her window pane. Th
poor woman had glanced innocently at the window, glimpsed
bloody hand slowly rotating there, uttered a terrified shriek and dive
under the bed, where we found her cowering and yelling blood
murder. Father had sauntered onto the scene to enquire at th
commotion and was soon heaping scorn on her story. She gathere
her possessions in a huff and left that very night, swearing that sh
would not work another minute in a haunted house.

So Father wasn't at all impressed by the sight of an enormou
green limb crumpled under the tree on a windless day, and he wasn'
about to put up with the servants' standing around and gawking.

That was on Wednesday. On Saturday he was dead from a hear
attack.

Five days later I saw his ghost.

His death had thrown all of us into such stark terror that we wer
too petrified even to sleep in our own rooms. Days after the funeral w
were still huddling at night on Mother's king-sized bed—all seve
children—trying to snatch a little sleep among a pile of bony elbows
gouging fingers, and stinking feet. One night I decided that I coul
stand it no longer. I pried a big toe out of my nose, hoisted a leg off my

belly, and staggered into my own bed, muttering that I didn't care if the devil himself was in my room, tonight I would sleep in comfort.

I fell asleep as soon as my head hit the pillow.

An hour later I awoke to find Father, dressed in the clothes he had been wearing at the hour of his death, sitting in a chair beside my bed and peering intently at me.

I blinked, rubbed my eyes, and looked again. He was still there. Still staring.

"Daddy," I blurted out, "what you doing?"

"Take care of your mother," he said.

The odd thing was that his lips did not move. Yet I heard him say distinctly, "Take care of your mother."

Then he was gone, leaving a faint smudge of blue smoke coiling lazily in the dark open doorway.

Father had good reason to be worried. Mother was nearly forty and pregnant with her eighth child, and his death had left us pauperized. We had been living from hand to mouth ever since he'd lost his last job, were lodged in a rented house in Kingston, and owned nothing except the clothes on our backs and a few worn sticks of furniture. Only in the forty-fourth year of his life, father had died intestate and without insurance, bankrupt without a penny to his name, and left us so poor that we could not even afford to bury him. Some uncles chipped in and bought him a coffin and a burial plot. He died on a Saturday, and we had to move into my maternal grandfather's old house that Monday, when the rent—which we could not pay—became due.

Father also appeared to Lascelles, the gardener, who had been sent to collect a few remaining things left behind in our vacated rental house. Lascelles arrived late at night and, since his bed had not yet been moved, decided to sleep in the old house. But Father's ghost came ranting into his room and woke him up. Lascelles reported that Father flailed around the room cursing that something was wrong with his eyes and he couldn't open them up, but vowing that once he could, he intended to give Lascelles a kick in the backside for laziness. After that incident, Lascelles refused to go back to the house even in broad daylight.

And Father also came to the priest in a dream. The priest saw Father stumbling from cottage to cottage in a driving rain, banging on doors and begging to be admitted, but no door would open up to him. Two nuns in the dream who shared a miserable hovel took pity on him and gave him shelter under their roof. The priest said that the dream meant that Father had squeaked into the slum section of heaven and now shared a makeshift and humble abode with two fallen sisters.

After Father's sudden death these stories circulated among us and were listened to with much oohing and aahing. No one ever said they didn't happen or that they were hallucinations made up by grieving relatives. Father was definitely tramping about among us, and our culture had prepared us for fitful glimpses of him.

But what always troubled me about what I had seen was the glimpse of smoke in the room after Father's ghost had vanished. Had he been smoking? I do not think so, but I distinctly remember smoke coiling in the doorway. Many years later an aunt who had a lifelong interest in the occult sent me a book titled *Communication With The Spirit World*. I leafed through it and came across a lengthy and somewhat garbled explanation of how beings in the next world are occasionally able to make contact with those souls left on earth. The propellant for these visits, said the book, was a substance called "Od" that must be consumed for materializations to take place.

It continued: "The odic current, when only slightly condensed, looks like a cloud of smoke...."

Grandfather was always seeing ghosts. Many a night he scared me out of my wits by suddenly stiffening, fixing his wide-eyed stare at some vacant spot in the drawing room, and following the movements of an invisible presence with his riveted gaze. He claimed to keep company with a familiar whose name he said was Ida and whose earthly life had once been partly lived in the tiny bungalow he shared with Grandmother. Ida did not know that she was dead, according to Grandfather, and was still intemperately fond

f human food, for she was forever padding to the refrigerator and
rying vainly to open the door with her ectoplasmic hand. She was
qually fond of Grandmother's pantry, which she often
unsuccessfully tried to raid.

Unhappily transplanted for life to Jamaica, poor Grandmother
uffered endless embarrassment at the hands of Jamaican ghosts.
When she was a young woman, one of her daughter's teenage suitors
decided as a prank to dress up in a skeleton costume and come
triding down her walkway. Grandmother peeped out the window,
aw a skeleton brazenly tromping towards her veranda, and
catapulted out of her chair with such violence that she fell and
ractured her ankle. Grandfather grabbed his gun and pointed it at the
apparition.

"Don't shoot, Missah Winkler," the skeleton blubbered. "Is me,
ah! Is only me!"

Grandmother was on the floor wailing and shrieking with pain
over her broken ankle. The skeleton ripped off its skull mask and
rushed her to the hospital, where her ankle was set in a cast. For the
next three months Grandmother hobbled around on crutches, sullenly
replying to anyone who asked about her injury that she had suffered
a mishap. Her sense of dignity would concede no more to that
ridiculous incident.

But it was mainly when she threw a tantrum and rushed headlong
into the darkness, as she often did, that Grandmother encountered
Jamaican ghosts. Then they would take a demonic delight in driving
her ignominiously back to the domestic battleground from which she
had just petulantly fled.

When Grandfather died, Grandmother went to live with her only
daughter, carrying with her a lifetime addiction to domestic turmoil
and intrigue. She immediately engaged her son-in-law in periodic
bouts of sulkiness over what she perceived was his callous
indifference to her person. She warred with maids over imagined
slights and insults. She bickered with her daughter and squabbled
with her grandchild.

Her effect on the family was poisonous. Maid after maid

resigned in a huff. Her grandchild began to get bad marks in school. Her daughter took to drink. Her son-in-law became impotent. Ill feelings mounted and finally splattered all over the veranda one night in a noisy power struggle between Grandmother and her daughter over who was mistress of the house. Grandmother wailed to the skies that Grandfather had abandoned her to the mercies of uncaring wretches. She vowed that tears would fall upon her death, whose killing blow she felt coming on this very instant. Then she clutched her head and pretended to be sinking into a coma. But her daughter was obdurate in laying down the rules of the house. Unable to bear the sound of wicked regulation being rattled off any longer, Grandmother fled into the dark overgrown back yard that fringed an ugly concrete gully.

Exactly what happened then has been garbled in the telling, but it came out later that a malicious ghost either pushed poor Grandmother into the dark gully or fiendishly lured her over its edge. For the next thing she knew she was sprawled on the bottom of the gully with no bones broken but no hope of climbing out. Eventually a squad of garden boys and maids who heard her screaming for help came pouring out of back doors and servants' quarters to mount an ignominious rescue operation. One garden boy manhandled Grandmother halfway up a ladder while another climbed down beside her, placed the top of his bushy head squarely against her rump, and flipped her over the lip of the gully with a debasing plop.

She was so mortified by the experience that for weeks afterwards she would not show her face in the neighbourhood during daylight.

Her other encounter with a duppy occurred one rainy night at our house. Grandfather was dead and gone, and Grandmother had hardened into a chronic hoarder of treats. It was a detestable habit she had had even before Grandfather's death and widowhood made it worse. She squirrelled away candy, chocolate bars, cinnamon buns, Easter eggs, caramel chunks, anything sweet and tasty. She hid her treasures in every imaginable nook and cranny throughout the house. She stuffed cinnamon buns wrapped in wax paper under loose floorboards. She found niches and holes in the walls for gumdrops and paradise plums. And she was so clever and sly about finding hiding places that her comestibles were usually safe from gluttonous raiders.

But not in our house. There were eight of us by then, everyone a remorseless plunderer of sweets. Treats were safe only when cached in a private colon. Otherwise they would be found and eaten. This ruthless law was applicable to every inch and every inhabitant of the household. No one was to be trusted.

During a brief stay under our roof, grandmother had meticulously sought out obscure rat-holes for her treats and secretively stowed them. But when she returned to her trove for a nighttime munch, she found everything gone. Picked clean. Stripped down to the slurped wrapper. Not even a crumb left.

Her reaction was predictably volcanic. She stood in the drawing room and squawked so loudly that everyone came running to see who had died. And when it was discovered that she had merely not hidden her treats securely and they had been found and eaten, the gawkers shrugged callously and drifted back to their predatory practice of jungle law. It was too much for Grandmother. She threw an explosive tantrum and flung out into the darkness during a roaring rainstorm.

A few minutes later she came scurrying back onto the lighted veranda as if she had seen the devil. She was shaken, splattered, and quivering with white-faced terror.

"He was behind a tree," she managed to gasp when I asked her what was wrong.

"What, Grandmother?"

"A duppy. I saw one hiding behind a tree."

"Maybe it was a dog."

"It was not a dog! I know a duppy when I see one."

"Where was it?"

"In the vacant lot down the road."

"Sometimes dere's a cow tied up down dere. Maybe you saw a cow."

"You are not going to make me look ridiculous," she snapped, shaking the rain off. "This was no cow. It was a duppy."

She turned and marched for her room.

"Thank God I'm going to Juliette's home tomorrow," she said with a grateful shudder. "This house is a den of thieves. My grandchildren are a pack of crooks."

She departed the next morning with an indignant swish.

CHAPTER 17

We continued suffering government by jawbone. It went like this: Mr. Manley would wake up one morning with an urge and decide to give a speech about it. Everyone would sit up and take notice and wonder what the speech meant and what the devil the government was up to now. And more people would become sufficiently agitated to spark anew another rush for visas.

An example of this jawboning occurred one morning when Mr. Manley decided that a shameful elitism lingered in the public school system and that steps should be taken to reform it. He announced a crusade to democratize the schools, proposing a vague sharing of authority among students and teachers. Typically grandiose and filled with utopian bombast, the initial announcement provoked a tepid editorial in the *Gleaner* and sent the teaching profession scurrying for rebutting pen and ink.

Indignant letters from educators all over the island poured into the papers protesting the plan, though no one really knew what it entailed. The staff at Longstreet frothed at the mouth with contempt and disgust at the very idea of enforced equality between faculty and students.

Typically, Mr. Manley was again both right and wrong. In perceiving that hierarchical practices were entrenched in the island's schools, contradicting the equality preached by socialism, he was assuredly right. But he was wrong in thinking that the remedy was to pound the offending institutions over the head with governmental jawbone.

This time I was watching him and his government carefully and grasped once again that democratic socialism was too Sunday-schoolish and well-meaning, too filled with dogmatic rectitude. If he had been clever, Mr. Manley would have quietly instructed his Minister of Education to examine ways for democratizing the school system. But that was not Mr. Manley's personal style, and it certainly was not the operating procedure of his government. According to his followers, Mr. Manley wielded what they gleefully called a "rod of correction," and they expected him to periodically chastise someone or some group with it. One night at a political rally he had appeared with this rod of correction, which vaguely resembled a riding crop and swished it about for emphasis during a speech. The sight of their leader symbolically smiting evil men and traditions inflamed the imagination of Mr. Manley's supporters, who dubbed the crop "the rod of correction" and made it the emblem of democratic socialism.

So now the teachers were being whacked with the rod of correction. And Mr. Manley was justified in his criticisms of the elitism rampant in the educational system. But he didn't have to be so insufferably righteous just because he was right. The schools hadn't hatched overnight like windblown mushroom spores. They had grown out of our worldview and ambitions; they were deeply rooted in our culture and self-concept as a people.

One of the fatal flaws of the Englishman, which has helped to strike him from his place on the world stage, is his confusion of accoutrement with accomplishment. In the Jamaica of my boyhood professional accomplishment among the English carried with it a certain accent, deportment, and glibness. I never met an English professional who dropped his "h's" or did not speak impeccably grammatical sentences. They did not dangle participles or use improper tenses.

Occasionally they would rear up in conversation and browbeat you with a terrifying subjunctive.

At first I thought that every Englishman in the world had been flawlessly created by God and sent among us stumbling Jamaicans to cow us with their superiority. It was an awful feeling living under the rule of these perfect men. Even their women and children made you feel gawky and cloddish.

But one night I came across a group of English soldiers stranded in a gas station and muttering over the open hood of a stalled car. Since I then fancied myself an expert backyard mechanic, I offered to help.

"Blooming car just won't go," one of them muttered.

I stared at them with wide-eyed wonder. Bad English out of the mouth of Englishmen. Had I died and gone to heaven?

"Oh," I said primly. "You mean to say that you can't get it started?"

"Bloody bloke who sold it to us is a thief. Ain't he, 'Arry?"

"Seems that way."

Meeting them worked a very bad effect on me. I became snobbish and exacting in my replies to them, making it clear that I would not partake of their vulgar English. Having started their car and turned up my nose at their clumsy offer of a tip, I withdrew in triumph like a rajah who had just bagged a tiger.

They turned out to be ordinary foot soldiers stationed at a nearby camp, and encountering them that night taught me a valuable lesson about my English masters. Their cannon fodder dropped their "h's", confused their tenses, belched in public, and were remarkably like us ordinary folk.

Nevertheless, you could live to be a hundred during the Jamaica of my boyhood and never meet an English professional whose manners were crude or whose spoken language was ungrammatical. Those who ran the affairs of the Empire came from a homogenous class that practised the same manners and spoke with one accent. The effect of this homogeneity on us native Jamaicans was to make us confuse manners, accents, and glibness with competence. We thought that professional, scientific and business skill was inseparable from the accoutrements of the upper class. We became convinced that to be a professional in any field meant to become an upper-class Englishman, and this mistaken belief was translated into educational axioms and vested in the island's curriculum.

That was what was wrong with our schools. We had learned the wrong lessons and now taught the wrong lessons. We were not realistic in what we taught, and our educators were too preoccupied with aping the Englishman's obsolete and backward ways to devise a better system for students.

Even our elitism was nothing more than empty mimicry of our colonial masters' faults. On campuses all over the island it was indeed plainly understood that students were an underclass and teachers were their betters. Students were required to stand in the presence of a tutor, unless given permission to sit; to stand when answering a question from a tutor; to stand when a tutor entered a room; to eat at separate tables; to use separate washrooms; to end every question or answer to a tutor with either "sah" or "ma'am;" and overall, to cringe in the company of their betters or be regarded as bumptious. This was all very English, but carried out to a degree worsened by our mimicry.

Even so these practices would not disappear merely because Mr. Manley was a socialist. Over the years the Jamaican and West Indian tutors had grown rather fond of bootlicking from their students and would not willingly give it up. So when Mr. Manley decided that enough was enough and proposed putting student representatives on the governing boards of schools, a cry of outrage and derision arose from the teaching profession. Some of the densest among us, the older tutors who paraded across the campus dragging a bogus air of gravity and learning behind them, exploded with anger and outrage.

"Now I must sit side by side wid student and treat him like him and me is friend!" one of these pedants wailed in the staff room one morning.

"When dat day come, doomsday is near," another replied dourly.

"Who Manley think him is, eh? God? Him must think him is God! Him can just say such and such is de case and such and such miraculously become the case!"

"So de socialist dem go on, me dear," the other clucked. "So dem think."

"But you ever hear anything so out of order in all you born days, though?" the first asked with rhetorical indignation, looking around the staffroom as though he expected to see a nasty student rabble encamped beside the wastepaper basket.

"Dat's why me migrating, me dear," the other rejoined tartly. "When dem come, dem can have me share. Me will be in another world across de ocean." A timid knock revealed a student cringing in our doorway.

"Come in, man," the first tutor said sarcastically. "Barge in. Don't knock. Mr. Manley say everything is equality now."

The student tittered. "Yes, sah?"

"You don't read de paper, eh? Is equality time now. Tutors and students break bread at the same table. You don't have to knock anymore."

"Please, sah, I looking for Mr. Robinson."

"Mr. Robinson over in de cafeteria."

"Thank you, sah."

The boy shuffled off.

"What is dis world coming, to, eh?" wondered one of the griping ancients. "Somebody can tell me dat? What is dis world coming to? Winkler, you know what de world coming to?"

Winkler was in a grumpy mood. "Don't bother mad up me brain with philosophy dis morning, you hear, sah. I have a whole heap o' paper to grade."

"But Winkler, you don't hear? Dis is equality. Grading gone out de window. You don't need grade paper anymore."

Sarcastic sniggering from all present.

Of course, nothing came of the grand plan for democratizing the schools. Some weeks after Mr. Manley's speech, a bloated memo from the Ministry of Education crammed with abstruse bureaucratic suggestions for making schools equal flew over the transom and plopped down on the principal's desk. It circulated briefly in the staffroom, where it eventually provoked Derrick Smith to write an essay on the subject for the *Gleaner*. Like the Ministry's document, the essay waffled back and forth about equality and discipline in dense scholastic prose and drew another spate of irate letters from annoyed teachers.

Then the whole hubbub died down and was forgotten.

Americans do not practise the Englishman's witless association between class and profession, finding the whole notion superficially undemocratic and abhorrent to their egalitarian way of thinking. Because of this distaste, it is virtually impossible to judge accomplishment or ability from the way an American talks.

When I first arrived in America I made the mistake of thinking that the people I worked for were idiots because they were so faltering and inept in their speech. My first job was as an insurance clerk working for a man who often groped for words, and when he couldn't find the right one, would use the expression "set-up" as a substitute. So he would ask me to look into the "set-up" of a certain policy, when he really wanted to know whether its coverage extended to a particular risk. He would send me into the back room to "set up" the files when he wanted them alphabetized. "What's the set-up?" could mean anything from "What happened while I was out of the office?" to "Where are you going for lunch?"

Accustomed to English managers who expressed themselves with bullying precision, I thought my American boss a hopeless nitwit. But he wasn't. He simply reflected the countrified manners and folksy diction he had acquired from a childhood lived on an Iowa farm. That he had risen from the cornfield to ownership of a major insurance brokerage in California was proof of his business shrewdness. He had a wonderful memory for details and was able to spew out nearly verbatim the exact coverage of a policy he had written ten years before. But his manners and speech gave absolutely no indication of his abilities or that he was a monied gentleman with a prosperous business in Pasadena and a mini-mansion in the ritzy suburb of San Marino.

After watching American leaders for some years now I am even convinced that many of them deliberately stumble in their speech because they think that doing so makes them sound more sincere than if they volubly said what they meant. A suspicion of smooth talking runs deep in the American character, making it smarter for the politician to hem and haw before his constituents and seem one of the boys than to unwittingly discomfit them with an invidious glibness.

I have often thought, too, that the American's reputation for practicality might in some obscure way be related to his distaste for class accoutrements. The upper-class colouial Englishman often seemed to be squinting at the world dimly through the clutter of superstitions and protocol inherited by his membership in a privileged group. He seemed perpetually blundering about in a fog of rigidly correct English, etiquette, and a doltish worldview. In old movies we often see him standing stubbornly erect and in a heroically disciplined line on the battlefield just as he is about to be skewered in his red-coated belly by a Zulu spear. It never occurs to the fool to abandon his dignity and duck or lie flat. The American would assuredly have ducked, not because he is more cowardly, but because his mind is uncluttered enough by class codes and expectations to be practical.

That is why the American is today riding space shuttles while the Englishman is wondering how he happened to fall off his high horse.

The sad fact was that many of the tutors at our school, especially the older ones educated in Jamaica or England, struck me as out-and-out boobs. Many had only a smattering of understanding about their discipline. Many could not write a decent sentence if escaping the gallows required it, and many could only pass on in parrot fashion what they themselves had been force-fed as students. The Englishman's rote learning had wreaked a terrible destruction on their minds while carving only a narrow slug's path through the mysteries of their disciplines. Here they inched forward in fear and dread that some precocious student would come along and knock them off the dimly lit track and into the surrounding darkness with a question.

Some of these elder ones annoyed me incessantly. I could not endure their sanctimoniousness, their standing on ceremony with students, their pompous air of dignity. I found myself bickering constantly with them, arguing against this and that idiotic classroom tradition.

Among the company of these elders my hackles rose too quickly. I became arbitrary, perverse, often contradictory, and went out of my way to show my irreverence for their snobberies. I thought I was revelling in my American side, and so did they, but with noticeable disdain for it. I caught myself more than once playing devil's advocate with them, and I always scolded myself afterwards for acting like a brainless firebrand or a plain ass. The truth was that they reminded me too much of the classroom tyrants of my own childhood, for whom I hold an unabated hatred to this day.

Many of the teachers of my boyhood were hardened beaters of schoolboys who openly relished their dirty work. For the most part they were not university-trained but had been unleashed into the lower grades after completing only the equivalent of an American junior college education. Then as now, there simply weren't enough educated men and women willing to work for the pittance teachers were paid. Those prepared to endure the long hours and miserly pay were either of a decided academic bent or such a lazy temperament that they found the promise of long summer holidays irresistible. I am also firmly convinced that many of them were drawn to teaching because they liked being able to cane the small boys entrusted to their care.

Caning is a diseased import from England which Jamaican teachers of my era adopted and practised with a born-again zeal. You had to bend over and grab onto your legs just below the knee, presenting your arced rump to the master's cane.

Theoretically a master was not allowed to raise the cane any higher than his shoulder when he whacked a boy, but in practice most masters would hoist the cane to the ceiling and a few would even take a running jump just before they blasted your backside. Caning stung excruciatingly and slashed tender welts across your buttocks that made it painful to sit for days afterwards. But even worse than the physical agony was the degrading humiliation that a caning inflicted. You walked away with hatred and fury burning inside but too cowed and ashamed to give vent to either feeling. And this hurt and humiliation was often inflamed by the unmistakable impression that many of these child beaters loved their work.

There was one especially nasty martinet, for example, who liked

o play a fiendish trick on terrified small boys sent to him for a first-
ime caning. He would reach behind his desk and take out two canes,
which he would place officiously on the desk before the wide-eyed
and trembling boy. Which do you prefer? He would ask with a
wicked leer.

One of the canes was thin and flexible, irregularly jointed, and
made a serpent's hiss when flailed through the air. The other was
thick and bumpy like the green limb of a sapling and made a hollow
whoosh when flailed about. To the petrified boy the choice seemed to
boil down to the equally ugly alternatives of being clubbed or
switched, and in his half-witted state of terror, he would nearly
always choose the switching.

But that was the wrong choice. The thick cane looked worse than
it really was while the thin one looked deceptively better. Being
whacked with the thick cane felt no worse than being hit by the flat
side of a ruler; but the thin one sliced into the flesh of your buttocks
like a razor. Sometimes this particular master would pause midway
through his cruel labour to gloatingly ask the quivering boy how he
liked his choice.

In the school that I attended, a boy could only be caned by the
headmaster or his house master. The house is something of a tribal
division allowing intramural competition among all the boys in the
school. Houses vie against one another on the playing fields and in
various academic endeavours. We competed in elocution contests
and generally struggled to convey the superiority of our membership
to a doubting world. But mainly the system of dividing the student
population into houses ensured that every master on the staff would
have his fair share of boys' bottoms.

The house to which I had been assigned was headed by Mr.
Brim, a skinny brown-skinned man who covered the school grounds
with lanky strides while perpetually scowling about him as though
provoked by a stench. Although he was a devout Catholic, his cruelty
and disciplinary harshness were legendary on campus, and the boys
whispered extravagant myths about him with the grudging
admiration that boys often have for a bully. And he took an early and

bitter dislike to me.

I could not understand what had sparked this antipathy in him because I was a timid boy who always tried to avoid trouble especially with masters. I grovelled with the most supine of my chums and was as enthusiastic a toady as any student who ever walked the hallways.

I had him for Chemistry and Spanish, and although I was naturally good in neither subject, I tried as hard as I could to compensate for my lack of understanding with a vivid memory. Whenever we were assigned a lesson I devoured it word for word, line for line, page for page. I would lock myself up in a room and eat every word until I could spit out the lesson down to the last comma. Most of the time this brute force memorization got me through with my other teachers. But not with Brim.

He would find some question to ask that I could not answer, which was easy to do since I usually did not understand what I had been taught, and when he saw that I was stumped, he would snar with a wicked glower, "See me after class, Winkler."

The first time he said those menacing words was over some silly mistake of mine that deserved no more than a scolding. I had an uneasy idea that I was in for it, but I did not know to what extent. Then I found out. He caned me in the staffroom. Since I thought was being wrongfully punished, I made up my mind not to cry no matter how hard I was beaten, and I remember tasting blood as I bit my lip to block out the pain. When he had finished his dirty work Brim nodded curtly towards the door and I staggered gratefully for it. But then one of the other masters in the room exploded in a jeering laugh and chortled, "But Brim, you light!"

It was a belittling taunt that Brim's caning had not been potent enough to draw tears from a first form boy.

"Winkler," Brim called to me in a dangerous voice.

I stopped at the door and turned, holding my breath.

"Yes, sah?"

"We're usually not too hard on little boys, Winkler," he warned venomously. "But the next time will be different."

"Yes, sah," I muttered.

I was only eleven then, but I vowed that there would be no next time if I could help it. I would kill myself with sheer effort to please him.

But there was no pleasing the tyrant. I swatted until I was blue. I kowtowed and grovelled and squirmed and bootlicked for all I was worth. But he always found a pretext for caning me. He caned me every Friday afternoon for a whole school year. Most of the masters liked to top off a Friday with a rousing licking to tide them over a weekend in the company of a wife who would most likely fight back if hit. So having me in class for the last period must have seemed a godsend to Brim, the only inconvenience being that I studied his lessons so hard that sometimes he was sorely pressed to find a pretext for caning me. He would pepper me with questions on the lesson, and I would answer them flawlessly. He would scowl and ask for the subjunctive form of an irregular verb, which I would fire back like buckshot. But he always managed to scrounge up some stupid excuse. Once after I had answered his every question perfectly, he snarled,

"You stammered on that last answer, Winkler. Kerr House boys aren't supposed to stammer. See me after class."

To curry favour with him, I even went so far as to post myself along with my textbook beside the footpath he took from his house to the school grounds every Friday after lunch. When he came strolling by he would see me sitting against a tree, piously absorbed in Spanish.

"Good afternoon, Mr. Brim," I would hail him piteously as he walked past.

"Good afternoon, Winkler," he would growl.

An hour later he would be grubbing around for a reason to cane me.

It became a hideous and inescapable encounter—this Friday afternoon caning—and nothing short of my dropping dead could have prevented it. No effort on my part could appease him. No cramming, no sitting by the path with a book, no simpering, squirming or toadying. I did not understand. Then it occurred to me that something else was at work other than my God-given ineptitude. These were prosperous years for our family: my father owned a sailboat, belonged to the yacht club, and we lived in a big house overlooking the ocean. We were white, upper-crust, and seemingly well-off. Brim was brown and lived in a modest cottage in the hills behind the school. He did not even own a car but had to ride a humble bicycle wherever he went. My belief was that he boiled over with class envy and hatred which he was taking out on me. It also occurred to me that something about my defenceless upturned rump excited the wretch and that caning was his way of exorcising this sickness within him.

In those days caning was considered necessary to toughen a boy, and my parents would have done nothing if I had run crying to them. The headmaster would have thrown me out by the ear if I had accused Brim of beating me because I was white. I was trapped.

So I accepted the inevitable. Instead of killing myself over Spanish, I began taking sensible precautions to lessen the Friday afternoon ordeal. Every Friday morning I showed up at school wearing no fewer than eight extra underpants. But the maids soon discovered what I was up to and began complaining that I was deliberately making extra work for them. Doris, the washerwoman, was especially vehement.

"Why you have to wear so much brief on Friday?" she growled suspiciously at me one Thursday night as I was rummaging around in the hamper for padding.

"Me need extra pant," was all I would say.

"Why? You goin' wash dem? What you doing wid extra drawers on Friday?"

"Nuthin'. Me not doing nuthin'."

"Go 'way outta de room, den, and leave de drawers alone."

Doris was an enormous woman with arms as sinewy and thick as the trunk of a full-grown elephant, and there was no getting around her when she became stubborn. She stood menacingly in the doorway gesturing for me to get out of the laundry room, annoyed at the idea that I was maliciously intent on making more work for her.

"Doris!" I wailed. "Me need some drawers."

"No! Get outta de laundry room!"

I began to sob. She melted instantly and hurried over to kneel beside me.

"Wha' you bawling 'bout? Wha' you want drawers for?"

"Because me goin' get a beating tomorrow," I wept.

"Beating? Who goin' beat you? Wha' you do?"

"Me don't do nuthin'. But every Friday me Spanish teacher beat me."

"Why him beat you?"

"Him don't like me."

She stood up and sighed loudly.

"Why you don't put a piece o' cardboard under you pants?"

"Because him will know from how de cane sound."

"Damn teacher dem," she mumbled with the disgust of one who had also suffered a childhood of Jamaican teachers. Then she waved at the hamper of clothes.

"Gwan! Take de drawers dem."

And so I took them and next morning showed up in school fortified against the expected caning.

The dimwit never caught on, either. Once after he had given me six strokes of the cane, he shot me a glowering look of suspicion.

"Winkler, how many pants have you got on?"

"One, sah. Only one. Want to see, sah?" I bluffed, reaching for my zipper.

"No, no," he growled, turning away quickly and dropping the cane in its storage place behind the desk. "That'll be all."

For a year I endured these weekly canings at his hands. Then I advanced a form and mercifully lost him as a teacher. Shortly after I had been expelled from school for refusing a caning by the headmaster, Brim left the teaching profession to become a policeman.

My experience with him was not unusual. Many colonial schoolboys grew up being battered by teachers such as Brim. The evident and sadistic delight he took in caning small boys was commonplace then among teachers. But what astonishes me is the

nostalgia for these harsh pedagogues some of my generation fee
They look back fondly as though the experience has had a fortifyin
effect on their adult character; many even have a dim sense c
gratitude and appreciation for what they endured at the hands c
these tyrants.

But I am not among them. Caning schoolboys accomplishes nc
one whit of good. It is not instructive. It does not improve mora
character. And it leaves behind in the adult a lingering and permaner
sense of anger at being subjected to such merciless mistreatment as
child. In some this anger becomes an adult sense of fair play and
stirring hatred of injustice. But more commonly it survives only as
perverse and cruel desire for revenge—to give as good as one gc
when one was small and helpless.

Caning teaches nothing but cruelty, callousness, and meannes:
Some of the beaten boys grow to themselves become teachers, and t
do unto the young the same wickedness that was done unto ther
And so the cycle is repeated endlessly and pointlessly throughout th
generations.

CHAPTER 18

Murder stained the island. We heard horrifying tales of hushed-up decapitations and rapes, of slaughters that the police had deliberately concealed from the public, of wholesale butchery of entire families by gunmen breaking into houses at night. Jamaicans have always been intoxicated by rumours, and the gory stories that circulated among us were told and retold with hushed insistence on their truthfulness. Someone always had an important cousin or an uncle or an aunt who knew the score.

But for all the ugly rumours and gossip the countryside remained steeped in its ageless placidity and rhythms. Every morning we awoke to the wayward country bus honking and bellowing for a palpitating instant. Shortly afterwards we would hear the playful burbling of wild canaries splattering in the scummy water of the reserve tank outside our window. Then a tremulous stillness would flutter over our drowsiness, broken only by the distant lowing of cattle and the wing-beats of egrets furrowing the dawn mists on their way to the feeding grounds. We would arise and find that once again we had gone to bed and left the ignition keys in the car.

Yet a bloody war raged across the island, characterized by a distinct brand of island buffoonery. We were told the story about one of its skirmishes by a man who had killed a thief.

The teller of the story was a transplanted Welshman, the manager of a northcoast resort of villas where foreigners love to come and winter. The villas, scattered over a hilly stretch of coastline that tumbled in shaly folds down to the sea, were not opulent by American standards, but to the dwellers of the surrounding shanties and huts in the bushland they must have appeared palatial.

One night this manager was driving patrol on a ridge road that wound through the property when he glimpsed a shadowy figure crouched under the windowsill of an occupied villa. The manager, who was armed with a pistol, drove past the house for several hundred feet, then quietly pulled over and doused the lights of his car. Clutching his revolver, he stalked back to the villa where he had glimpsed the thief.

He was sneaking around a gloomy hedge, intent on surprising the interloper, when a figure suddenly exploded out of an inky shadow and hurtled across the street and into the thick underbrush that blanketed the hillside. The manager spun and fired at the blur and thought he heard the thief groan as he crashed pell-mell into the thicket. He cautiously nosed his way to where he thought the wounded thief had fallen, but his probing flashlight illumined only a bruised path of crushed bramble slowly uncoiling among the shrubs. The manager decided to summon help. He drove to the police station in the village and roused two corporals who were sleeping in the back room to help him with the search. Returning to the property, the three of them decided to hide in the dark clumps of shrubbery spaced along the roadside from which they could bushwhack the thief if he had the gall to show himself again. They flitted into the overgrown embankment and settled down to wait.

That should have been that, and in any other universe but this one the ambushers would have had nothing to show for their lonely vigil but lumbago and crick neck, the thief being more than content to slink home and count his blessings. But in this universe some thieves were not only obdurate, they were also blindly stupid. This one came back. At three o'clock in the morning, he skulked out of the shadows and scurried across the road, padding for the villa where the manager had originally spotted him, and got as far as the driveway before the manager felled him with a single shot.

The manager and corporals scrambled out of their hiding places and raced over to the figure crumpled on the pavement. But even though he was bleeding heavily from the gunshot wound, the thief was still strong enough to make a nuisance of himself by wiggling as the manager struggled to snap handcuffs on his wrists.

"Damn it!" the exasperated manager finally barked over his shoulder to one of the corporals. "I can't get the handcuffs on him!

He's wiggling about too much and getting blood all over my clothes. Put a round into him, Johnny."

"Move you head, Manager," advised the corporal named Johnny, taking careful aim at the squirming thief and cocking the revolver within inches of the manager's bobbing head.

The gun went off with a thunderous blast at point-blank range.

"Rass!" the thief yelped, lurching violently at the shot.

He hurled the manager onto the pavement, leapt to his feet and took off down the road with a furious burst of speed. Cursing and swearing, the manager jumped up and gave chase, but the thief was already bounding into the surrounding darkness of the bushland.

"Damn it to hell, man!" the manager raged, "I tell de man to put a round into de thief, and him shoot him in him foot!"

"Me shoot him in him chest, Manager! Me no shoot him in no foot!"

"If you shoot him in him chest, how come him get up and run away like a damn schoolboy on a football field?"

Grousing at one another, the three stalkers trudged down the hillside road, occasionally kneeling to read the splattered trail of blood that marked their quarry's flight down the darkened road.

They came across the shadowy body of the thief slumped against an embankment, his hands clutching the bramble of a bush.

The corporal crowed with triumph.

"Wha' me tell you, Manager? Don't me tell you me shoot him in de chest? Don't me tell you so? A-hoa!"

The conclusion of the manager's tale more or less summed up the attitude of the police towards this brutal vigilantism that was sweeping the island. A week or so later, after the thief's body had been claimed by relatives for burial, a police superintendent made a special trip by chauffeured limousine to congratulate the manager on the killing.

"That fellow was wanted on twenty-three charges," the superintendent reportedly said, warmly shaking the manager's hand. "That was some job of work you did that night, Manager. Some job of work."

A streak of callousness ran in our people. It sprang from th
capriciousness of our history, from the wearying and brutalizin
poverty whose stench was constantly in the wind. Even in th
countryside where the land was luxuriant and rich and where frui
grew bountifully everywhere the eye looked, we saw children wit
distended bellies, their bodies clothed in rags and tatters, their face
stamped with the whorls and scabs of ringworm. You passe
disfigured men and women in the streets, some with the jellylike sa
of a goitre slushing off their necks, others with the scars and sore
that bespoke years of desperate neglect and want. The signs o
hunger, hardship, need, were scribbled wantonly over the soile
black and brown faces everywhere you looked.

You did not see such sights in America where the people drifte
past in the clean translucent aquariums of spacious malls looking a
torpidly content as well-fed carp. Misery and pain existed there, too
but it had been swept into dark corners for tending by specialists.

But you could not escape seeing the poverty, the grinding want i
a third world country such as Jamaica. To arrive at any shoppin
plaza in a motor car was to be surrounded by a cloud of unkemp
beggars who flew at you from corners and walls with clamourin
cries and grimy outstretched paws. To stop at a traffic light drew
hordes of spindly urchins who swabbed your windshield with rag
and sponges and then thrust a bony palm under your nose for money.

Want was everywhere, even in the opulent hotel in which yo
stayed, where it nibbled at the carpet, the bedsheets, the doormat lik
unseen vermin.

You could not avoid the sights and sounds of suffering. The
wounded, the homeless, the mad shuffled to your very doorstep an
bayed under your window.

My brother, for example, owned a palatial house on the brow o
an affluent mountain suburb where even in a blistering summer th
nights were freshened by a breeze. One morning on a walk I nearly
stumbled over a madman crumpled in a dishevelled pile of bones and
rags at the gate. He was muttering to himself, scribbling gibberish in

the dirt, and hardly looked up at the white man who calmly stepped out of the driveway for a morning stroll. You were torn between the impulse to gawk and cry, "My God, who did this terrible thing to you?" or mutter a polite "Good morning," and go about your business.

So a rind of insensibility hardened over your heart. You looked on misery and grief and found humour. You laughed at suffering, traded banter about the ghastly daily sights you had witnessed. As part of your tropical seasoning, you became almost religiously serene in your acceptance of horror.

A wretched beggar used to squat on Duke Street near the insurance office in which I worked.

Because of hideous bone deformities, he could neither sit nor stand upright, but was perpetually twisted with his head drooped between his knees and his mouth dripping inches off the ground. When I walked past he would hoist a wordless supplicating hand above the rubble of flesh and bone like a snake head sniffing for fresh meat.

Thirteen years later I returned home to teach and encountered this same beggar in an uptown shopping mall, his hair singed with grey at the edges, his face chiselled with fissures of age.

"I used to see you on Duke Street," I remarked, handing him a bill.

"Yes, sah," he chuckled, squinting up at me, his head grotesquely twisted next to his feet. "Me used to be dere."

"Hey, man!" a gruff voice barked from a boutique behind us. "Don't I tell you not to sit in front of me shop and trouble people?"

I turned and saw a beefy brown man standing menacingly in the doorway of his shop, glowering at us.

"Me not troubling nobody, sah," the beggar cringed.

"Me say, move from me shop, man!" the shopowner raged, waving his hands angrily.

"Yes, sah. Yes, sah."

The beggar glanced up at me.

"Goodbye, sah! Hope fe see you soon."

"Damn people are everywhere, man," the shopkeeper groused a me as though we were united in municipal revulsion against this public nuisance. "Everywhere you look, de damn people dem come trouble you customers! What is dis damn island coming to, eh, when a man can't even go inna mall and shop without de damn wretches troubling dem?"

The beggar trundled down the sidewalk on a wheeled platform, a ruined wrack of meat and bone suitable for exhibit in the Chicago Art Institute as an expressionist's demented vision of a man.

A burly taxi driver is standing beside his opulent American limo scanning a newspaper as he waits for his tourist passengers who are shopping nearby. A ragged lunatic wanders from the street and explodes beside the taxi driver in a sudden spasm of madness. The madman twitches and howls and flecks his foaming mouthwater with every bellow. A vengeful and wicked-looking crease hardens over the fleshy mouth of the driver, who obdurately ignores the lunatic.

Then the madman makes the mistake of executing a clumsy pirouette and brushing lightly against the fender of the taxi.

"Touch me rass car one more time if you name man!" the taxi driver shrieks, all pretence to calmness abandoned.

"Dem is too out of order!" a female sidewalk vendor trills like a frightened bird. "Dem is too out of order to come touch up de man car when de man goin' 'bout him business and not troubling anybody."

"Jeremiah! Obadiah! Ezekiah! You don't know dem! Dat is what dem tell me yesterday. Jeremiah! Obadiah! Ezekiah!" the madman chants, the bulging whites of his eyes bursting out of their sockets like half-shucked oysters.

"Me say, don't brush up against me car, you rass, you!" the taxi driver bellows, "or is dead you goin' dead here now!"

He scurries over to an embankment and returns brandishing a heavy stick.

"Touch me car and I bust you rass head open!" he threatens,

aising the makeshift club.

"Jeremiah! Obadiah! Ezekiah!" the madman howls wildly.

"No matter where you go today," another vendor wails, madman come trouble you. No matter where you walk. None is safe n Jamaica today! None!"

The madman is like a wild bird in a frenzied mating ritual. He whirls and darts around the car, spinning and gyrating while creaming in a nightmarish rasp. The driver settles against the fender s motionless as a sunning turtle and resumes reading the newspaper while the lunatic's body splatters jerkily about him. Everyone—the igglers, passersby, the driver—studiously ignores the whirling and hrieking madman, who is careful in his dervish dancing not to brush against the car.

With poverty and want come the intrusion of anomaly that can at ny innocent moment blast apart your placid schedule with the disrupting violence of a lightning bolt. You go about your business as a clerk or a teacher or a salesman and suddenly an incident brings ou face with face with the abyss. You step back, unsure of your ooting, haunted by the absurd onrush of tomfoolery into your life. It s merely the intrusion of anomaly, as must inevitably occur where vastly different lifestyles—from the rectitude of the bourgeois to the lisarray of the vagrant—are compressed and lived out side by side in a small space.

I went to New Kingston to transact business at a bank. No sooner ad I parked my car and gotten out than there was a ragged and dirty black man whispering at my elbow with a menacing intensity.

"Boss man! We love you, you know, sah! We would kill for you! Dat's how much we love you!"

"Thank you very much," I muttered. I hurried on my way, acting ike a man on a purposeful errand who was being buzzed by a wasp. There was a fat cheque in my pocket and I wanted to cash it.

"Boss man! Me goin' wait on you. We have business to do! We ove you, sah! We love you!"

The man blasted this parting shot in my ear as I vanished into the bank whose doorway was barred against him by a hard-eyed guard. Settling on the kerb with the fussy deliberateness of a dog, the vagrant scrutinized my every move through the plate-glass window with burning eyes.

I found the manager, shook his hand, and sat before his desk.

"Be careful of that fellow, Mr. Winkler," he warned. "He's dangerous, somewhat deranged. He just got out of the asylum. I wouldn't trust him if I were you."

"But how the devil am I going to get out of here now?" I asked, flicking a glance over my shoulder at where the madman sat waiting on the kerb. He met my gaze and gesticulated furiously, pointing alternately from himself to me as if we were conspirators in a dark plot.

What was I to do? Linger and delay—that seemed the best strategy for the present. Chat with the manager about cricket matches and football games. Row about the government. Fuss about the budget. Eventually the barracuda would become disgusted and drift off in search of more likely fish.

Ordinarily that would have worked. But as bad luck would have it, the bank's biggest depositor just then waddled in through the door, causing an outbreak of clerical and managerial fawning from every quarter. Dour tellers sang out to her as though she gave them daily bread. Even the stony security guard, who had been giving his impression of a statue at the door, became animated and effusive. I was hustled away from my perch before the manager's desk and pawned off to the mercies of a birdlike clerk. Where my bottom had formerly been agitatedly squirming, the copious rump of the biggest depositor now settled with a self-satisfied squish.

The clerk briskly attended to my cheque. She fished out the notes from her drawers and counted them out plainly on the counter while the madman, cemented to the kerb like a sea creature on a reef, stared. I managed to shift my body between him and his view of the money so all he could see was the clerk's head (or so I hoped) and not the rows and rows of twenties she was fastidiously plunking down on the counter.

When she was done counting, she glanced through the glass wall and murmured, "Dat madman seem like he's waiting on you, Mr. Winkler."

"Waiting on me?" I pretended surprise. "Oh, no, you're mistaken. He can't be waiting on me."

"Now he's waving," she said cheerfully.

"Not at me, you can be sure."

"Oh, yes, Mr. Winkler. I'm certain he's waving at you. Now he's pointing, too."

"Maybe he's waving and pointing at you."

She wrinkled her nose at this preposterous idea.

"Not dis madman. Some madmen are funny, you know? Dey either only trouble women or dey only trouble men. Dis one only love to trouble men."

"I'm not an expert on madmen, and I don't think you are either," I said stuffily, walking away to a corner of the glass wall that was partly shaded by the unfurled drapes, offering me a moment's respite from the madman's stare. He got off the kerb and trekked in an inquisitive tilt down the sidewalk until he had a better angle and could glimpse me again. Then he resumed his ghastly sitting and waiting.

The absurd choices seemed clear to me now. I could be cowardly and simply refuse to leave the bank as long as its local madman lurked outside its door. But I thought that would be unbecoming.

Or I could accept the manager's offer to have the security guard walk me to my car. But I didn't want the madman roughed up, which was a distinct possibility if I agreed to be escorted by the guard.

Nor did I even resent paying the madman a pittance. In a third world country like Jamaica you must be prepared to pay reparations to bands of scavenging sufferers. It is more than alms-giving: it is a kind of unofficial exacting of tribute. There are vastly more of them than of you, and they could rise up at any minute and drown you and yours in an unrelenting tide of class retribution. But they don't, even though it is painfully obvious to them that your lot is happier and more content than theirs. For this forbearance, you pay spontaneous toll in the streets.

But the question was, would the madman be content with money? Would his madness not goad him to a more insatiable and barbarous demand? What exactly did the fellow mean when he said he had business with me?

I took a deep breath, transferred a ten-dollar bill into a separate pocket, and walked gravely out of the bank.

The madman was on me in a blink.

"Boss man!" he jabbered, stinking right at my elbow. "We love you, sah! Read dis, sah! Read dis!"

He stuck a scruffy piece of brown paper, torn from a grocery bag, into my hands. Scrawled on it in indelible pencil was the ominous note, "For a specified sum, I kill anybody you want kill. My name is Brown. I kill good."

I glanced behind me at the door of the bank.

With a sudden burst of speed I could probably retake it. But a flight either to the bank, which was behind me, or to the sanctuary of my car, which was some fifty feet ahead, would have required abandoning all dignity, and there was no assurance that I would make either one before the madman, who suddenly struck me as unreasonably robust and fit for one lately out of the asylum, ran me down and grappled me bodily from behind. I thought of handing the note back to the madman, together with the ten-dollar bill, and blubbering that while I didn't want anyone killed at the moment, if the need should arise later, he would certainly be the first to get my business. I even thought of feigning an outbreak of madness myself and shrieking at him, thinking rather unclearly that if there was anything a madman should dread it would be assault by another madman. But this was only panic and its attendant fuzziness.

I was about to make some lame reply, my fingers dipping despairingly into the pocket where the madman's ten-dollar tribute lay crushed, when an expensive car pulled up right behind mine, hemming it in. Ignoring the fact that his car was now selfishly blocking mine, the nattily dressed driver clambered out from behind the wheel clutching a briefcase and wearing the distracted air of one n his way to transact some weighty business.

"I have a favour to ask you," I said conspiratorially to my
madman, reaching into my pocket for the ten-dollar bill.

"Yes, sah!" his eyes were afire with expectation.

I handed him the bill and pointed to the gentleman who was
lready locking his car.

"Dat man car over dere is blocking me," I said. "Will you please
sk him to move it?"

The madman swivelled his head from me to the man at whom I
ointed, uncertainty and doubt wrinkling his features. He glanced at
he ten-dollar bill I'd just pressed into his hands, at the man in the
uit who was already walking away. Then he sprang into feverish
ction.

"Oyyeh, man!" he roared, racing after the suited gentleman.
You blocking me boss car, man! Move you car!"

The man with the briefcase nearly jumped out of his skin as
nomaly suddenly exploded into his life. He was bustled back to his
wn car by the jabbering madman, who planted himself officiously
n the middle of the street and began directing traffic.

The lunatic held up a line of cars so I could reverse out of my
arking space, then waved cheerily goodbye as I drove away. In the
ear-view mirror I could see that as he maniacally waved the suited
entleman into the parking space I had just vacated, the madman was
till eagerly brandishing between his fingers the grimy scrap of paper
ag on which his offer to commit murder was scribbled.

CHAPTER 19

Then we roasted the rat. We did not mean to roast it. We meant t
roast a chicken for my two sisters, who had promised to drive ove
from Kingston for dinner and a visit. We trekked into the village
chose a chicken from the butcher's shelf, and brought it home for it
appointment with the roasting rack. Then we bustled about preparing
Sunday dinner.

But somehow the rat had managed to squirm its way inside th
oven and die there in a dark corner. When we turned on the flame
the dead rat began to roast and the house filled with a sickly stenc
of singed hair and charred rodent flesh. We hurried to the oven an
peered inside but couldn't find the rat, although from the billowin
smoke it was obvious that he was being broiled by the flame of th
burner.

Cathy was in hysterics. We couldn't cook dinner, she declare
vehemently. We simply couldn't. Why not? I wondered. If I foun
and retrieved the dead rat, surely we could go ahead and roast ou
chicken. No, we could not, she yelled. We could not roast a chicke
in the same oven where we had just broiled a rat!

Why not? We didn't mean to broil the rat, we meant to roast th
chicken. Once we'd cleaned the rat out of the oven, why couldn't w
roast our chicken?

She threw her head back and practically screamed i
exasperation.

All right, I said, trying to calm her down. We would just have t
get to a telephone and call my sisters and tell them not to come.

The only telephone was a single callbox some fifteen miles awa
across a mountain in another village, and we hurried there in
domestic frazzle to head off my sisters.

"I go to cook a chicken and instead I cook a rat," Cathy i
muttering inconsolably over and over as we drive through th

chequered countryside.

"It's not your fault," I assure her. "The rat had no business being in the oven to begin with."

"That's not the point," she grates. "I can't stand the idea of ever again cooking food in an oven where I cooked a rat."

"So you cooked a rat," I consoled her. "What's so terrible? I'll clean it out and nobody'll ever know that you cooked a rat."

"Leave me alone," she mutters grimly.

Then one morning we awoke to a splatter of news that the island's flour supply had been poisoned and that people were dropping dead after eating bread, sugar buns, and particularly dumplings. The poison was nearly instantaneous and death had struck within minutes after the contaminated food had been eaten. One poor fisherman in an eastern parish had lost nearly his whole family after a meal of fish and dumplings.

Stranded as we were in Longstreet, news was difficult to come by and always fragmentary. But terror was rampant on campus that perhaps our flour supply was also poisoned. That morning at snack time there was none of your usual run-amok stampede for the piles of buns and tarts laid out neatly on the tutor's tables among the shiny teapots and porcelain pitchers. Instead, everyone milled about and watched edgily to see what his neighbour would do.

"Go ahead, Winkler," an education tutor named Miss Buford crooned wickedly, "have a tart."

Usually Miss Buford behaved like a famished water buffalo at the snack table, goring every bun or tart within reach of her fork and shovelling it down into a bottomless belly. But this morning she was the model of daintiness and restraint.

"Winkler," Daphne Dickson murmured at my shoulder with bogus concern, "you not eating today?"

"No. Are you?"

"I just not hungry this morning," she sighed treacherously.

But everyone was thirsty, though, and eagerly sipping tea or the matron's patented bellywash—a muddy brew of brown sugar, water, and lime.

This was nonsense. I announced that I intended to ask the matron point-blank about the flour.

"Do it, Winkler! Do it, man!" several of the tutors urged.

Feeling rather heroic, I traipsed into the kitchen, elbowed my way past gloomy rows of vats and giant pots, squinted through the mist rising from bubbling soups and stews and found the elderly school matron in her cubicle poring over her account books.

"Miss Hubbard," I hailed, "good morning!"

"Good morning, Mr. Winkler."

She stared up at me, a finger impatiently tapping the desktop.

"I can see you busy this morning, so I goin' come straight to de point. Nobody eating bun this morning, Miss Hubbard. Nobody eating tart at all."

She looked disgusted.

"So dey think my flour poisoned, eh?"

"Oh, no, Miss Hubbard. No such thing. But, of course, under de circumstances..."

"Well, you may tell de tutors for me, Mr. Winkler, dat dat flour is from de same bag dey've been eating for the whole term. So if dey not dead yet, something other dan my flour will have to kill dem."

"Thank you for de reassurance, Miss Hubbard."

"You're welcome, Mr. Winkler."

Her head bobbed under the wash of figures in her account books, signifying that our interview was concluded.

Returning to the table where the expectant and silent tutors still sat glumly among the untouched piles of pastry, I chose two shiny tarts, hoisted one to my mouth and bit into it with dramatic flourish. The tutors stared with morbid interest and foreboding.

"It's quite good," I declared, taking another bite.

After a few minutes Daphne Dickson sniffed, nabbed a tart, and took a tentative nibble. Miss Buford charged the piles of sweets and gobbled down two tarts in a blink. The other tutors snatched greedily at the thinning sugar buns.

They were all contentedly and busily chewing when I gasped,

lutched my throat, and pretended to be stricken. Miss Buford
creamed. A bolus of half-chewed bun spewed out of her mouth in a
wobbly arc and splattered on the table with a vulgar plop. Daphne's
and flew to her mouth. Eyes popped open and mouths collectively
aped.

"Damn it!" I cried peevishly. "I forgot I'm giving a test to 4B this
norning!"

"Winkler! You wretch!" Miss Buford howled, scooping up the
asty wad she had spat on the tablecloth and plugging it back into
er mouth.

"Damn you, Winkler!" yelped Daphne. "You nearly make me
hoke!"

"What a brute, eh?"

A few tutors snickered.

But it was no laughing matter. The government later announced
hat the flour had been found to be contaminated by the deadly
oison parathion. Speculation was that the poison had accidentally
eached into the flour during shipment to Jamaica aboard a cargo
hip. Whether this was what had really happened, or whether it was
he evil handiwork of the CIA as some of Mr. Manley's supporters
ater charged, was never proven. But for weeks afterwards everyone
vas hesitant to bite into even a slice of bread if he didn't personally
now someone who had eaten from the same loaf and not dropped
lead shortly afterwards.

For nearly eight months now I had been teaching at the college
nd still my salary had not been adjusted by the Ministry of
education. I continued to earn the pittance paid an untrained teacher.
The Ministry used a series of Byzantine categories to classify tutors
nd determine their pay. None of us at the school really understood
he classification system, but every month the bursar translated its
teps into a penurious check that barely paid the rent. It was expected
nd hoped for by every tutor that sooner or later the Ministry would
roperly classify us on the higher steps and our salaries would take a
ealthy jump. All the new tutors grumbled at the bursar on payday

about the awaited classifications. When would we finally b
classified and given our rightful pay? She did not know. Consult th
Ministry if you want to. It wasn't any of her business.

One day Derrick Smith took her at her word: he announced tha
he intended to drive into Kingston and see someone at the Ministr
about his pay. He did exactly that, returned in triumph with a nev
letter of classification for the bursar's books, and on the next payda
appeared in the staffroom crowing over a fat cheque.

I had not come home to teach for the money. Yet it began t
gnaw at me that I was being so ill-used by some uncaring oaf in th
Ministry. Didn't they know that teachers had to live, too? Didn't w
have to eat? My pay came to seventy-five dollars per week. Our rer
devoured more than half my cheque. By the time the electricity bil
was paid, we were left with little or nothing. Without Cathy's salary
we would have had no money for food.

To compound my sense of grievance, one night Mendoza, th
Canadian math teacher, invited us to dinner at her lovely seasid
home. You wound down the sheer side of picturesque rock on
wooden stairway and slipped into the Caribbean from your ow:
swim platform. Every bedroom window was filled with
breathtaking view of precipice and ocean, and every room freshene
by a cool sea breeze.

As we sat down to dinner at Mendoza's table, I began to fee
aggrieved. It didn't seem fair. Even if I had moved back home lock
stock-and-barrel bringing with me all my royalties now secretl:
cached in American banks I could not have afforded to live a:
opulently as Mendoza did. We were both tutors at the same school
yet she was revelling in a palatial house on the Caribbean whil
Cathy and I were stuck in a cramped former servants' cottage on th
fringe of a smelly cow pasture. Mendoza didn't have to dodge lew
bulls and horny cows on her way to work in the mornings. She didn'
have to put up with croaking lizards grunting like nightlon;
fornicators under her very window. She didn't have to endure th
Mongolian hordes of bugs and insects that swamped our screens an
whined and shrieked and hissed and breathed in our ears. When sh

had finished riding her doltish husband, Mendoza could get up and bathe in the sea. If she was in the mood, she could even soak in a hot bath, complete with warm water and bubbles. We, on the other hand, had only a tiny shower stall and a hot water tank with such a meagre capacity that if we did not hurry our bathing the water would turn brutally cold and lash our naked flesh with icy needles.

But the worst injustice of all was that Mendoza had her own telephone. The entire village of Longstreet had none; the college had none; but Mendoza had one that sat on a table in her drawing room and had had it so long that she had become callously uncaring about its preciousness and could be heard mumbling about "that damn phone always ringing" as she tramped down the hallway to answer it.

Under Mr. Manley's regime if you were possessed of Mendoza's comfort and wealth you were encouraged to pay the piper with feelings of guilt.

But Mendoza felt no guilt. Mendoza had contempt for socialism, despised charity, loathed poverty, and was openly scornful of all public benefaction. Mendoza did not give at the office, at home, or in the street. She did not give, period. Mendoza haggled with the scruffiest urchins trying to sell her fruit on the street and was known in the market to drive such a pitiless bargain that higglers grew stony and suspicious when she approached lest she badger them once again into selling their wares at cost. Mendoza was in Jamaica only because the island's blood was rich and plentiful for her sucking. And because Mendoza was paid in Canadian money which she always changed on the black market, the more Mr. Manley ranted and raved about capitalism and bourgeois selfishness the higher the rate of exchange shot up and the richer she got. Every time Mr. Manley gave a speech to parliament, Mendoza made another bundle.

This evening Mendoza was chatting as usual about everything under the sun except anything that mattered while her nitwit husband occasionally babbled Spanish cautions to their toddling daughter between bouts of slithering his eyes up and down the ridges of Cathy's Polish cheekbones. And I couldn't help thinking, I'm just as bloody good a teacher as Mendoza! Why shouldn't I be paid what

I'm entitled to? What the dickens is fair about this?

By the time we left Mendoza's house, I was in the mood to do battle with the Ministry of Education. Like Derrick, I would storm into the Ministry's building and lay siege to the bureaucrats until they reclassified me on the pay scale.

The next morning I sprang eagerly out of bed. I had a day off from my classes and instead of staying home and pecking at *The Painted Canoe*, I took the tortuous two-hour drive into Kingston and stalked boldly into the Ministry of Education's office.

Standing on pillars opposite an ugly grassless park as though its architect feared flooding from the Caribbean some two miles down the road, the building occupied by the Ministry of Education wears the grubby and hardened look of a government office inured to the cruel labour of repelling supplicants and beggars. It is perpetually grimy and stained and for as long as I can remember has been treasured by no one but the generations of pigeons who use it for target practice. Among the island teachers the Ministry's building is regarded as a hateful and unending source of capricious regulation and a mere glimpse of it arouses the urge in many of them to reincarnate as Jamaican pigeons.

When I explained my business to a gate guard there, he sent me to the third floor where I was waylaid by another guard and sent tooling down to the first floor. But here I was nabbed by yet another guard and directed rather brusquely to go the second floor. From there I was referred again, this time with uncouth emphasis, to the first floor, whose guard got vexed at the very sight of me and demanded to know who kept contravening his instructions and misguiding me to the wrong floor. I explained that the guard on the second floor had insisted that my business could only be done on the first floor.

"What him name?" the guard demanded, opening an official looking ledger.

"He didn't tell me his name."

"Go ask him his name!"

"But I don't have anything to do wid dis man's name!"

The guard's face took on an obdurate and surly look.

"Widout a name, dis business can go no further," he said stubbornly, turning his head away.

So I trudged up to the second floor and was immediately accosted by its guard.

"What's your name?" I asked. He became instantly suspicious.

"Who want to know me name?"

"De guard downstairs say me to ask you you name and come tell him."

"What him name?"

"I don't know."

"You go and tell him dat if him tell you him name I tell you mine."

"But this is madness!" I yelped.

"My name don't have nothing to do wid you business. Him is out of order telling you to ask me my name. You business is on de first floor."

I trudged back down to the first floor, stymied about what I should do next, apprehensive that this could quickly lead to a lifelong career of trudging back and forth bearing venomous messages between Ministry guards, when I ran into an official from the Ministry's external examiner's office whom I had met on nis accreditation visit to Longstreet. I explained my difficulties to him and he took me under his wing and rode the elevator with me to the fourth floor. We bustled past the guard and entered an enormous cavern lit with embedded banks of overhead fluorescent lights that threw a gauzy illumination over rows and rows of desks behind which were seated jumbles of clerks reading the morning *Gleaner*. He pointed to a desk in the far corner and identified the fat female sitting there as the person in charge of tutor classification.

Soon I was standing within a few feet of her desk, twitching, clearing my throat, coughing, and scratching my head noisily in an effort to attract her attention while she continued imperturbably to read the *Gleaner*.

"Good morning," I finally said. She did not stir.

"Good morning!" I said again, this time so heartily that two o
three clerks several rows away automatically mumbled "Goo
morning" into the thick of their open *Gleaners*.

But mine had not winced.

I opened my mouth and was about to bellow "Good morning!
when the clerk grasped that I meant to raise a clamour and elevate
her head sufficiently high to gaze pugnaciously at my kneecap.

"Yes?" she glowered.

I explained to her that I was a tutor at Longstreet, that I had bee
at the school now for some seven or eight months and still was bein,
paid the lowest provisional salary, that I had come to get my prope
classification and carry it back to the school's bursar.

A stony silence followed. Then she mumbled for me to take
seat while she got someone to fetch my file.

That was more like it, I gloated inwardly. I sat down in triumpl
and waited.

And waited. And waited. And waited.

Occasionally my clerk would stand and seep sluggishly acros
the room, heaving with such a gait and ponderousness that I hal
expected to see a shiny stain uncoiling after her. Lunchtime rolle
around and freshets of waddling clerks purled out of the room. M
own clerk lurched to her feet and joined the river of clerical flesl
flowing out the doors.

So I also went to lunch then hurried back to await her return.

She trundled in half an hour later, weighed down by postprandia
gloom, and buried her face with a philosophic sigh of futility into
legal-size dog-eared document.

I walked over hopefully.

"Excuse me, have you gotten my file yet?"

"Dey can't find your file."

"Can't find my file? Who can't find my file?"

She chiselled at my kneecap with her eyes.

"De filer."

"But why didn't you tell me that!"

"Oh, you know where de file is, sah?"

"No, of course I don't! But to keep me sitting here waiting!"

"I tie you to de chair, sah?"

"No, but you led me to believe that if I sat here and waited you'd see to my reclassification."

"I lose you file, sah?"

"I drove all de way from Longstreet!"

"I make you drive from Longstreet, sah?"

She had driven me over the brink.

"Yes! Yes, you did! And you tied me to de chair. And you lost my file!"

"Lawd have mercy! I tie you to de chair, sah?"

"Yes!"

"Jesus peace! I lose you file, sah?"

"Yes! You same one! And you made me drive from Longstreet!"

"Kiss me neck! What is dis, now? I tie dis man to de chair! I make him drive from Longstreet! I lose dis man file! Me poor poor sinner!" she bawled vituperatively to no one in particular.

"Miss Wiggins," a clerk a row away interposed saucily, "why you love to tie man to chair, eh?"

"But Miss Simpson, don't you know I have nothing better to do wid me time? I must lose people file! I tell dem to drive from Longstreet! I tie man to chair! What else do I have to do wid me time?"

Plainly I had exhausted my welcome with this clerk. I tromped grimly across the room towards what I assumed was a supervisor's cubicle.

Inside was a matronly woman who was peering intently at a folder gutted open messily on her desk. I pushed my head into the room, got her attention, and explained my business with the indignant air of one unjustly used.

She listened patiently, nodded, and asked me to have a seat while she investigated my complaint.

Then she went over to the far side of the room, huddled in conference with the fat clerk, and reappeared a few minutes later.

She sighed plaintively.

"Mr. Winkler, your file cannot be found. And you have annoyed Miss Wiggins by accusing her of tying you to a chair. So for the sake of peace and quiet I suppose I will have to see what can be done."

It took her nearly three hours of being absent from her desk to see what could be done. While she was away the afternoon newspaper was delivered and the rows of arid desks suddenly flowered with blossoms of tabloids open to pictures of the latest bludgeoning. Tea was served and the thick air of the room filled with the sound of clerical sipping and teatime chatter. Then suddenly it was five o'clock and a stupendous wave of civil servants reared up off the shoals of desks and battered against the front door, splattering into spumes of humanity that rolled down the stairways and flowed out into the street, and the enormous floor was left desolate except for one or two grim zealots who clung to their desks while occasionally peeping around to see if anyone in authority had noticed that they remained piously absorbed in Ministry business after regular hours.

Wedges of darkness were hardening in every corner of the room when the supervisor finally appeared clutching a scribbled-over document. She looked dispirited and grim as she faced me in the doorway of her cubicle.

"Mr. Winkler, I spoke to the undersecretary. You have been reclassified as a pretrained teacher."

"Pretrained teacher? What does that mean?"

She fidgeted and looked embarrassed.

"Your degrees are academic ones, Mr. Winkler. You have no formal training in education."

"But I have taught! I have written textbooks!"

"But you have no formal training in education, have you?"

"Well, no. I've never taken any education courses. I've never needed to..."

"So, that's the difficulty here!"

"But still...I can't be at the lowest step of the pay scale," I clung to the delusion of hope. "I mean, I must be at least one or two steps higher."

She pursed her lips.

"You're quite right there. You're not on the lowest step of the scale. In fact, you're off the scale."

"I'm what?"

"You should not have been paid by this scale in the first place. You should have been put on another one that begins with a lower step."

"What are you trying to say?"

"Mr. Winkler, I'm sorry. I know you came a long way and you've waited all day. But it turns out that you've been overpaid these past seven months. You owe the government money."

"I owe the government money!"

"It's not a large amount. Some few hundred dollars. If you hadn't brought it up we might never have noticed. But now we will have to inform the bursar of your school."

"You're going to inform her that I owe the government money!"

"Try not to take it so badly, Mr. Winkler. It's not a large sum, as I have said. Just three or four hundred dollars at the outside... I can't even say that I blame you for laughing about it. In these trying times, what can we do but laugh?"

CHAPTER 20

More and more I was wracked with misgivings about what we were teaching in the classroom. The college's emphasis on pedagogical formality drove me up the wall, and much of the literature I was obliged to teach mystified my students to the point of stupor. I slogged dutifully through an abridged edition of *Wuthering Heights,* labouring every day before the same rows of attentive but plainly indifferent faces while I vainly groped for fresh metaphor that would translate this English melodrama with its suppressed and stilted sexuality into terms my Jamaican students could grasp. It was hard and merciless toil trying to make these constipated English characters understandable to my students. Nor could I truthfully say that the students under my care were learning to write either although I was struggling mightily to impart the basic principles of composition.

Teaching writing is probably the most thankless and futile job anyone can tackle. You cannot teach writing the way you might, say teach riding a bicycle. There never comes a point when you can say Ah ha! You've finally got it! and watch with pride and joy as your students pedal off into the sunset. Far more likely is the hint of glacial improvement, not noticeable in a single essay, but glimpsed against the backdrop of months of submitted work. Over the long haul you might notice that an egregious grammatical error which used to be the unfailing trademark of a certain student has been slowly disappearing from her papers. One day you may get a decent essay from an unlikely student and greet it as a sign of fresh triumph. But the very next essay from that same student is likely to sink into horrendous relapse. It was hard to get away from the nagging feeling that I was accomplishing precious little good. My students cared no one whit more about literature or the written word because of me. I huffed and puffed mightily in the classroom, but for all my efforts I had managed to uproot only or two picayune errors of style from endless rows of students' sentences. I could come home and say, well, Jennifer Smith no longer puts a semi-colon between coordinate adjectives as she used to, and Gladys Jones no longer thinks it necessary to misplant a comma after every dash, and Cynthia Brown now understands the difference between an adjective and an adverb, but none of this smacked of pedagogical glory.

With my A level students I was tormented by similar misgivings. We had finished the syllabus and were in the middle of a review but I still wasn't confident that either of my students had a realistic chance of passing. Of the two, Mavis was the better student and seemed to have the clearer shot at a pass, but even so a lot would depend on the luck of the draw. Jeanie struck me as having a slim, a very slim chance of eking out a passing grade. Yet we continued to meet four times a week, as we had all year, in an empty classroom to swat our heads off. Although I prepared my lectures with as many secondary sources as I could scrape off our meagre library shelves, some nights I felt so pitifully threadbare in my offerings that I would trudge back up the pasture wondering what the devil I was doing and what on earth had ever possessed me to tutor A level students.

Then came spring and the field trips to observe our students teach elementary school, the final climactic event of our academic year.

Like a dramatic play, a school year features characters, dialogue, complications, breaks in the action, and a moment of ultimate resolution when everyone walks off the stage and goes home. Stars emerge over the course of the term as does an obligatory train of spear-carrying plodders who beat their brains out all year to mumble a few perfunctory lines and earn the lukewarm applause of a C. There is humour, subplot, punctuated moments of hysteria, stretches of calm and relief, and always the foreboding sense of the administration hovering like fickle fate on the darkened edge of the stage ready to intervene with capricious wickedness. There is suspension of disbelief—God knows that my students practised it with a vengeance as they grappled with *Wuthering Heights*—carping critics, declamatory windbags and shrinking violets. And there is the inevitable climax, the moment all the players—teachers as well as students—have been waiting for and labouring to produce.

For our school the grand finale of the year would be the field trips to elementary schools during which all tutors of the college would take part in evaluating the classroom performances of the students. It was a critical moment in the careers of the students as fledgling teachers, for if the tutors decided that any one of them couldn't carry her weight in the classroom, she would not be certified and allowed to graduate, which meant that the government would not employ her as an elementary school teacher at its annual pittance and the whole two years she had spent labouring over the scholastic asininities we had been pounding into her would have been for nothing. It was a climax that had been hinted at in the plot for months now, and suddenly it was upon us with a whimper of meetings. We met at the staff level, at committee level, at departmental level, got assignments to different schools and planned carpools. We were addressed by the principal, by the vice principal, by a ream of smug education tutors gloating visibly that for the moment their specialty had finally triumphed. No one told us exactly what to do except that we should observe our students teach and grade their performances. Although there was some babbling of pedagogical mumbo-jumbo from the education tutors, we were given no criteria about what to look for, about how we should grade the students, about what to expect.

Then we scattered into the countryside with the hopeful air of a departing safari to observe our students teach.

The first school I visited turned out to be indistinguishable from the second or the third or any of the other score of schools to which I and the rest of the tutors wearily tramped for the next three weeks.

It was a cinder-block concrete building upended over the dead air of a gully, a sullen and grimy structure with a flat roof, louvreless windows, and no interior walls or partitions. It squatted low-slung nd ugly in the middle of trampled and grassless grounds looking as f it had been flattened into the earth by a giant thump. Its outer walls vere painted a dreary grey stained with splotches of mud and grime. 3ecause the building had no interior walls, the classes within were eparated merely by the arrangement of desks. A row of desks and enches lined side by side and facing the east marked one class; a econd row that faced the west, another. Within the single cavernous oom seven or eight classes were so separated by the arrangement of lesks and benches and by blackboards placed to serve as crude artitions.

It was not the repelling aesthetics, the overall grimy and airless gliness of the concrete building or even the dimly lit and stiflingly ramped conditions that wore on your nerves and grated all livelong lay at the teachers and students. It was simply that without walls to hysically separate the different classes you could not hear yourself hink in these suffocating bunkers while school was in session ecause you were awash in a continuous and unabating blare of oise. It was sometimes a roar, constant and deafening like the ndless blast of a waterfall; sometimes a splatter of wild cries and hrieks and yells from odd nooks and corners of the echoing uilding; but most often the regulated and disciplined chants of entire lasses bellowing out separately and all at once multiplication tables, istorical dates, and irregular verb tenses.

"Twice times one are one, twice times two are four, twice times hree are six, twice times four are eight," thirty children would be owling three feet away, while the class which you observed from an ncertain perch on the edge of a bench, would thunder in reply,

> Ring rang rung
> Sink sank sunk
> Sing sang sung

A few feet away another thirty children would be screaming a itany of historical dates:

In 1494 Columbus discovered Jamaica
In 1655 the English captured Jamaica
In 1692 an earthquake destroyed Port Royal
In 1865 the Morant Bay rebellion 'appened

Sometimes the history teacher would lead the chant with a play
of humour and Socratic questioning, and you would hear a
exchange that went something like this:

"What happened in 1494, children?"

"Six times five is thirty," a clutch of banshees would shriek ju
then from across the room.

"Columbus discovered Jamaica!" the children would choru
happily.

"Very good," the teacher's voice would sing above the tumu
like the cry of a gull over the crash of breakers.

"Then what happened in 1655?"

Hesitation and confusion. Part of the class ventured a defiant an
singsong answer,

"The earthquake destroyed Port Royal!"

But a claque of dissenters blasted out in contradiction,

"The English capture Jamaica!"

"No! No! Is not de English capture Jamaica!"

"Ring rang rung! Sing sang sung! Slink slunk slunk!"

"Children! Children!"

"The boiling point of water is 100 degrees centigrade! Th
boiling point of water is 212 degrees Fahrenheit!"

"So what 'appen in 1655?"

"Hush you mouth, Howard. You don't even know wha' 'appe
yesterday!"

"Go 'way!"

"The English capture Jamaica!"

"How dat again, class?"

"Think thought thought! Bring brought brought! Fight fough
fought!"

"The English capture Jamaica, Miss!"

"Five times four is twenty! Five times five is twenty-five! Five times six is thirty!"

Suddenly a jet plane taxied menacingly towards us, its turbines whining out diphthongs,

"Oooouuu, aaaaiiii, oooiii!"

"So what we say 'appen in 1655 again?"

"The English capture Jamaica!"

"You sure about dat, class?"

"Six times one is six. Six times two is twelve. Six times three is eighteen."

"The English capture Jamaica, Teacher!"

"A-hoa! I just want to see if you sure 'bout dat."

I made notes about my treks to these country schools. I kept a journal on the students I visited and jotted down the grade range of effectiveness in which they seemed to me to be teaching. But I had already made up my mind that nothing short of repeated, egregious and unrepentant errors in the subject being taught would cause me to flunk a student. The thing our students were being asked to do was simply unachievable by human effort, and it did not matter how puffed up and vainglorious the education tutors became about the tommyrot written in their unreadable books. You could not effectively teach pupils who couldn't hear you, and that was that. Freud, Piaget, Skinner, none of that pontifical lot had had anything intelligent to say about how to teach a class that was squished into an cavernous and airless bunker infested by bad gully air and simultaneously blasted by the decibel equivalents of chorusing banshees, taxiing jetliners, and shunting railway engines. And all the academic drivel that the college had been drip-feeding the students had so studiously ignored the horrible reality under which they would have to teach that our whole programme, the entire year of academic and pedagogical training which we had been pounding into our hapless students, struck me all at once as a sick and wrong-headed joke.

Forget the cramped and stifling conditions of these pathetic government schools, which were caused by poverty and want and could be remedied only by money, which our country did not have. To live in a third world country like Jamaica is to suffer and encounter poverty at every level of life, institutional as well as private. But where the college was grievously wrong was in not accepting things as they were and then setting out to realistically teach students how to cope. Instead of arming our students with practical schemes, visual lessons, mnemonic aids, and useful devices that would permit at least a modicum of teaching to take place in these overcrowded and blaring classrooms, we had spent a whole year bandying about the sophistries of grammar and punctuation that even under ideal conditions mattered to no one but the professional hair-splitter. We had been playing at being tutors but hadn't taught a single lesson that was applicable, practical, or useful to our students, to whom we must have appeared as inept as any bunch of bombastic humbugs.

What the devil did *Wuthering Heights* have to do with these nightmarish classrooms in which my poor students were doomed to vainly labour? Why had we wasted the whole blasted school year blundering about in a schoolmarmish fog teaching moronic rules about "shall" and will" and picky subject-verb agreement—none of which mattered in the least, counted, or could even be taught under these ghastly conditions? It was the episode of Dr. Levy and the stupid lizard during my interview with him all over again, which now struck me as a kind of primal symbolic encounter that summed up and anticipated the ruinous mindset dominating the school, the island, the warp and woof of Jamaican culture. Even as a lizard had wallowed among the Ministry's precious papers scattered over his desk and threatened to nibble his finger, Dr. Levy had persisted in acting the straitlaced part of the dignified headmaster, pretending for all the world that the reptile under his very nose did not exist. This was no "the show must go on" bravado. It was a more ominous kind of self-deception, one that simply and altogether repudiated any reality regarded as vulgar and unseemly. And it was a pretentious self-deception Jamaicans had learned at the feet of their English masters, who are hardened practitioners of it.

Keep the upper lip stiff and dignified, the pants creased and pressed, the crinoline starched and billowy, enunciate your "r's" and slow your Received Pronunciation "h's" down the gaping gullets of the unkempt rabble. So the Zulus, the Arabian dervishes, the riotous Punjab Indians are charging, eh? Steady lads, don't flinch. They may butcher us but only because they are prepared to behave like an uncouth mob. There was no lizard. There was no bedlam in the elementary classrooms, no chronic overcrowding, no higgledy-piggledy clutter of desks and chairs and benches, no howling and shrieking and stupefying din that made teaching and learning nearly impossible. And there was no need to teach our students how to cope with these hellish conditions because, like the presumptuous lizard, we simply ignored them. Yet the thought of all the energy and talent and potential among our children being laid waste and squandered by our rigid adherence to this asinine and pretentious worldview goaded me into an unspeakable fury.

So I kept notes about what I observed and I steadfastly refused to flunk any student teacher who tried and whose teaching of the subject matter was not impossibly garbled. And I seethed inside that I'd wasted a whole year—a whole year!—on trivialities when I might have been devising guerrilla tactics that would allow lessons to be taught even in the madhouse.

The educational tutors had swept through the field leaving behind the strict rule that all classes should have a public notice board on which must be daily posted items of news contributed by the children. So the first thing you saw as you entered a class was either a makeshift cardboard plaque hanging off the blackboard on which was scribbled the news, or a portion of the blackboard itself clearly chalked off for this purpose. But what items my students wrote there! Some were gory, some unintentionally funny, most absurdly out of place. Many years later I still have the notes and impressions I had hurriedly scribbled down as I observed my students struggling to teach with pandemonium roiling all around

them. My notes are transcribed below, along with the gist of a qui
talk that I always made a point of having with the student afterward:

Student: Karlene Smithson
News: Sophie said that a thief shot a girl in the head.
Lesson: Where our parents work.
Notes: Talk louder, damn it, they can't hear you. Introduction
lesson abrupt. I think she's nervous. Misspelled "guest" as "guess
and "barber" as "baber"—wrote on the blackboard: "Some of you
parents take care of guess at the hotel, and some work as babers in
shop." Take her aside and explain that with the airport on her rig
and the railway station on her left she has to talk louder.

Karlene, don't you think that news item was rather an alarmin
one to put up on the board?

Mr. Winkler, it was the only news we had all day, sah. Dat's wh
me put it dere.

You must talk louder, you hear? De children in de back can't hea
you.

But de education tutor tell me, sah, dat sometime when you can
get a class attention, it work better if you lower your voice.

Yes, Karlene, dat would work if you were teaching in a churcl
But you have to remember, you holding you class in a bus station.

Yes, sah. Is true.

And if you don't raise you voice for de students to hear over th
background noise, dey won't hear you at all.

Yes, sah. Is true.

So how you doing, anyway?

Lawd God, Missah Winkler. It so noisy, sah!

You did all right, you hear. Just try you best.

Yes, sah. Thank you, sah. Sometime de pickney so rude so der
just make me head hurt all day.

I know. I know.

Student: Cornelia Buchanan
News: Brian got hit down by a bus.

Lesson: Science, Metals and non-metals.

Notes: What the devil does it mean to say that some metals are iron, some are steel, and some are spoon? She's waving about that bloody spoon far too much and will soon bash some child's head in the front row with it. Wood is heavier than tin? Always? "There is some things that is metal, and there is some things that is non-metal. Who can tell me what is non-metal?" Child in the back row immediately thrusts his hand into air. "Yes, Colin?" "Me exercise book not made of metal, Teacher." "Very good, Colin! Can you tell de class what you exercise book made of?" "Paper, Teacher!"

"And where does paper come from, Colin?" "From de Chinaman shop, Teacher." "No, Colin, dat's where you buy paper from. But anybody know where paper come from?" "From Kingston, Teacher!" "No, not from Kingston." "From Montego Bay, Teacher?" "No, class. Paper come from wood. Dey make paper from wood. So even though it don't look it, we have metal here" (waves spoon) "and wood here" (waves paper). (Look out with that blasted spoon, Cornelia! You almost clouted that little girl who's chucked so close to you that she's practically on your lap.) Talk to her about speaking louder.

Cornelia, why did you tell de students that metals are iron, steel, and spoon?

Lawd God, Mr. Winkler, I was so nervous! Afterwards I say to meself, look what you tell dem now, eh? Dat's not what I meant, sah. But de noise in de room confuse me lesson plan.

All right, Cornelia, so long as you realize your mistake.

Yes, sah! Me know it from it jump outta me mouth, but me just couldn't concentrate to stop meself.

All right, Cornelia. Don't worry about it. Just clear it up next time. If you can, bring two spoons with you, one wooden and one metal, and say something about the difference in the substance each is made of.

Yes, sah. Me will do dat next week.

By the way, who is Brian?

Brian, sah? Oh, he's a boy in de class dat a bus lick down dis morning.

Good God, Cornelia, if he's in dis class, why you put dat on de board den?

Is no news, Mr. Winkler?

Is he goin' to be all right?

Me no know, sah. Him modder carry him to de hospital.

Cornelia, do me a favour. Use better judgment next time before you write down something like dat on de news board, eh?

If you say so, Mr. Winkler.

Student: Gwendolyn McBaugh
News: Sylvia saw an accident this morning.
Lesson: Religious Education.
Notes: Finally, someone who talks loud enough. She practically bellows. When the class behind her begins its multiplication chantey she drowns them out with sheer lung power. Effective lesson, too except for the part that compared Oral Roberts with Jesus Christ. Did she really have to regale the class with that long-winded story about seeing Oral Roberts make a lame man walk on television when she was in Miami last year? And is it fair to liken what a modern preacher does on a television show, which could easily have been rigged, with what Jesus was reported to have done in Galilee? And wasn't it a bit much when she bawled out Roberts's command, "I say to you sinner, get out of your wheelchair and walk!" three or four times, with her eyes bulging out of her head (I think she may have watched too much corny American television while she was in Miami). Give her credit, though, with all the chanting and shrieking going on in the room, the class was utterly mesmerized. One little girl in the corner even started to cry.

Mr. Winkler, I make up my mind dat my students in my class must hear me. If I have to bawl all day long till I have no voice left, my students must still hear me.

Well, they certainly heard you, Gwendolyn.

Dem must hear me, Mr. Winkler. You think I goin' stand before my class all day and just because dem reciting de times tables next oor my students not goin' hear me?

Well, you did a wonderful job of making yourself heard.

My father was a preacher, you know, Mr. Winkler. And I myself ee wid dese two eyes when my father preach in a village where dey vas having a dance right next door with music playing on sound ystem dat have four o' dem big loudspeakers, and not a man who ome to listen to him couldn't hear him, you know, Mr. Winkler? You hear what I say, sah? Not a man in dat village who wanted to near my father couldn't hear him! A-hoa!

Gwendolyn, you're talking too loud.

Is de one thing I learn from my father, Mr. Winkler. Dat if God ;ive you a loud voice, you must use it to spread de word. Use it, sah! You must use it! Wha' you saving it for?

Shhh! Class is over, Gwendolyn. And you did a good job.

Thank you, Mr. Winkler. You like me news item, sah?

Yes, I do. At least it's not like some of the others I've seen.

Yes, sah. Dem tell me you don't like read 'bout too much violence. So I put dat one down just for you, Mr. Winkler.

Oh, is that what dey say?

Yes, sah. Dey say Mr. Winkler don't too much love news 'bout le violence.

Well, they're right.

You should come hear me teach mathematics, sah. When I teach bout de number line, dey can hear me down in Trelawny. A-hoa.

I observed one class in which something educational seemed to nappen. It was a class taught in St. Ann's Bay just after a cloudburst. This particular school had a zinc roof, and every raindrop pounded he zinc like a drumstick. The effect was one of being trapped inside ι bongo during a frenzied solo. Speech was out of the question; no one could hear or be heard. Some few classes were caught in mid-:hant, but soon the voices of all the children petered out and everyone in the enormous room, children as well as adults, sat and listened to the thunderous roar of the rain, darting occasional wide-eyed glances at the naked zinc sheets overhead. The roof began to leak and water dripped onto the floor and desks and benches. Some children complained, others snickered and used the puddles to draw makeshift sketches on their desktops. Gaiety and fun were in the air drawing exasperation and scowls from some teachers, helpless resignation from others.

The storm passed and the chanting resumed from every corner of the building, which now felt muggy and clammy enough to pickle a mummy. The student whom I had come to observe suggested that the class go outside under a tree, and we all trooped after her. She settled the class down under a tremendous flame heart tree whose boughs and leaves were thick enough to have kept the surrounding ground dry from the rain, and she began to tell a story.

She told an Anansi story and told it with such power and feeling that the children were quickly mesmerized and riveted on the spot, staring up at her. And she told it in patois, which is the way such stories are known to Jamaicans in folklore. I do not remember exactly what the story was about, but in it Anansi was up to his usual tricks.

In Jamaican folklore, Anansi is a spider who lives by his wits, does not particularly like to work and spends a great deal of his time trying to dupe his neighbours out of their possessions. Sometimes his schemes backfire and he is caught in his own trap, but mostly his deceits serve him well.

The children clung to every word. They stared and leaned forward from the effort of straining not to miss a syllable. And when the story was done, there followed the hushed silence of slow digestion.

The recess bell rang from the school building, and still no one stirred. Usually the children had the good sense to fly out of a class as from a revival tent, but this time they stayed put and asked questions and begged for more. Then one by one they reluctantly got to their feet and staggered off in pairs and threes.

Right before my eyes, the children had learned something. What I couldn't say. But right before my eyes I saw the lesson of the story sinking in, impressing them. The experience gave me a glimpse into what we might have accomplished if we had had the imagination to draw from our own folklore and use such creatures as Anansi, a character beloved by every Jamaican child, to animate lessons in arithmetic, geography, history, and English.

It was only a thought and a very fleeting one at that. For when the bell rang again I found myself back inside the steamy interior of the schoolroom watching another student stand before a class teaching a lesson on adjectives. "I have in my hand a *pretty* book," she said, emphasizing "pretty." The children stared and intoned dutifully, "I have in my hand a pretty book." And I scribbled in my notes, Damn it, that's a frigging index card you're holding in your hand! Couldn't you at least hold up a real book?

And yet most of the student teachers did heroically well. A few wilted under the blast of noise and confusion and at the end of a day looked as if they might simply drop dead in their tracks. But most of them held up in good spirits and accepted the pandemonium with infectious humour. The errors they made were venial ones that came from inexperience in the classroom and misjudgment of the children's backgrounds.

As I drove from school to school my respect and admiration for these slaving and beleaguered students mounted. They seemed to me stalwart, unselfish, and heroically enduring. Most of them had amusing anecdotes about the classroom to share at the end of a day, and the horrible conditions they confronted daily seemed to bring out the best in even the weakest of them. They should have been bad-tempered and irritable and complaining, but for the most part, they were not.

"Don't tell the children that the noisiness described in a certain poem was like the noisiness of a circus," I suggested to one girl. "These children have never seen a circus."

"Never see a circus, sah?"

"I'm sure of it."

"Never see a circus!"

"Have you seen a circus?"

Giggle.

"No, sah."

"So, neither have the children."

"Is true, sah."

I advised another girl not to ask such broad and unanswerable questions as she had done during a science class. She had asked the children to close their eyes and listen.

"What do you hear, children?"

What she intended to draw out of the children was that they heard the sounds of the countryside.

But they couldn't hear the occasional birdsong or the faraway mooing of a cow or the bleating of a goat kid cropping futilely at the trampled-over hollow of the school grounds because of the deafening background din from the other classes. The children said they heard the multiplication tables being recited behind their heads and capitals of the West Indian islands being broadcast on their left, but not one of them could hear the birdsong or the moo or the bleating goat. In desperation the student finally blurted,

"Who hear goat?"

Twenty hands shot up in the air.

"Me, Teacher, me!"

"Ask me, Teacher!"

"Me hear Missah Brown goat!"

"Who hear cow?"

But by then the cow had stopped its mooing and nothing could be heard that even vaguely sounded like a cow.

"Wha' cow?"

"Me no hear no cow, Teacher."

"Cow, Teacher? You hear cow?"

"Teacher, Winston mooing in me neckback!"

"Winston!"

"Take them outside next time," I suggested afterwards, "where there's peace and quiet. It's no use trying to teach nature study inside this chicken coop."

"Is true, Missah Winkler. I make a mistake."

" I like your lesson plan. It's very good."

"Yes, sah?"

"And I like the control you have over your class."

"Thank you, sah. I dunno why I never think to take them outside."

"Never mind. You did well."

And I found, on my second pass through the schools, that my presence had had an editorial effect on the tone of the daily news bulletins.

Richard saw a cow jump over a wire fence.

Jehovah said that a truck overturned on a bridge (no injuries, however).

Precious saw a helicopter last night.

Sandra saw a car hit a dog (but the dog was unhurt).

And one evening after I had trudged through some four or five schools, I made a final call on a school that clung to the slopes of Mount Diablo and found the student teacher wearily sitting behind her bench while a boy in the back row of her class pored studiously over a dog-eared book. The teacher was the same girl who claimed to have seen the duppy. She was asthmatic and usually whiny and had struck me as lazy. At the end of this day she wore the frowzy and beaten-up look that comes from teaching thirty-five eight-year-olds.

"Oh, you still here, Gloria?"

"Yes, sah."

"I didn't know it was so late. What are you still doing here?"

"Me waiting on Richard, sah. He want to finish reading de book."

"Oh. Why don't you let him take it home with him?"

"Him house don't have electric light, sah. Plus him have to help him father and mother wid de goat."

Purple shadows from the big mountain were slowly draping the schoolgrounds when I left them, the boy monastically immersed in concentration on the book, his silently moving lips slowly chewing its words and sentences, while his weary teacher sat and waited for him to finish reading.

CHAPTER 21

Our academic calendar was inching to a close with the tutor
visibly relaxing and the students in a continuous whirl of chatterbo
gaiety at the prospect of approaching holidays. It was hard to get an
real work done in class during these final weeks.

Qualifying exams loomed only days away and the second-yea
students were jittery with excitement and anticipation over thei
pending assignments by the Ministry to elementary schools. We me
in classes everyday as scheduled, but after a feint at the assigne
material, I usually gave in to the surge of chatter that swirled aroun
every subject under the sun but *Wuthering Heights*. With my A leve
students, however, there was no letting up. Our exams were als
weeks away, then quickly, only days away, and we plodded on wit
our final review and study. I was beginning to have hope that perhap
Mavis had a realistic chance of passing the A level exam. Sh
belonged in the university—more and more I became convinced c
that, and it would be a cruel waste if she were not given the chance
She was quick-witted, articulate, and intelligent. The quality of he
writing had taken a quantum leap during the year. I graded her wor
mercilessly and did my best to coax the best out of her, and sh
responded by outdoing herself on every assignment.

I had gotten to know both girls well, had given them rides t
their homes in Kingston, and had met members of their families
Jeanie had three children and shared a squalid tenement off th
Spanish Town Road with her mother-in-law's family. Mavis lived i
a lower-middle-class concrete-block house on the outskirts o
Kingston in a district notorious for its high crime rate and politica
murders. The houses in her neighbourhood were attractive enough t
lure gunmen but modest enough to be defenceless against any gun
toting thug. Jeanie's neighbourhood was so pitifully poor that excep
for the risk of an occasional sneak thief fishing for a purse throug

an open window, the residents could sleep in safety behind flimsy doors.

We plodded on. Five days a week. Two hours every evening. Through Shakespeare and Shaw and Swift and Donne and Chaucer. We read and analyzed and studied and made notes. I lectured and explicated the text and tried to give them a flavour for the kind of academic exegesis they would be expected to write. We pored over the ruminations of critics, forewords by famous scholars, afterwords by the authors and their contemporaries, footnotes by interpreters, endnotes by anthologizers and compilers. Many a night it took all my self-control not to hurl the books against a wall and scream, "Piss on Swift and Donne and Dryden, piss on the whole lot of them!" We plodded on. Day in and day out. Moonlight, humidity and thunderstorm. Croaking lizards and whistling frogs and whining mosquitoes. We met in the same empty classroom, sat in the same chairs, faced the same scribbled-over blackboard, and read the same authors over and over and over.

Then, with the sneakiness of a glacier, our time had suddenly come. The exam was tomorrow.

My A level students and I had had our final meeting, had closed the books once and for all, and had spent our last study hour or two congratulating ourselves on work well done. Since the girls did not have the entrance fees for the exam, I had scraped together the hundred dollars and lent it to them. The A level exams would be held in Kingston and would coincide with the week of island-wide qualifying exams administered to all graduating teachers by the Ministry. There was to be much frenzied shuttling back and forth from Kingston to Longstreet, and the girls were going to be in for a gruelling week of sitting for both the Ministry's and the A level exams. But as we wandered out of the classroom that last night, the dormitory buildings blazing with the lights of last-minute crammers and a cool mountain breeze fanning us with the blossoms of the flowering poui trees, we felt as lighthearted and giddy as underground miners getting a first glimpse of the clear night sky after a long shift.

"The exam tree blooming," Mavis said, sniffing the air with pleasure.

"Yes," Jeanie said softly."When the poui blossom, exam time come."

And the pouis were blossoming in all their fleeting and triumphant glory during these soft days, carpeting the earth with fallen petals.

Another generation of Jamaican children were being summoned to the bar.

Dr. Levy called me into his office early in the morning. He had lately moved his administrative throne to a remote rear room on the second floor of a concrete annex recently added on to the old wooden administration building. You walked up the stairs and entered a tremendous anteroom so austerely empty of furniture that your footsteps echoed as if in a fog, and it was guarded by a trio of two glum typists and the doctor's secretary. Three small desks with battered manual typewriters were moored in an ocean of pastel tile, and the tang of barely cured concrete and freshly applied whitewash immediately tickled your nose. The typists generally had little or nothing to type, and the secretary, who had no phone to answer, spent most of her time reading magazines or sticking her head out the window to scold the boisterous labourers below whose profanity occasionally drifted in and buzzed her ears. Because of ill-fitting dentures that stretched her lips and gave her an ugly overbite, she wore the grimace of a seasoned battle-axe and seemed sour and bad-tempered, but, in truth, she was a soft-spoken and sweet-natured woman whose only quirk was a Christian aversion to blasphemy and bad words. I had scarcely settled in the straight-backed chair before his desk when the doctor, looking officious and abnormally solemn, broke the news. The girls would not be allowed to sit for the A level exams.

At first I thought I had heard him wrong, so I asked him please to repeat what he had just said.

The girls would not be allowed to sit for the A level exams, he said again, this time with a flinty grimness. The A level exams conflicted with the Ministry's island-wide exam.

"But you knew that last year, sah. You knew that six months ago. I asked you about that before I agreed to tutor them."

Nevertheless, they would not be allowed to sit because of the conflict in the scheduling.

"Conflict? What rass conflict? You knew about the rass conflict ten months ago!"

I do not know how he did it, but right before my eyes he increased in volume and girth and cubic capacity until he had swelled into a mountainous presence of offended dignity.

"You dare use that word to me?"

"Rass? You think dat word is all I going use? I teach dese two students for a whole rass year with your permission, and now you tell me dat dey can't take de exam?"

"You have the nerve to address me in that tone, sir!"

I used other words, too. I was in such a blind and uncontrollable rage that I could hardly talk. I cursed and swore until the profanities seemed to lacerate my lips as they spewed out my mouth. Then I stormed out of the room, leaving him sputtering.

"Him is a dirty rass!" I roared at the head of the stairs, the obscenity caroming off the freshly laid walls as if bellowed in a grotto.

This was not America. Here rass mattered.

Here rass was virulent and cathartic.

"Lawd God, Missah Winkler," the doctor's secretary cried in horror, her hand flying to her mouth. "Lawd God, sah!"

I stomped downstairs and broke the news to my two students, who were dressed and waiting with their pencils and pens and exercise books to journey to the examiner's office in Kingston. Jeanie stared out the window and shrugged with heavy resignation. Mavis narrowed her eyes, leaned forward and spat evilly at me,

"Don't I tell you, Missah Winkler? You remember when I tell you dat, sah? You don't remember, sah?"

"I remember," I mumbled. "I can't believe he did this to us. can't believe it."

"I believe it, yes!" she crowed with boundless malice an vindication. "Is so a Jamaica man do him own people. I tell you da already! You don't remember?"

"I remember," I capitulated abjectly. "I remember."

We left Jamaica the next week. I stormed home after th interview and in a mindless, headstrong fury announced to Cathy tha we were selling out lock, stock and barrel and leaving the island. I was a rash and impulsive gesture, the kind you commit only whei you are heedlessly young and your wronged heart smoulders with righteous and unrequited rage.

Cathy was ecstatic at the sudden whirl of events. We sold ou furniture, our car, our personal effects to a tutor for a single lumj sum, and two days after my explosion in the doctor's office battered old truck nosed through the pastures and the tutor and he brothers gingerly loaded it up with all our meagre possessions. turned in my grades the next day, passing every student, ani immediately stopped attending class. A few students trudged up th pastures to say farewell, and a few more stopped me on th walkways of the college and whispered quiet and sorrowfu goodbyes. Word of my rash departure had spread quickly. Secret were impossible to keep on such a small campus as Longstreet, ani even the workmen and maids from the kitchen, all of whom hat heard about my row with the doctor, turned and stared inquisitivel as I walked past.

Only three days after my outburst in the doctor's office, Cath and I mounted the steps for a jetliner bound for Chicago. Second after the plane took off, it banked, and the serrated mountain rang that encircles Montego Bay was lightly flicked off the left wingti into the vast emptiness of the heavens leaving nothing to be seen bu a white sky sectioned into wispy rectangles by the jetliner'; windows.

I went into the bathroom, carefully locked the door, and wept.

Grandfather died when I was eleven years old. He became stricken while my brother and I were vacationing at his small cottage, and Grandmother spitefully blamed us for the fatal blow that killed him.

We were innocently playing cricket on the front walkway, my brother and I, and Grandfather was sitting on a stump, watching us.

"Come, Grandpop! Come bat!"

He waved us off. He was too old, he grumbled.

"No, Grandpop! You not too old! Come bat, man! Come bat!"

He couldn't remember what it was like to even hold a cricket bat.

He lumbered off the stump and gamely took his mark on the makeshift crease we had drawn in the earth. I bowled to him and he clouted the ball over the fence. Then he clutched his heart and patted it with his open palm as if he had an itch deep within his chest. He trudged back to the stump and put a pill under his tongue, and leaning on his knees with a reflective and faraway look in his eyes, he watched us play.

That night he was stricken. The room in which I slept could have been a chamber in the underworld, it was so pitilessly dark, and I remember groping my way to the door and inching down the narrow hallway that threaded between the rooms. Grandfather's door was ajar, light streamed through the crack, and the ominous sounds of solemn adult muttering drifted into the hallway. I paused at the door and peeped in. A strange man leaned over Grandfather's bed as Grandmother stood helplessly in a corner and fretfully watched. Grandfather was sitting up in bed, clutching his chest, his face twisted with pain.

Just then our eyes met. He straightened, winked, and made a feeble effort to wave. Grandmother flew to the door and bustled me back into the underworld chamber. When I awoke the next morning, Grandfather was gone.

Grandfather died badly. Years later I heard the story from my aunt who had been at his deathbed. He lingered on the verge of death for two days, and when it became clear that he was dying,

Grandfather began a loud and blasphemous cursing that brought alarmed nuns scurrying into his room.

He cursed God for making him sick. He cursed God for letting him die. Worms would eat him because of God's cruelty. He became graphic and obscene in his vituperations against the Almighty. The priest was sent for and tramped into the room with an unforgiving scowl. But Grandfather would not be hushed. He raised his voice against the Almighty so violently and vehemently that a decision was made to sedate him for the good of his immortal soul. Although he struggled with what little strength he had left, Grandfather was overpowered and given an injection. While he slept the priest administered Extreme Unction and prayed to God to forgive the blasphemies of this desperate and terrified sinner.

Grandfather awoke with a start, peered groggily around the room, and immediately fixed his stare on a far corner. Grandmother hovered over his bed, wringing her hands and weeping.

"Mother!" Grandfather whispered, reaching out to the empty corner.

"I'm here, Lou," Grandmother said, bending over to stroke his forehead. "I'm here!"

Grandfather waved her away.

"Mother!" he said insistently. "It's Mother!"

He tried to sit up and reach out for his invisible mother. Then he was gone.

Grandmother left the hospital, came home and recriminated with us for the death of Grandfather. If we hadn't inveigled him to play cricket with us, she glared, he might have lived. Weeping bitterly, we denied that we had killed Grandfather and were sent home grieving on the evening train.

That next day she put a match to Grandfather's thousand-page unfinished novel and, sobbing, watched it go up in smoke.

EPILOGUE

Many years have passed since I went home to teach, and many changes have befallen the people who lived this story.

Almost to a man the foreign tutors left the college within a year or two and returned to their own homelands. Melissa Richardson, the ugly Englishwoman, found a husband, settled in Europe and bore two children. The Canadian do-gooder Evelyn Moon went to America and worked for a while as a missionary teacher among New Mexican Indians. Then she dropped out of sight. Peter Matheson, the piano-playing Englishman, drifted to Chile, where he taught for a year or two. Then he wandered away to Africa.

Among the Jamaican tutors, migration took a heavy toll. Many left for America, some for Canada, a few for England. Two years later when I returned to the school for a visit, there was almost no one left on the faculty with whom I had taught. Those Jamaican tutors who did not migrate abandoned teaching for other positions that paid better.

Dr. Levy rose in favour with the Manley government and worked for a while in a highly placed ministerial post. Then he got ill and died and received a state funeral complete with pompous eulogies and officious testimonials to his illustrious life.

My A level students never sat for their exams. Jeanie drifted away from the campus and disappeared. Mavis went into teaching, served a grudging year in some far-flung village school, then broke her contract with the government and went into other better paying work. For a while we corresponded and she remained as callous and waspish as ever. A persistent theme of our early letters was, Why did he do it? Why did Dr. Levy sabotage the academic dreams of two of his own students and ruin their slim hopes for a better education, a better life? Mavis thought she knew: It was because of sheer unstinting meanness. He had acted on the illiberal and mean-spirited

cautions passed down from the slave generations that warn again
letting anyone but your own flesh and blood through the Massa
front door and into the cushy parlour. That view of the doctor fits
well with her cynical opinion of Jamaican society. Some thirtee
years later, much battered and beaten from hustling as a
international higgler, Mavis eventually made her way to th
university. Through her own tireless labour and frugality she ha
painfully and carefully accumulated the money she needed and ha
gotten a foot in the door. Later she went to law school.

Jameson, the prosperous farmer from whom we rented ou
cottage, came to ruin. Shortly after we left Jamaica, the Manle
government accused him of hoarding "idle land." This phrase wa
then a well-known shibboleth that preceded confiscatory action b
the government. Jameson argued in vain that his land was for grazin
not for planting and pointed to his annual beef yield. But th
government was unwavering and threatening. Fearing the loss of a
his property, Jameson panicked and sold all his land at a fraction o
its value to a Kingstonian well-placed in government circles. Then I
and his wife migrated to Canada. It was a decision he bitter
regretted. The land had been in his family for generations. His enti
life had been spent in Longstreet. He was gone no more than a ye
when he returned begging the man to whom he had sold his proper
to sell it back. But the man said no and Jameson vanished foreve
among the forlorn hordes of exiled Jamaicans who pass their lives
distant places hungering for their lost homeland.

The Canadian math instructor, Mendoza, who to my min
provides a mini-moral to this tale, fared better than Jameso
Mendoza was mercenary; Mendoza was avaricious; Mendoza wa
uncharitable. Mendoza despised Manley and socialism, stoutl
rejected the gospel that every man was his brother's keeper. She wa
keeper solely of her loved ones and laboured only for gain that woul
better their private lot. Yet Mendoza outlasted every foreign tut
who has ever taught at Longstreet out of philanthropy o
humanitarian love. She did not serve merely a year or two as di
itinerant missionaries such as Evelyn Moon or global nomads such a

Peter Matheson. Mendoza taught at Longstreet for ten rich and productive years. Worldly gain, pure and simple, was her only motive, and for this grubby reason she trained hundreds of teachers and bequeathed the school the legacy of an innovative math curriculum. Years after I had served my own fleeting altruistic term at Longstreet, Mendoza remained behind doing useful work.

Her career in Jamaica ended on a stroke of happenstance and bad luck. One day a bureaucrat in Ottawa accidentally stumbled on her file and gasped, "Good God! We've been paying this teacher all these years under the wrong scale!" Mendoza's salary was cut to the prevailing missionary pittance. She immediately resigned, sold her mansion to the fiery socialist Raymond Hunt, and left Jamaica.

Mendoza's story is rich with biblical paradox and offers a tentative explanation of why socialism failed in Jamaica, of why Manley's well-meaning and humane government was so bungled and futile. Manley failed because his socialism lacked the attraction of betterment.

Betterment was what Mendoza found in Jamaica, what kept her there. When she left Jamaica she was richer by far than when she had come. Betterment of this sort is what human beings universally want for themselves and their loved ones. The idealistic appeals of socialism that call for unselfish sacrifice in exchange for the collective betterment of one's nation are too remote and monastic to stir ordinary hearts. Humans crave betterment that is personal, exact, measurable in teaspoons. Yes, yes, we want a better nation; but first we want a better hat. Many scowling Russian old men find this lust ugly and rage against it, but the craving to better oneself is in the blood and will persist to the end of humanity's days.

Soon after I fled Jamaica the slurry of uncles and aunts inherited from my mother's side died off in a wanton reaping of generations. Corpulence, a love of brown and black female flesh, took their toll on the profligate uncles. Many strangled to death on a rind of fat around gluttonous hearts. The aunts perished of unslaked sexual hungers, of wicked husbands, of female drudgery and toil. Cancer darted among them like a barracuda and drew blood. Madness struck at least three of them and for years they stumbled over the land in occasional dementia. On my father's side there was only one aunt who survived, and one cultured uncle-in-law whom I loved and helplessly watched succumb to a lingering illness. Then there was Grandfather.

Grandfather was lost to me for many years. I could not even find his grave. I knew that he lay in the cemetery of a church at Matilda's Corner in Kingston with Grandmother at his side. But the graveyard is weedy, unkempt, littered with rotten stumps of tombstones and fissured slabs. Then one day I set out with determination and found it. I was searching among the ruined and abandoned graves when the caretaker of the cemetery wandered over and asked me what name I was looking for. When I said "Winkler," he furrowed his brow like a knowing librarian, immediately stalked off to a far corner, clambered atop a solid hump of tangled weeds and began a furious kicking until a faded grave-slab surfaced through the scuffed foliage. "Winkler" was chiselled on it.

"Me clear de grave for forty dollar, sah," the caretaker said shooting me a shrewd glance.

"No, man! Forty dollar! You a madman or what?"

"Is hard work, you know, sah!"

"Forty dollar, man! Wha' happen to you? You catch too much sun?"

He chuckled and braced for a good haggle.

"All right, sah. Me see you love you daddy."

"Me granddaddy."

"Me see you well love him. Since is love, me do it for thirty dollar."

"Twenty."

"Twenty dollar, sah!" he scoffed. "You no see all de weed and vine 'pon de grave?"

"All right. Thirty dollar. If you clear de one beside it too. Him wife suppose to be dere beside him."

"Lawd God, sah! What a hard man, dis, eh? Chew me down ten dollar, now want me to clear two grave instead o' one!"

"If you clear one, you may as well clear two."

He laughed.

"All right, sah. Mek me get me machete."

He bounded off the grave and headed for his shack standing at the edge of the grounds.

A few minutes later he returned and began slashing away at the weeds with a shiny machete.

"Come, Granddaddy," he muttered. "Time you see de sun again."

He chopped and hacked away at the bush, the sweat beading off his face and forearms. Black muscle and sinew and sweat pitted against weed and heat and bush—the primeval theme of Jamaican history enacted once again in a ruined cemetery. The weeds and creepers and vines yielded before the sexton's machete and Grandfather's grave-slab soon bared its scarred breastbone to the sun. Grandmother's rose up beside him sprouting a makeshift ruff of freshly chopped weeds. I paid the sexton. He waved his machete and trundled off between the cracked tombstones, whistling happily.

Grandmother lingered unhappily for some fifteen bitter years after Grandfather's death. She became impossible to live with, a chronic complainer who moaned endlessly about her loneliness and troubles. Her daughter put her in a nursing home and she pined away there still caching sugar buns and candies in secret nooks and crannies throughout her tiny room even though no children remained who might have been tempted to filch her riches. She longed for America, saw her daughter-in-law and various grandchildren go there, but was never to return home herself.

Growing old and feeble, she died a slow and painful death from stomach cancer among aged and abandoned strangers.

Now both of them lay side by side at my feet, with the tendrils of weeds and vines tapping at the edges of their graveslabs: Grandfather where he belonged, Grandmother webbed forever in a land she hated.

Cathleen was the title of Grandfather's unfinished novel that Grandmother destroyed. Its plot told the story of young lovers in Ireland who wanted to marry but faced the disapproval of their

parents. A separation occurrred, during which the girl wa
mistakenly informed that her beloved had been killed. She renounce
forever the secular life and entered a nunnery. Eventually she wa
sent to Jamaica as a medical missionary at the outbreak of Worl
War II and posted to a hospital as a nurse. She had been at th
hospital only a few months when a freighter was torpedoed off th
coast of Jamaica, the wounded crew brought to the hospital, and sh
recognized one of the survivors as her lost beloved. She fell in lov
with him all over again and was confronted with the agonizin
dilemma of choosing between love and the church.

Grandfather waffled at the end, I am told, but finally cast his lo
for life and against the church. Cathleen renounced her vows an
returned to Ireland with her beloved.

A book very like Grandfather's had already been written lon
before he worked on his own opus, but since he was not
particularly avid reader, he might not have known about it. Its title i
The Cloister and the Hearth and it tells a similar story except that i
it the young man becomes a Dominican monk while his belovec
thinking him dead, mourns and raises what she thinks is thei
fatherless child. But in that book, when the mistake is discovered, th
young man chooses the church over his bride, and the two unhapp
lovers die of broken hearts.

· Grandfather would never have chosen such a sanctimoniou
ending for his lost version of that classic plot. He was not one to b
duped by bogus doctrines that regard the flesh as necessarily an
absolutely antithetical to the spirit. That venomous teaching of th
Dark Ages lingers still with us among the fire and brimstone sects.

But such specious doctrines were not for Grandfather. He woul
have chosen love. He would have chosen life.

ABOUT THE AUTHOR

Anthony C. Winkler was born in Kingston, Jamaica. He was educated at Mount Alvernia Academy then Cornwall College in Montego Bay, and California State University in Los Angeles. He is the author of several textbooks in English and Public Speaking which are widely used in American colleges and universities.

His first novel, *The Painted Canoe*, was published by Kingston Publishers in 1983, followed by *The Lunatic* in 1987 and *The Great Yacht Race* in 1992. American editions of the first two novels were published by Lyle Stuart in 1986 and 1987 respectively. All three novels met with international critical acclaim, and the movie *The Lunatic* was released in 1990.

Mr Winkler currently lives in Atlanta, Georgia, with his wife and two children.

Printed in the United States
2110